Society, Caste and Factional Politics

Conflict and Continuity in Rural India

Society, Caste and Factional Politics
Conflict and Continuity in Rural India

Masaaki Fukunaga

Manohar
1993

ISBN 81-7304-038-9

Published By
Ajay Kumar Jain
Manohar Publishers & Distributors
2/6 Ansari Road, Darya Ganj
New Delhi - 110 002

Laser Typeset by
Ankit Computers Inc.
Flat No. 56
85 Trilokya Adarsh Kunj,
Patparganj, Delhi - 110 092

Printed at
D.K. Fine Art Press
C2/9 Community Centre
Ashok Vihar, Phase II
Delhi

CONTENTS

ACKNOWLEDGEMENTS

My foremost debt is to the people of Cakra whose life, culture and activities provide the substance of this study. Beginning with the winter of 1981 when I first entered their community until fall of 1983 when I left India for Japan, I experienced their vitality, vividity and contrasts with generous hospitality, affection and kindness. Their names, as well as the name of their village, have been changed in this study, but I am sure they would easily recognize themselves and their village. I hope that the study presents a true and balanced picture of the political life of Cakra.

It was ultimately in the highly stimulating intellectual atmosphere of Banaras Hindu University, that this study took its final form as a doctoral dissertation (1989). I am grateful to my colleagues in the Department of Sociology, Banaras Hindu University, for their constant support while I was conducting this empirical study: special gratitude is due to Prof. S.K. Srivastava, Prof. G.S. Nepali, Prof. S. Tripathi, Dr. O.P. Gupta and Dr. Anand Kumar for their critical, but fruitful comments.

The initial inspiration and encouragement for this work came from my former teachers and colleagues at Tokai University, Tokyo University and Takushoku University, Tokyo, Japan. I am grateful to Professor Teiji Sakata in particular, for the institutional and personal support he has provided me in all phases of my research.

I will be failing in my duty if I do not express my sentiments for my esteemed friend and collaborator Dr. Rana P.B. Singh,

Reader in the Department of Geography, Banaras Hindu University, for his overall concern and patience in helping me at different stages of this work, and also for its final editing.

(Late) Dr. Rudra Dutta Singh, a resident of Senapur village and my informal teacher has helped me in the field study which I would always cherish.

I am extremely grateful to Prof. Sachchidananda, Ex. Director, A.N. Sinha Institute of Social Sciences, Patna, who has very kindly spared some of his valuable time in writing a foreword to the book despite his heavy schedule.

Numerous persons have offered their critical comments on various parts of this work. Of them Prof. Bernard Cohn, Prof. Leela Dube, Prof. S.C. Dube, Prof. S. Epstein, Prof. Hiroshi Ishii, Prof. S.N. Mishra, Ms. Fumiko Oshikawa, Prof. A.M. Shah, Prof. Otoya Tanaka, Prof. Hirokazu Yamaguchi and Prof. Haruka Yanagisawa are notable.

The officials of the Block Development office and District Magistrate, Jaunpur were extremely courteous and generous in providing all the necessary help and information for the study. I express my sense of obligation to them.

A grant from Toho Gakuen in Tokyo, Japan supported me in updating some of the data and preparing the manuscript by word-processor.

My heartfelt thanks are due to my friends and colleagues for their valuable suggestions incorporated in this work. I would like to make a special mention of Mr. Ram Advani, Mr. K.L. Chadha, Mr. and Mrs. H. Devas, Mr. Taigen Hashimoto, Dr. Hisayoshi Miyamoto and Mr. and Mrs. Hiroshi Nakagawa in this regard.

Further, I want to express my sincere gratitude to Professor Yasuyoshi Fukunaga, my father and a distinguished sociologist of Japan, who showed me the first light and right track to observe and think sociologically. Additionally, the sense of confidence has been instilled in me by my mother, Mitsuko Fukunaga; she has made all efforts to enable me to pursue my studies by providing her blessings in various ways. With sentiment and feeling of utmost gratitude and deep regard I dedicate this study to my parents.

In the end, let me express my thankfulness to my wife Miyoko, and my sons Tetsuhiro and Noriya who sacrificed their contingent comforts in difficult times with a view to helping me complete this study.

Chofu, Tokyo
August 20, 1992

Masaaki Fukunaga

FOREWORD

The dawn of independence ushered in many changes in Indian villages due to the emergence of various socio-economic and political forces. One of these was the introduction of Pachayati Raj. It brought the democratic political process to the doors of villagers. The abolition of landlordism (zamindari) and the advent of agricultural development which was the key to the all round development of the village envisioned under the Community Development Programme, ushered not onyl an awareness of a better qaulity of life but also brought about a shift in the balance of power. Elections to panchayats gave the people a taste of power which they had not been used to earlier. This phenomenon gave social scientists an opportunity to study political behaviour at the grass root level.

The new forces generated feverish activity among all sections of the society belying the image of the village as an intergrated, peaceful and cohesive unit. Indian villages presented the spectacle of a vibrant community with competition, struggle and factional politics for control of power and resources. The interplay of caste, class and power at the village level was witnessed by a Japanese sociologist for two full years in the early eighties. He went to the field with an open mind without preferences and prejudices of any kind. After establishing rapport with the villagers and learning the local language, he observed their behaviour, interacted with them, gathered data and analysed it.

There have been several sociological studies of the Indian social scene by foreign scholars. This study is particularly welcome as it comes from a sociologist from the Far East who looks at the Indian village not from the Western but from the Eastern perspective.

Such studies may not only bring together sociologists from Far East and South Asia, but also provide insights for sociological studies of rural areas. Shared concerns may also lead to joint work by Indian and Japanese scholars.

Dr. Masaaki Fukunaga has put Indian sociologists in a deep debt by unraveling the complexities of village politics in an east Indian village. This debt can only be repaid when an Indian scholar makes a similar study in Japan.

Sachchidanada
former Director, A.N. Sinha
Institute of Social Studies,
Patna
and
former Vice-Chancellor,
Ranchi University, Ranchi

PREFACE

When a foreign traveller looks out of the window of a running train, he glimpses the village scene of any part of India. He might think that every Indian village is an identical unit. This is an illusion because each village records some uniqueness, some contrasts and similarities in terms of the life, culture, people, and overall environment.

Individual and daily life in an Indian village is the main concern of the sociological perspective of the area studies. Every villager adopts his own way of life, particularly in reference to profit-seeking behaviour as a political actor in the community. The factional conflict and tension appear over the arena of the village scene.

The general outlook of the Indian village is cohesive and friendly for an outsider, but there also exists the 'real human life' where people are involved in competition, struggle, upgradation and relationships, to achieve political goals at a given time.

In the above purview, this is the study of an Indian village where people have the typical life style representing northern India, especially in reference to their political life, i.e. dynamics of rural faction.

The introduction highlights the major problems of the study; while justification and theoretical framework of the study are discussed in Chapter Two. The approach, methodology and evaluation of data are presented in Chapter Three.

For understanding the political activity, intra- and inter-jati groups of factions in the context of the total village situation with emphasis on socio-economic structure are focused in Chapter Four.

In Chapter Five, the institutional study of Panchayati Raj system, particularly in Uttar Pradesh has been presented. The Panchayati Raj elections (specially village Pradhan election) in the given community have been the main concern of this study, hence they have been described separately in Chapter Five.

To understand the present political situation in the village, a historical resumé of political affairs is presented in Chapter Six.

Chapter Seven recounts the main analytical observations of this study, where the case of major factional conflict, i.e. Pradhan election in 1982, is narrated in detail. The last Chapter highlights the findings and their critical appraisal.

Without tending to make undue claims, let me express openly that while this work, may not open a new vista of research, it does provide a new way of looking at the complexities of the village political structure and behaviour through direct observations and description of the experience and actual happenings.

LIST OF FIGURES

LIST OF TABLES

INTRODUCTION

During the pre-independence period, observers had presented the Indian village in a romantic light. The general conception about an Indian village was based on its status as a survivor of a glorious past and living symbol of simple, rich, peaceful and harmonious life.

The Indian society has undergone far reaching changes since Independence in 1947. However, such a generalization may not be equally applicable to both urban and rural areas.

In the field of sociology and social anthropology importance has been given to rural investigative research which has brought about a large number of remarkable studies [see, Institute of Development Studies, 1976; Mandelbaum, 1970: Bibliography 1-37; Vidyarthi, 1978: 1-75].

Researchers have used politico-sociological methods in studying rural political environment. Their works are mostly concerned with subjects like the internal rural leader and his control structure, the Panchayati Raj, administrative development planning and its actual process, voting patterns, and also conflicts and tensions between the various jatis.

Subsequently, a number of village studies carried out have clearly broken the myth of an 'Indian village'. The reason of such a shift was the impact of dynamic forces permeating the village situation. It is true that the reverse situation is more conspicuous nowadays.

The rural India which is visualized under the deceptive and surface appearance of calm and harmony, in fact has been bubbling with conflict and hostility. The researchers have been told repeatedly that suspicion, jealousy, deceit and inter-personal rancour are a common phenomena. Moreover, Indian villagers also feel that they are not face-to-face communities; the typical posture is back-to-back.

Among the research works on rural political behaviour, concentration has been upon the trends of intra-jati and inter-jati factions which received attention in the 1950s-1960s [Baviskar, 1974]. Typically, one of the studies considered that rural India is a "faction society" [Baljit Singh, 1961:4].

In the rural investigative papers on North India, Oscar Lewis has recorded in detail the structure, participation and function of factions, and also their importance and "group dynamics". According to him, the jati's residence in a village, shows a tendency to form smaller groupings which depict ramifications of cooperation and opposition. He has interpreted the smaller grouping of the jati called *"dhar"* by villagers as faction [Lewis, 1954; 1955; 1958]. Even, the term "faction" has come to be used in the analysis of the Indian rural political structure and this is recognized as being "deeply significant in analytic research, and expansional concept" [D.F. Miller, 1965:17].

In India, faction is an important and universal feature of the local level politics. There are many village level research studies on socio-political life, referring to faction and factionalism as a widespread phenomenon, and describing the numerous ways in which individuals and groups form alliances with each other and are engaged in mutual conflict of one kind or the other. Each emphasizes different ways in which factions perform in different situations, that generate a large range of relationship among leadership, voting patterns, political party organization, clan structure etc. In the relationship between rural politics, social tension and opposition an analysis of factionalism has been made.

There are, in general, two ways of analyzing factions that highlight equally important phases of the phenomenon. One approach focuses on conflict between factions, the others stresses on the organization of factions. However the term "faction" has been used inconsistently by researchers inspite of its distinct conceptualization.

If one takes a general research trend in reporting faction, it can be said that after 1970s, it has been taken up as an object for research only a few times [Baviskar, 1974; Brass, 1984; Carvas, 1972; McDaull, 1980; Mandelbaum, 1970; M. Sharma, 1979; M.L. Sharma, 1984; Chaudhary, 1987]. This does not mean that there is a progress concerning change in consciousness towards Indian social studies. It shows that the complex rural political structure analysis has been avoided in recent research. In fact, there has been a tendency of gradual withdrawal in sociology to study castes in India. Keeping aside the relationship between trends in research and actual rural conditions, it cannot be said that there is further drop in the study of faction, because there has been a decrease in the number of research papers in this field.

The North Indian villages are faced and pressured by the modernization of the 1980s, and hence research should be taken up on their political structure and behaviour [Berreman, 1979; Beteille, 1974a, 1975b, 1983; Cohn, 1979; V. Desai, 1988; D'Souza, 1982; Gupta, 1988; Kohli, 1987; Rao, 1978, 1979, 1984; L. Rudolph and S. Rudolph, 1987; Y. Singh, 1977; Srinivas, Seshaiah, Parthasarathy, 1977; Terence, 1988].[1] It is only when the internal matters of the rural areas are made clear that the necessity arises for an analysis of society and the political structure and the projection of the actual picture of the villages. As factions are essential elements of political process and also seem to activate the process of modernization, today it is important to re-examine and verify as to how political processes and activities of factions are performed within a given community.

I have used the English term "faction" so far. As already mentioned, Lewis has used this term to express the smaller groupings making up the jati. In actual practice, however, people who live in villages do not make use of the term "faction". In the eastern part of North India, where this study was made, the people of the villages use the term "*parti*"[2]; thus it has received a place in the vocabulary of village people.

To project the society and current political behaviour of the North Indian village on personal investigations, perhaps it would not be proper to use the term "*parti*"— a term that is used by the village people. I prefer the term "faction" so as to give more importance to the academic terms common among scholars.

Faction refers to a political conflict group that can be identified.

as it is basic in rural society and political structure, and is made up though a vertical tie. It is also effective in rural social research as an important analytical concept, helpful in understanding the rural people.

By the 1980s, faction had transformed the shape and background of the village activity and at the same time strengthened the activational force in the daily life of the villagers in North India. Specially the members of the lower jati who were the subjects of discrimination played a positive role in political activity: additionally the improvement in the economic status had shaken the structure of political control by the dominant caste in the villages. It is considered that after Independence the faction itself has been responsible for encouraging intensification of enmity and disputes and also the widening of cracks within the society.

The internal split in the dominant caste, cooperation and combinations beyond the framework of the jati groups and the tensions and conflict in the village originate from a background and stage activity of political conflict or faction. It is considered that the political structure of the villages and many of its facets are often biased by the trends and tendencies of the factional dynamics. In this sense, faction bears a significant place. It is the faction which is problematic as it gathers or disturbs the village people. In other words, sometimes it scatters the stability, unity and cooperation within the same jati, while at times it brings reconciliation beyond the framework of the jati groups. This shows the composition of village politics, where opposition among the different jatis leads to the faction. It shows a complex pattern of the composition of village politics.

This work while placing importance on such trends in the faction, deals with the tension and conflict occurring in the election of the village Pradhan (village headman) of a Panchayat in a North Indian village.

More specifically, the objectives of this research are:

(i) to understand the operation and emergence of factions over time, particularly their increasing numbers in the post-Independence period ; (ii) to analyze the causes of the mushrooming growth of factions ; and (iii) to understand the nature, scope and functions of these factions in the local level socio-political structures.

Notes

[1] The introduction of the Panchayati Raj system of legislative control as implemented in mid-1989, has opened a new subject of research under village faction.

[2] This term has its origin in the medieval period referring to a smaller grouping of people of a clan. Originally the word was derived from Persian.

2

FACTIONS AND CONFLICT IN AN INDIAN VILLAGE

I. Theoretical Study

After the publication of Oscar Lewis' *Group Dynamics in a North Indian Village* (1954), sociologists started paying attention to the phenomenon of faction in order to analyse the Indian village politics. Lewis was a pioneer in studying factions and credit goes to him for inviting attention to a very important aspect of the socio-political life in the Indian village.

Most of Lewis' assumptions and conclusions have been questioned by scholars, because they tended to give them a substantive reality and permanence which they did not find elsewhere [Baviskar, 1974: 441; Benedict, 1957: 338; Mayer, 1957: 328; D.F. Miller, 1965: 17; Nicholas, 1963: 22-33; Pocock, 1957: 297]. The findings of researchers who did not mention about Lewis' conception, nevertheless contradicted this. For example, Beals found that "the basis of factions cannot be established by reference to previously existing groupings. The factions need not represent opposed caste, a conflict between progressive conservative, or a conflict between economic groups" [Beals, 1959: 443].

One can recognize various conceptual types of factions in the studies on Indian local level politics; these were considered by different scholars in their own way. Firth defined factions as "groups or sections of a society in relation of opposition to one another, interested in promoting their objects rather than those of the society as a whole and often turbulent in their operations" [Firth, 1957: 292], while Mayer refers to them as "temporary groups recruited over particular disputes" [Mayer, 1960: 121]. Srinivas opines that "factionalism was different from other units of the structure in that membership was to some extent voluntary unlike with caste and lineage" [1979: 221]. Nicholas also defines factions as conflict groups, and the conflict as political competition for public power; factions are not corporate enduring groups, members are recruited by a leader and drawn for diverse reasons and principles [Nicholas, 1965: 44-46; 1966: 52-57]. The difficulty in describing factions is narrated by many scholars like Berreman [1963: 265], Dube [1968], Hitchcock [1956: 262], Karve and Damle [1963: 45] and R. N. Sharma [1979: 122].

Thus, the term faction has been used inconsistently by sociologists, mainly due to the lack of a proper definition. Significantly, the fluidity and ambiguity of clear boundaries lie among the salient features of a faction. For the purpose of complete understanding of the term in such a difficult situation, it seems proper to re-examine the whole problem.

Some important issues that appeared in the studies of Indian village factions are (i) permanence, (ii) composition of membership, (iii) openness of membership, and (iv) political role of factions.

First, Lewis defined the permanence of factions that "they are both relatively inflexible in membership" [Lewis, 1954: 14]. Pocock [1957: 296, 300] says that "factions are not permanent but are expedient groupings temporarily created through a coincidence or conflict of interest, the resolution of which automatically terminates the faction's *raison* and therefore its existence". Eventually, Lewis' description of permanence feature has been denied, as the faction exists only for short term. However, the short term existence means the "ephemeral changing their composition with the issue" [Benedict, 1957: 337; Nicholas, 1965: 27-29; and also Pocock, 1957: 295-296].

Secondly, the membership composition, or the alliance of a faction is the only feature which was found to be constantly changing. The membership composition of a faction is changing whenever different issues occur. Contrary to this composition stables the core element in the faction. The core element, or the nucleus, of the factions remains relatively steady.[1] Beals and Siegel [1966: 397] found that only wealthy men were able to maintain a relatively consistent number of followers while the membership composition of the opposed factions was found to have changed three times during a short period of three months. The faction is generally made of a few core families, rich and powerful enough to generate a field of influence and withstand challenges from other families. It is important that the core element does not have to be always constituted by the wealthy men, instead it is only large, influential and well-to-do families which make up the core [Berreman, 1963: 266].

According to Lewis, factions are necessarily "small cohesive groups within castes" or "primarily kinship groupings" [Lewis, 1954: 14]. But other researchers [Hitchcock, 1956: 258-259; Beals, 1961: 34; Berreman, 1963: 267] noted that village people provided political support within the intra-group of kinship or jati as a natural tendency.

Thirdly, as for the extension of membership, factions cut across kinship and jati lines. However, factions also tend to provide a common platform of action to the members of the different jatis and kinship to bring them together. It provokes the individuals to enter into inter-personal relations that cut cross the boundaries of established groups. Lewis mentions "instance of members of one joint family joining up with opposite factions" [Lewis, 1958: 148]. Several other scholars also indicated the same situation, e.g. Epstein has observed in a South Indian village that only one man of the dominant caste had associated himself with a faction other than that of his lineage [1962: 130]. Pocock too reported [1957: 298, 300] that even brothers were potentially members of opposed factions; Berreman [1963: 267] also noted a case where brothers belonged to different cliques. It is clear that extension of factional membership is not identical to kinship and jati groupings. Especially, the fact that faction membership cuts across jati lines has been noted by Baljit Singh [1961: 9] and Khare [1962: 212].

Fourthly, the political role of factions is the issue which makes the difference between Lewis' conception and the findings of subsequent researchers. Lewis [1955: 159] has noted that factions served no political functions and it was one of the major distinctions that he described between North Indian villages and Mexican villages. However, the later researchers emphasized that factional behaviour is one of the most significant indications of the political process existing in the village. As political activity is organized resulting in conflict over power and prestige, factional behaviour becomes political. Pocock [1957: 296] noted that "the behaviour of a faction is such that it attempts to bend the power and potentiality of the whole, of which it is a part, to its own particular interests and dominate the other faction or factions which are similarly motivated". Even in the case of a conflict, the beginning may involve a purely economic quarrel between two individuals with hardly any political implications but it does not remain so for long. The conflict will involve factional interests very soon, and the original issue becomes a test of strength, prestige and resources between the opposing factions.

One can understand that all the factional behaviour arises out of political interests. The political process of faction indicates that factions feed themselves, keep alive and moving. The only important goal is "bringing down" of the opposing faction, and the initial economic consideration, if any, becomes secondary. In fact, the factions involved endure much economic expenses in order to get their final political goals. Opler [1959a: 141] reports from a North Indian village that at the time of village elections, the two factional leaders picked up their own candidates for each of the twenty-eight constituencies, paid the required fees on their behalf, and cleared up their tax arrears. And besides, the high expenses often incurred on court litigations are generally out of proportion to the economic considerations involved; this can be explained only in terms of the political motivations of the warring factions.

I have examined herein four important problems of Indian village factions, but there still lies another aspect of factional politics which deserves attention. This other aspect is that factionalism is not a conflict between the "haves" and "have-nots", nor is it a conflict between higher and lower jatis. The jati groups formed the sharp line of cleavage from time to time, or at least their core elements are drawn from within the dominant caste of the village. This dominant caste is the supreme position of the main land-owning group which has traditionally controlled most of the economic and political power in the community. The village studies from various parts of the country indicate that this dominant group has managed to be resilient in the face of various changes which have been introduced during the last forty five years.

So far as factionalism is an expression of the conflict for political prestige, it has been limited especially to the dominant group. McComack said that "....open factional allegiance is... limited to economically independent households, in which the head does not fear physical assault from members of (the) opposed faction" [1956: 10, 1959: 440-441]. It is also found that the dominant group of Rajputs in a Himalayan village was the only group large enough to permit its members to form factional alignments [Berreman, 1963: 265]. The size of the dominant group has other effects on the nature of factions. For example, Nicholas [1963: 19] found in a comparative analysis of three West Bengal villages that in two of the villages where the dominant group was also the majority group, political action on the part of any member of that group was likely to meet great resistance, because most of the people in those villages were equals to his jati. And then, there are villages where the economic and political power is shared by several jatis. In such a situation the core element of various factions may be spread over these various groups. Beals studied 30 villages in a small region of South India and concludes that villages with a single dominant caste had conflict within that dominant group whereas villages which lacked such dominant group had conflict between jatis [1961: 33-34].

It is clear that the above studies could not indicate that jatis groups other than the dominant caste have remained outside factional politics. The lower jatis, the group which are usually not dominant in the village, have been gradually involved in the village factional politics because of the introduction of several new large-scale political, social and economic changes. Naturally, as even earlier, the traditional *jajmani* system which tied several different jatis' families to those of the dominating group provides means and mechanism for support and alliance across jati lines. Berreman [1963: 265] reports that although major clique alignments were limited to the dominant Rajput group, members of other groups were also tied in, sometimes despite their own efforts to remain neutral. But, the low jati groups have always been mere passive subjects to the political tactics of factional leaders. Because of their low social and economic status, they have not wielded much political power. However, if an opportunity occurred they did not fail to make use of it in their own interests. Opler described in his study of village elections as to how the members of the low jatis tried to gain various concessions from the contending parties [1959a: 143]. Rowe [1960a: 349] provides another account of a low jati members exploiting an election situation by extracting cash rewards for support to the contestants in the dominant group. According to these evidences, the observation of Nicholas [1963: 53] that "members of subordinate caste may be merely 'human resources', (and) not participants in the political system" does not appear to be very tenable.

The above significant characteristics of factionalism in Indian village are documented by the empirical findings of several scholars. These may be presented in the form of generalizations:

1. Factions are not permanent corporate groups. Their membership composition is fluid, and their boundaries are seldom, if ever, clearly defined.
2. Factional membership is not necessarily limited to jati or kinship groupings.
3. Factionalism is not a class conflict; it is neither a conflict between the "haves" and the "have-nots" nor is it a conflict between higher and lower jati groups.
4. Factionalism is an expression of political struggle for power and prestige within the group of dominant caste(s), and tends to reach into other jati groups for support and alliance. Economic considerations, when present, tend to get overshadowed by political considerations.
5. The subordinate jati groups are not necessarily passive participants in the village factional conflict. Whenever possible, they make use of the factional strife to their own advantage.

The extent to which these generalizations hold true in the village of this study is a subject of investigation here.

II. Explanations for Factionalism

The preceding summary of research findings shows that we have come a long way from Lewis' original conception of faction. Many dimensions have also been revealed to suggest the dynamic nature of factional behaviour. However, inquiry into a social phenomenon is not complete by simply describing its nature. We have to go beyond that to search for those causal factors which can 'explain' the phenomenon. This search is particularly challenging when we realize that factionalism, perhaps universally prevalent in Indian villages, does not constitute the totality of the village scene. As noted in the following section, the phenomenon of factional conflict has to be viewed within the context of numerous modes of mutual cooperation which is an equally significant aspect of village life.

Most of the literature on the Indian village has been largely descriptive, providing only insights into the forms and processes of factional behaviour. Theorization about factionalism, as and when it was done, has either been limited to sharpening the definitions of factions and other related concepts, e.g. what a faction is and what it is not (something of a kind we have attempted in the preceding section), or has resulted in taxonomies, distinguishing one form of behaviour from the other. Nonetheless, a few attempts to look for possible explanations have also been made. It is possible to discern two different approaches in these attempts.

1. First Theoretical Approach

The first of these approaches tends to find the explanation for factionalism in such external factors as acculturation, stressed from outside the system, monetization, intervention from the central governmental authority, and similar aspects in the system. This explanation rests on the assumption, implicitly or explicitly, that until a few decades, or at the most a century ago, the Indian village was a picture of perfect peace and harmony, with little room for competition or conflict. It was a well-knit social organization where every unit, every subsystem "formed an interlocking and mutually reinforcing unity" [Beals, 1954: 234]. It is further argued that this harmony and unity was gradually disturbed by the coming to power of the Britishers and by the introduction of several new measures which interfered with the autonomy of villages. The following two paragraphs substantiate this line of thinking:

For several decades, as a well-knit social organization the

village community has been slowly but steadily declining. As the pursuit of individual interest within and outside the village has become more common, the influence of the community over its members has diminished. In this situation conflicts of interests within the village have sharpened and the process continues [Singh, Tarlok, 1955: 203].

The breakdown of the community spirit which is what faction implies, the absence of enlightened leadership, the increasing influence of jati and communal friction, the apathy of villagers and their feeling of haplessness and dependence on outside government agencies for effecting improvements in their lot – it is these factors which are characteristic of the village in a state of decadence brought about by the changes of the last one hundred years [Jayaram, 1947: 138].

Talking about a Pakistani village, not very far from the Indian border and part of the same socio-cultural milieu, Inayat Ullah [1958] says that only twenty years back Tarawala was a village with peace, harmony, and cooperation, despite the fact that its population was even more heterogenous, McCormack [1956: 11] attributes the growth of factionalism to such factors as shift from subsistence type farming to cash farming and direct government interference in village affairs. According to Rao [1963: 13], the recent administrative measures have opened up "new areas of conflict.... resulting in the loss of the traditional basis of harmony".

On the other hand, there are others who have categorically stated that factionalism is not a new phenomenon in Indian village society; Baljit Singh's statement on this issue was noted earlier. Hitchcock [1956: 69-73] writes about the "tradition of lawlessness" in Khalapur village which included cases of faction, feuds, robberies, cattle-thefts, etc. Cohn [1954: 136], too, notes that in Senapur factionalism, rivalry, jealousy, and friction between groups had always existed and often found expression in open fights, killings, and house burnings.

How, then, can this issue be resolved? Beals tries to do so by making a distinction between regulated and unregulated conflict. Unregulated conflict, according to him, is one which has very few rules governing it, few efficient mechanisms for controlling it and it thus, remains unresolved. It is this kind of conflict which he calls factionalism, or pervasive factionalism. About Namhalli village he says: "It cannot be stated categorically that Namhalli in 1900 was without factionalism, but there is evidence that the village possessed a high degree of autonomy and well developed capacity for resolving and regulating such conflict as occurred within it" [1954: 235].[2]

This approach raises many questions. First, is it proper to limit factionalism to only those conflicts which are 'unregulated' and 'unresolved'? If a conflict is resolved, it is not factional. But, as pointed out by D.F. Miller, [1965: 18], most of the conflict is periodically or temporarily resolved. Yet the conflict continues, perhaps on different issues, along different dimensions, and involving different persons. It seems that by so limiting the definition, one only tends to deny a reality which has perhaps been always there.

Secondly, this approach relies, for obvious reasons, on the memory of a few old people living in the community. Beals does not make any secret of the fact that he got the information about conflict in this pre-1900 Namhalli from the older people of the village [1954: 235, also Beals and Siegel, 1966: 46]. It is on the basis of such evidence only that he concludes that in those days "there was warm and reassuring sense of solidarity, mutual support and order" [1954: 235]. The extent to which a researcher can rely on the "recall" of a few of his respondents is a relevant methodological question. But besides that, those who have worked in Indian villages are quite aware of the fact that there is often a tendency on the part of the older villagers to glorify the past. Hitchcock [1956: 72-73] reports, for example, that despite the general tradition of lawlessness in Khalapur, it is the tradition of peace and harmony to which the Rajputs look with pride. Evidence of this kind is even more questionable when it is used as a key foundation on which to build one's theoretical argument.

There is no doubt that the villages in India enjoyed, till very recently, much autonomy and the picture which emerges from this past is one of self-sufficient, peaceful, and harmonious village life. But one has to keep in mind that this picture emerges mostly from the impressionistic accounts of early British administrators like

Munro, Elphinstone, Metcalfe, Maine and others,[3] who know what went on inside the villages. Bailey [1965: 4] puts it: "We have no means of knowing how consensus was reached in those days, or on how many occasions it was not reached".

It could also be argued, as done by Tinker [1963: 68] and Mayer [1958b: 193] that the solidarity, cohesiveness, and harmony in village life, as observed by the 18th and 19th century British administrators, was perhaps a reflection of the peculiar historical factors of that time. That period is widely known as *gardi-ka-wakht* ('time of troubles'). The Central government had collapsed and new powers were rising at different places. A sense of insecurity prevailed over the countryside. Local communities had to fend for themselves against marauders and the exaction of local tyrants, who were trying to exploit the situation of political instability. It is not surprising that in the face of such constant external threat the villages adopted a front of internal solidarity and cohesiveness.

This is not intended to imply that the developments of the past one or two centuries had no effect on the political life of the villages. The various inroads into village society like the establishment of legal courts, intervention by centres of governmental authority, improved transport and communication, and more recently, land reform measures, community development, establishment of statutory panchayats, etc. have been very important developments.[4] But as far as the internal politics of the villages is concerned these inroads have been primarily instrumental in changing the nature of either the political goals of village people or of the means to achieve these goals.

Factionalism, as we have noted earlier, is an expression of political struggle for power and prestige. Whether or not a given conflict is resolved is not important to understand factionalism. What is important is that it is a dynamic process resulting from the continuously shifting alliances and coalitions which people make with each other to achieve what they might think as their political goals at a given time.

In view of this, the question as to whether or not factionalism in Indian villages is a recent phenomenon could either be fruitless or naive. It is a fruitless question because the kind of processual data we need to answer it could never be obtained for the historical period. This is naive because to assert that factionalism is a result of the recent changes in the outside world tantamounts to suggest that before such changes occurred, the villagers did not vie with each other for political power, or that this never resulted in open confrontations, or that these confrontations did not require forming alliances and getting or providing support. Such assumptions seem only unwarranted.

In conclusion, it may be said that the external factors can, at best, "explain" the increase in the factional behaviour because they have provided the villagers inducements, and have added new dimensions to local politics.[5] These factors cannot explain why factionalism occurs in the first place. For this we shall have to stay within a village society.

2. Second Theoretical Approach

In its search for causal explanations, this theoretical approach looks at the way village society and its economy are organized. Several factors are mentioned in this connection. "Amoral familism" – as an ethos, forming a pattern of syndrome – has been provoked by Banfield [1958: 10-11] to explain "the inability of the villagers to act together for their common good". Speaking in the context of a 'backward' southern Italian village, Banfield goes on to present a list of seventeen "logical implications" of his rule [85-102]. Many of these implications can be found in Indian villages too. Familism is definitely an important theme in Indian culture. Opler [1959b] spent the entire length of an article to show how even most of the calendric rites, rituals, and festivals in Senapur village revolved around family needs and aimed to foster family ties. Berreman [1963: 323-324] picked out these very propositions of Banfield and examined them in the context of Sirkanda village. Although he found instances of behaviour which were not quite consistent with Banfield's implications, he still found "enough 'amoral' preoccupation with, and loyalty to, the extended family that it (was) a serious obstacle to community action and (led) to most of the ramifications which Banfield (had) listed as 'logical implications' of amoral familism" [324].

But then, how do we explain "amoral familism"? Even if we disregard the moralistic tone implicit in the terms, we cannot regard it as the ultimate answer. What causes "amoral familism"? Berreman takes another step and suggests [1963: 324] that " 'amoral' self-interest seems especially likely to occur in societies where insecurity is a pervasive factor". Insecurity, it is suggested, is caused by limited economic resources. Lewis [1958: 148] says that "one of the fundamental causes of factions is the insecurity of village life with its scarcity of land and limited resources". Baljit Singh [1961: 10, 15] further narrows it down: "Clearly, land is the issue that causes the major factional split among the dominant factions. Around the land problem lie the discord, an extreme disorganization of the village people..." Foster [1962: 47-57], after examining evidence from many parts of the world, including India, finds that "the villagers frequently are suspicious of each other, filled with envy, ready to suspect the worst about their neighbours, (and) distrustful in the extreme [50]; moreover, quarrels about property and particularly land ownership were the most frequent causes [52]. Foster continued to state that the peasant economy is essentially non-productive. The pie is constant in size and "there is no way to increase it however hard the individual works. . . . If some one is seen to get ahead, logically it can be only at the expenses of others in the village" [53].[6]

This line of argument gets further support from Coser [1956: 201] who suggested that " . . . if within any social structure, there exists an excess of claimants over opportunities for adequate reward, there arises strain and conflict". Insecurities undoubtedly cause anxieties. Scarcities generate competition. The basic hard facts are survival conditions and interpersonal relationships. Shall we say, then, that the factional conflict in Indian villages is caused by economic insecurities and limited opportunities? This may be partly so. But this position leaves many doubts. First, we have noted in our earlier discussion that factionalism is not necessarily an expression of economic struggle. We also noted that at times factional leaders even undergo economic expense to meet factional goals. We observed, moreover, that the core elements in the opposing factions were usually constituted by economically well-off families within the dominant group. Here, perhaps, writers like Foster would argue: it doesn't matter! Even these "well-off" families are still trying to improve their fate by cutting the ground from under each other's feet. This brings us to another question: where is the cutting point? At what level of economic well-being and availability of opportunities do people cease to be suspicious, envious, and distrustful of each other, and begin to work for each other's benefit? One could even ask: do they ever?

By asserting that factionalism is caused by scarcity of resources, limited opportunities, and unproductive peasant economies, it should follow that factionalism as a form of intra-group conflict does not occur in settings where resources and opportunities are not limited. Both empirical evidence and observations however do not support such a notion [see, for example, Coleman, 1957]. Factionalism in Indian villages does, in fact, assume a peculiar character but is not due as much to the limited economic resources and opportunities as to other, mainly sociological factors. We shall examine them in the following section.

Before we move on to the next section, however, it is necessary to point out an important pre-requisite for an objective study of factional politics in Indian villages: that is to free the phenomenon of factionalism from emotionalism and "moralistic" judgments usually associated with it. There is no doubt that it has some very negative effects on the village society, particularly in view of the heavy premium the new programme of development places upon a village's ability to act in unity. In a state of anxiety and frustration, there is a tendency to deplore this kind of behaviour. One would, wish there was greater unity among villagers and ability on their part to act above personal interests. But realities cannot be erased by simple wishes, regardless of how well-intentioned they are. What is necessary, therefore, is to recognize, following Simmel [1955: 14-15], that interpersonal conflict, as any other form of interaction among people, is a form of "socialization" because conflict cannot possibly be carried on by an individual alone. People disagree with each other just as naturally as they agree. This simple recognition is the pre-requisite for understanding factionalism, or for understanding other forms of human behaviour.

III. Framework and Perspective

The theoretical framework and the perspective to be suggested here draw from two important developments in the social studies. Of course both are remarkably similar in their perspectives, yet have seemingly grown independent of each other. The first one was introduced in England in the mid-fifties when a group of social anthropologists challenged what is often labelled as the structural approach, and began to emphasize a "processual approach" to the study of political behaviour and political processes in peasant and tribal societies. The second development began in the late 1950's in American sociology and has since come to be known as the "Exchange Model of Society".

1. Processual Approach

The development in British anthropology needs to be seen against the background of *African Political Systems* [Fortes and Evans-Pritchard, 1940] which remained for a long time the main source for political anthropologists in search of a theoretical framework. According to this work, political organization was viewed as "that aspect of total organization which is concerned with the control and regulation of the use of physical force" [Radcliff-Brown in Fortes and Evans-Pritchard, 1940: xxiii]. This conception of political organization began to be questioned in the fifties. In what looks like a case of defection, Schapera, for example, had himself contributed a chapter to *African Political Systems,* and observed in his later work that this definition was too narrow and inappropriate [Schapera, 1956: 217-219]. Schapera was soon followed by Barth [1959: 1] who found that at the different levels of Swat Pathan organization, physical force was not the only sanction supporting positions of authority. Other objections to this definition are implicit in the works of Leach [1954] and Bailey [1960, 1964]. Bailey also objected to the simplistic classification of acephalous and centralized political organizations offered by Fortes and Evans-Pritchard.

But more important than these questions about definition and classification is the one which relates to the theoretical assumptions underlying *African Political Systems*. The main concern in the perspective presented there was with order and stability and the function of political organization which became "...the maintenance or establishment of social order...by the organized exercise of coercive authority through the use, or possibility of use, of physical force" [Radcliff-Brown in Fortes and Evans-Pritchard, 1940: xiv]. The implications of this view are quite clear. Political organization is equated with the conventional definition of the state used in political science, and society is reduced to what Bailey [1964] has disapprovingly termed a "singly coherent structure of jural rules". The individual, as a political actor, is left with no choices. He belongs to a certain structural position, defined by his status-role set, and carries out the functions associated with this position. As Firth [1951: x-xi] has pointed out, an individual's behaviour in this perspective is treated as "primarily determined by structural considerations, the outcome of his place in a system of roles, relationships, groups, (and) social patterns". Deviation, which is considered a threat to the system, either does not take place because members have been socialized to conform to the norm, or if it does, "organized exercise of coercive authority" comes into play.

The field investigators of the 1950s however, observed a different kind of social reality in their research. Neither the conception of socio-political organization nor that of a political man as implicit in *African Political Systems* could adequately account for this reality. And a fresh approach to the study of political life began to emerge. The stage had already been set by Firth when in 1950 he first introduced the concept of social organization as distinct from social structure, and characterized it by the processes of individual choice, decision, and adjustment [Firth, 1951, 1954, 1955]. Under the influence of Gluckman's exemplary work [1954, 1955, 1956, 1965] a new School, the so-called "Manchester School", emerged gradually. Instead of "structure", the emphasis now was on "process", placing the individual actor at the central position. The importance of structural features is not denied in this approach, nor are the limits imposed by an incumbent's status-role on his behaviour underestimated. But despite these limitations, an individual is seen with a large range of choices within which he can manoeuvre his behaviour to suit his interests. Also, the society is not conceived as a single, coherent structure of jural rules but as consisting of "different sets of rules between which a member can pick and choose on different occasions" [Bailey, 1964: 1]. A Kachin in Highland Burma is, accordingly, found to occupy a status position in several different social systems at one and the same time. To him, "...such systems present themselves as alternatives or inconsistencies in the scheme of values by which he orders his life. The overall process of structural changes comes about through the manipulation of these alternatives as a means of social advancement. Every individual... each in his own interest, endeavours to exploit the situation as he perceives it and in so doing the collectivity of individuals alters the structure of society itself" [Leach, 1954: 8].

The Kachin is not an isolated case displaying such political ingenuity. Equally active are the Pathans in the Swat valley of West Pakistan who "find their place in the political order through a series of choices, many of which are temporary or revocable" [Barth, 1959: 2]. Barth also tells us that the Pathans clearly recognize the distinction between private and group advantage, and when faced with a choice they tend to consider the former rather than the latter. Furthermore, "... allegiance is regarded not as something which is given to groups, but as something which is bartered between individuals against a return in other advantages... The authority system, in both terms of the relations of dominance and submissions and of alignment of persons in groups, is built up and maintained through the exercise of a continual series of individual choices" [2].

A similar observation comes from Orissa, where Bailey found that behind a Kond's motive in giving his allegiance to a political group was his expectation to gain his ends. If, by experience, he found it more profitable to give the allegiance elsewhere, he would do so. The starting point of analysis for Bailey is, therefore, "the actor, certainly as child of his social environment and bridled by training and sanctions, but also as an active person who makes use of this social environment, and who exploits its uncertainties and ambiguities" [Bailey, 1960: 11].

The remarkable similarity in the above observations of these investigators does not necessarily mean that the overall approaches followed by them are also alike. There are some basic differences, but what is important to note is that they all depart significantly from the former approach to political organization and provide a fresh outlook. We find here the emergence of the individual actor, not detached from the social structure, nor completely free from the demands of social norms, but still perceiving, manipulating and shaping the social realities in his own ways.[7] Working within the restraints of his structural position, he is consistently and consciously trying to maximize his gains, which could be economic benefit, political power, or social prestige. But he is not alone, nor are the resources unlimited. Thus, starts a process of give-and-take of social exchange in which every interacting participant approaches and withdraws in patterns that add to or subtract from his store of power and prestige.

2. *Social Exchange Model*

The recently developed Exchange Model in American sociology provides a similar perspective. In fact, one could go back to the 1880s when Albert Chavannes, whose name has almost been forgotten but who is believed to have edited and published the first sociological journal in America,[8] proposed the principle that "profitable exchange lies at the base of all relations of men to each other, and is the groundwork on which society is built" [Chavannes, 1901: 59-60]. But it is only in the 1960s that this principle is revived and made more vital. Homans' [1958, 1961, 1964a, 1964b] work is notable in this connection. Coleman [1964, 1966] tests the principle of social exchange in his legislative game and proposes a theory of collective decision. The principles of personal gain and social exchange are also present, although in a slightly different garb, in Gouldner's work [1960] when he hypothesizes the universality of the norm of reciprocity. They occupy the cardinal position in the theory of interpersonal relations and group functioning proposed by the social psychologist Thribaut and Kelly [1959]. Jones [1964], another social psychologist regards "ingratiation" and resulting process of social exchange as the crucial factors in understanding social interaction. The deductive theoretical scheme about conflict processes presented by Boulding [1962] rests, ultimately, on the same premise. R.H. Turner's [1962] attempt to substitute an interactional and "role making" approach to the role theory for the Lintonian status-role view is another example of this trend. And, finally, Blau [1964] builds his complex theoretical scheme about power and social life on the foundations of the profit-seeking individual and the process of social exchange.

Here again, it should be noted that these students of social behaviour differ greatly from each other in details and in terms of thematic emphasis. The common thread consists of their underlying assumptions and starting points, which places them together in the same theoretical framework. Their line of argument lends further support to the work of the British social anthropologists cited earlier and places it in the broader intellectual tradition cutting through disciplinary and continental boundaries, and suggests that the political processes identified by the British anthropologists are not exclusive features of the Kachins, Pathans, or the Konds, but are indicative of a universal phenomenon.

Societies, of course, vary in their structural complexity, organizational principles, and normative standards. Human behaviour, too, is bound by its own spatial and temporal dimensions, or by the "situation" in which it takes place. But despite these situational and structural variations, human behaviour everywhere, in some important aspects, is essentially the same. Whether it is in a primitive tribe, in a peasant setting, or in a highly complex industrialized society, man is everywhere seeking rewards and his own advancement.[9] In his interaction with his fellow beings he is using his discretion, regardless of how limited his range of choices may be. He chooses "between alternative potential associates or courses of action by evaluating the experiences or expected experiences with each in terms of preference ranking and then selecting the best alternative" [Blau, 1964: 18]. Social exchange thus becomes a central principle of social life which seems to run through all kinds of interaction patterns: a love relation between two persons (Blau); a dispute over a piece of land (Bailey); an incidence of lending support to one against the other political group (Barth); the game of legislature (Coleman); or a war between nations (Boulding).

When we view the political behaviour of Indian villagers in this perspective, we can begin to understand the phenomenon of factionalism. It is interesting to note that many of the researchers of the Indian village scene have themselves observed, inadvertently perhaps, that the primary force behind factional politics is the self-interest motivation of an individual actor. McCormack [1956: 10], for example, describes factions as ".... interest-holding groups which are formed through the working of personal opportunism". Talking about a major factional dispute in Namhalli, Beals [1954: 206] observed that "...the goals of each faction–appeared to be based upon the personal motivation of the individuals involved". Khare noted that in Gopalpur individuals "...constantly changed sides in their manoeuvres for exploiting some political problem or for gaining personal or group position". They were even found to "...affiliate themselves simultaneously with diametrically opposed power groups" to enhance their gains [Khare, 1962: 212]. "Personal animosity" and the "wish for personal gain and power" are reported to be the main driving forces for factions in Senapur [Cohn, 1954: 142]. From Khalapur Hitchcock [1956: 259] reports that alliances "...which have been formed to achieve different ultimate ends tend to be temporary and continue only so long as there is mutual advantage to be gained". Srinivas [1962: 113] suggests that "...even the 'same' facts are fitted into different configurations by different people". "A few strong self-interested men" were found to be asserting their personal authority in the ex-feudal village of Fetehpura [Carstairs, 1955: 4]. In a Pattidar village of Gujarat, the nature of faction membership "...depends entirely upon the circumstances and the interests at stake" [Pocock, 1957: 300]. In Govindpur, it is "...every man for himself in village politics" [Nicholas, 1965: 45]. After making a comparative analysis of factions in five cross-cultural settings, Nicholas concludes: "individuals align themselves politically with one another primarily out of self-interest; this interest may in some cases be primarily hostility, but obviously hostility alone cannot explain the factional alignments of all the persons in any political arena" [57].

Nicholas is right, individuals align themselves primarily out of self-interest. But he is perhaps not right when he says that this interest could in some cases be primarily hostility. It seems that the interest is not in hostility *per se*; it is in something else, mostly personal gain, the pursuit of which sometimes leads a person to hostility towards some people, just as it leads him to ally with others. It may even lead him to remain neutral. Mayer found, for example, that even kinsmen tended to remain neutral in factional disputes when their personal aims and interests did not coincide with those of the other members of their kin groups [Mayer, 1957: 324]. Pocock [1957: 300] even denies that there could be any such thing as a neutral faction "... so long as their interests ... are not involved they do not concern themselves". Opler [1959a: 147] also noted that the "neutral" compromiser, trying to pacify the differences between the two contestants for village headship in Senapur, was motivated to do so more out of his personal interests than anything else.

It is interesting to note the striking similarity in the empirical observations of so many different researchers. Yet, despite this uniformity in the empirical evidence supporting this proposition, it has not been given much emphasis by the students of village India. When conclusions in the form of empirical generalizations are drawn, this important fact is generally lost sight of. One illustration of this can be seen in the undue importance accorded to the role of faction leaders. For example, one of the five generalizations presented by Nicholas [1965: 28] is that faction members are recruited by a leader. Members can be connected to a faction, he suggests, only through the activity of the leader. A similar suggestion has been made by Firth when he says that "(factions)....are mobilized and made effective through an authority structure of leader and henchman, whose roles are only broadly defined and whose rewards in many cases depend upon the leader's discretion" [1957: 292].

Now, the importance of faction leaders cannot be denied, particularly in view of the superior position they almost invariably occupy in the village society of India. But to leave the membership and its rewards to the leader's discretion, and to suggest that the members are recruited by the leader, is not only minimizing the freedom and discretion enjoyed by the members but also denying the force of self-interests which motivates them to join one or the other faction leader, or none at all, evidence of which has already been presented. It is not a question of who is more important between the two. Both are complementary to each other; leaders do not need the supporters any less than the supporters need the leaders. The relationship is one of reciprocity. One is of course, in a better position by virtue of greater resources at his command. But the acquisition, and particularly the retention of this position requires legitimation in the form of continual acquiescence from the supporters. This acquiescence does not come automatically. What one gets from others normally depends upon what others are willing to give. And this "giving" is seldom, if ever, unconditional. The conditions vary with the range of choices open to an individual in a given situation, which, in turn, never seem to be nil because of the competition which goes on endlessly between the seekers of power positions.

3. Two Important Corollaries

The perspective presented here suggests two important corollaries. First, in villages each individual is potentially an important political actor. Decision-making on broad community wide issues is not an exclusive responsibility of the political elite. Every individual, directly or indirectly, participates in the process. This participation does not have to be active. Passive inaction is equally significant. It is a rightful exercise of a political choice which the actor thinks appropriate for the occasion. "Apathy" and "indifference" – the terms widely used to characterize Indian peasantry and held responsible for thwarting the progress of the programmes of planned change, when viewed in this perspective become deliberate and calculated "actions". These people are usually neither apathetic nor indifferent; on the contrary, they are keenly interested in whatever is going on in the village and are often aware of the issues involved. Their "indifference" lasts only until they realize that their own interests are likely to be affected one way or the other.

Second, this perspective also helps us understand better the phenomena of normlessness, lawlessness, lack of orderliness, etc., observed as part of the political processes by so many researchers. Beals [1954: 1] talked about the lack of rules which governed factional conflict, and also the lack of agreement as to what the rules were. Hitchcock [1956: 255-256, also see Hitchcock and Minturn, 1963: 260] suggested that the most evident and important aspect of political behaviour in Khalapur was its normlessness. He even noted some resemblance between the intra-village conflicts and a war between states. The legal courts, according to him, became a kind of battle-ground. In Senapur, "...bringing a false case is one of the most effective means of involving an enemy in difficulty and expense. The courts and legal systems are looked upon as something to be manipulated and used for one's own ends" [Cohn, 1954: 147]. Opler [1959a: 142] noted how the school records of an adamant low jati contender for village headship were changed to disquality him for election on grounds of age. A series of studies in the area of land legislation has revealed similar practices with regard to land records. Does all this suggest that the Indian village is a normeless society?; or is it that the people who live there do not abide by the norms any more? Affirmative answers to these questions would be an over simplification of a complex reality. What the aforesaid issue suggests, however, is that any conception of society with a single structure of jural rules and norms will not be an adequate one. Societal norms have to be conceived as constantly in flux, being shaped and reshaped by an interplay of actions which in turn are determined by the actor's perceived self-interests.

IV. The Context and the Limits

No incident takes place in a vacuum. Goals and self-interest need some kind of a yard-stick by which they get determined. Norms too, regardless of how flexible they are, emerge only in a social collectivity which upholds them. The same is true of "action" which needs a context to give it meaning and relevance. Despite all the negative connotation which have come to be associated with the term "factional behaviour" it could not have taken the kind of pattern which it seems to have taken without at least some degree of legitimacy in the society in which it takes place.

The village as a social unit provides the context, meaning and legitimacy to the behaviour patterns which are found to obtain there. It is in this context that the villagers perceive their self-interests and goals. In seeking explanations for factionalism in the external factors, the village has often been relegated to a passive role, as if it and its inhabitants had no identity of their own. Some scholars have even argued that the Indian village does not possess any substantive sociological reality [see, for example, Dumont and Pocock, 1957: 18, 26; D.F. Miller, 1965: 18-19]. This does not seem true.[10] The village, of course, functions within the wider social,

cultural, economic and political frameworks and is subject to many
of their pressures. But these pressures do not affect the life of the
people directly. The village as a collective entity serves as a buffer,
absorbing most of the initial impact. By the time these external influences get filtered down to the people, they have already been
translated into the local idioms as expressed in the symbols of
dominance, power, prestige, and a myriad other forms of interpersonal relationships. A road, authorized by an external governmental agency to pass through a village, for example, is not seen by
its residents as simply a mode of efficient transportation which is
likely to benefit the total community. Its merits are judged rather
on the grounds of personal gains, not economic gains necessarily
but gains in the local power struggle. The institution of Panchayat
is, for the villagers, not only a form of local government to plan
and execute programmes of village development, much as the
planners to plan at the state and central level would want it to be;
it also becomes a means to carry on the existing patterns of inter-
personal and inter-group relationships. As Opler once observed:
"The edicts of the village Panchayats are often interpreted as attempts of one group or another to seize power or seek its own
advantage" [1960: 195]. The failure of land reform measures to bring
the desired results was not due as much to their wrong conception
as to the fact that they lost much of their original meaning in the
process of "translation" by the villagers.[11]

The same could be said about almost every other measure of
change introduced by the "external" world. The point being stressed
here is that the village is a very real and significant social unit.
It is a world by itself and an arena which provides its own framework
for people to operate in. It is in the context of village life, village
history, village resources, village people and their interpersonal
relationships that factionalism and other modes of behaviour assume
meaning. To quote Marriott [1955a: 178]:

> If there were not compelling awareness of the village as a dis-
> tinguishable world, then why would people fight inside one
> village so intensely as they do through litigation and through
> ceremonies? Indeed, there is a local stage on which relative
> dominance and relative prestige must be fought out in the
> village. Few fights within castes but outside the village can

compare in intensity with these many local fights.

The above observations will be more easily appreciated if we realize that we are talking primarily about a traditional peasant society. This means a society which is "closed" in nature, with little history of inward or outward mobility except for the exchange of spouses within a small cultural region. This also means a society which has a functionally diffused and undifferentiated role-structure and primary-group type relationship pattern. All these characteristics of the society have their influence on the political behaviour of the people. The village, for one thing, becomes much more than merely a place to live. To use Marriott's explanation [1955a: 178] again, it becomes "...a focal point of reference for individual prestige and identification". People do not just live in the village; they belong to it. Almost all their life activities are centred around the village. The means of their livelihood, the sources of their joys and sorrows, the levels of their aspirations, the symbols of their prestige and status, all are somehow linked to the interpersonal relationships of the villages. In a society like this, factions or disagreements are not simply the expression of one or the other "rational" viewpoint, nor are they weighted by economic considerations only, but they also become the sources of personal satisfaction and means for achieving status.

Relationships in these villages are intimate and total. People not only know each other, they know "too much" about one another. There is hardly any detail in an individual's personal life or even in the history of his preceding generations which is not known to others. Inter-family animosities are inherited through several generations. Opler [1959a: 140] calls it the "heritage of inter-family rancour". This, coupled with the fact that the role-structure is so undifferentiated that in almost all the life activities one deals with the same set of people, makes it almost impossible to isolate a given issue of disagreement. As Bailey [1965: 5] has pointed out:

> You can quarrel bitterly with your neighbours if you live in certain areas of London, Manchester, or Leeds and still get on with the business of making a living, taking part in politics, worshiping your God, and maintaining amicable relationships with your kinsmen, because all these activities have nothing

> to do with your neighbours; but you cannot do this in Bisipara,
> Tikopia, or even Pentrediwaith, because some or even all of
> these activities are likely to involve you with the same set
> of people.

People are related to each other in so many different ways that no
single role gets specifically defined. Division of labour is there,
and quite an elaborate one, since most jatis have their specialized
functions. But it is not in the specialist's role alone that a person
is known to his fellow villagers. It is a society characterized by
what Gluckman has called "multiplex relationships" [1955: 19-20].[12]

Leadership, as it is understood in modern western world, does
not exist in a society like this.[13] There may be a few people with
greater resources and power at their command who, on that basis,
may also be able to exert a certain amount of influence over others.
But they would not be recognized nor would they overtly assert
themselves as "leaders". What Berreman [1963: 283] observed in
Sirkanda village is perhaps true elsewhere too: "...there is no
generally recognized leadership in the village. ...No man is in a
position to tell others outside his family what to do. Villagers found
it hard to conceive of an influential leader". In fact, leadership in
such a setting is "...considered to be a threat to the group, rather
than a necessary instrument for its functioning" [Foster, 1960-1961].

One would expect that in a society characterized by these features,
inter-group conflict will be far more intense, pervasive, cumula-
tive and will have far more serious consequences than in a society
where the relationships are factional and role-structure is highly differentiated. This is not saying anything new. About a hundred years
ago Simmel suggested a similar principle [1955: 43-45]. And, about
half a century later, the same idea appeared in Coser [1956: 68-
69]: "...in groups wherein ties are diffused and affective, engaging
the total personality of their members... there is a greater likelihood
that non-realistic elements will enter into realistic conflict situations, (in such groups) conflict will be intense and passionate".
The nature of political behaviour and political processes thus
depends upon the nature of society in which they take place.

However, the role of society, the village in this case, is not limited
only to providing the context and framework for its members within

which they perceive their self-interests and goals, or to determining the nature of their political behaviour and the resulting political processes. Society, through its structural features, plays yet another limiting role. It determines the range of choices open to any member by ascribing to him a certain position in the over-all social structure. This position is defined in terms of such structural features as age, sex, kinship network, and jati. An individual has no control over his structural position; it is ascribed to him by birth. He is born on a certain date which determines his age for the rest of his life and thus conditions his political role in relation to other members. The older a person is, the higher becomes his position in the status system of the community. Gender is important too, because it is the men who exercise most political choices, except perhaps in the case of a widow who heads a family. But here it is the male role of the family-head which gives her political status. Then, to be born in certain kinship group imposes its own restrictions on the alternatives available to a person. This works not only in his relations with other members of his own kinship group but also with the rest of the community. The heritage of land and other property as well as of inter-family animosities which a person acquires by belonging to a certain kinship group largely influences his political role and relationships. And, finally, there is the jati, whose restrictive functions hardly need elaboration because of the proverbial reputation it enjoys in sociological literature.

But these structural features do not dictate the political relationships which an individual possesses with his fellow beings. They only restrict the range of choices open to him. As pointed out earlier, an individual, because of his structural position, may possess a larger range of choices as compared to others and thus may enjoy a better bargaining position in his exchange relations. This unequal distribution of choices could also, at times, lead to a unilateral exchange[14] thereby resulting in the differentiation of power. This kind of exchange is not infrequent in a jati society where certain members enjoy an almost absolute command over most of the productive resources. But since these resources are not the monopoly of an individual but are shared by many who are constantly competing among themselves for greater personal command, and since those who do not share in these resources are trying, on their part, to improve their own bargaining position in order to get out of the situation of unilateral exchange, the political relations seldom, if ever, take permanent shape. They are contractual and revocable and are characterized by manoeuvres and shifting loyalties. This is further helped by the fact that individuals are related to each other in more than one way. A disadvantage in one field can thus be countered by an advantage in another.

There is yet one more important consideration which has to be taken into account before the argument is summarized. The discussion of social organization lies with the individual actors. The village as a collective site looks like a battle-ground where everyone guided by his interest-motivations is trying to edge out everybody else. But this is not a totally correct picture. We have already noted some of the restrictions imposed on individual's choices and behaviour by overall nature of society and by its structural features. But there is more to it. Society, whether it is the village or the larger unit of which the village is a part, is not a "sand dune" consisting of loosely organized individual units. It is marked by stability and continuity, sustained by its traditions and by its ethos. Values develop in it and become part of the total pattern. People tend to take many things for granted. Much of their behaviour — be it in the nature of conflict, competition or cooperation — is institution-alized, habitual and predictable. Not every action is therefore a calculated move to meet one's own self-interest. At times, it is only a spontaneous response to the demands which village society through its traditions, ethos, and values, makes on its members. It is these demands which make it feasible for the members to coexist and cooperate with each other while still engaged in competition and conflict. Competition and conflict, after all, do not constitute the totality of the village scene. Talking about the village Namhalli, Beals [1954: 25] once wrote: "In addition to those aspects of Namhalli which are dominated by conflict, there is another Namhalli, a Namhalli where people earn their living, practise their religion, and carry on together and in cooperation and essential processes of life". The same is true about any other community which is studied thoroughly. Conflict and cooperation are thus two equally real faces of society. Nor is it any more a question of personal disposition or value orientation of the researcher. The Redfield-Lewis debate

on the Tepoztalan material has already become old-fashioned.[15]
Thus, while on the one hand evidence from literature suggests that
villagers in India are constantly engaged in conflict behaviour, on
the other hand we gather from the same sources that people value
cooperation and unity and openly deplore the lack of it in their inter-
personal relationships [Hitchcock, 1956: 72-73; Mayer, 1957: 324,
399]. Evidence from literature also suggests that it is not bemoaning
alone which reflects these values. In numerous ways people extend
their hands to each other and add to each other's comforts and ease
in life. Everyone knows who are the people around him on whom
he can depend whenever the need arises. There are two other notable
modes of cooperation besides these instances of isolated individuals
and families helping each other. First, when a group closes its ranks
to present a united front against an external threat. This could occur
at any structural level: a family, an extended kin group, a jati, or
the whole village, depending upon where the impact of the threat
was felt. Secondly, there are cases where the issue involved is of
a traditional or sacred nature: marriages, death, festivals and even
epidemics which require invoking the blessing of the village deity,
are occasions when people usually put aside their internal rivalries,
at least temporarily, to engage themselves in cooperative venture.
It is in the context of these modes of cooperation that the phenomenon of factional conflict has to be viewed.

V. Summary

This study attempts to provide an analytical description of the
political behaviour in a peasant community of North India. By the
term "political behaviour" is meant all those activities through
which a man, in competition which others, attempts to retain or
enhance his public power. Since "power" implies control over resources, whether human or material, political behaviour includes
all those activities whereby a man tries to achieve or retain control
over resources, or men or both. The major political processes in
the village, like decision-making on community-wide issues,
factional alignments, exercise of political power, and submission
to it, are either direct consequences of or are largely affected by
this competitive activity.

Since factionalism largely characterizes the political scene, it receives a major share of attention. Two sets of questions will guide this inquiry; one, concerning the nature and form of factionalism and the other seeking an understanding of causes of factionalism. As far as the first is concerned, five summary generalizations have been presented earlier in this chapter. This study will examine the extent to which these generalizations hold true in the village.

The second question, concerning an understanding of the causes of factional politics in Indian villages, requires attention at two separate points of focus: first the context and second, the political actor. The context is provided by the village which serves at one and the same time several important functions. In provides the frame of reference – the arena – for its members to carry on the struggle for relative dominance and relative prestige. It gives meaning, relevance, and legitimacy to their behaviour. It determines their goals and self-interests and provides the channels through which they can reach these goals. Its traditions, ethos, and values enable the members to cooperate and coexist with each other despite the on-going competition for political power. Because of its peculiar organizational principles and structural features, (primary group-type relationship pattern and functionally diffused and undifferentiated role-structure), it determines the over-all character of the political activity in the village. The structural categories (age, sex, kinship and family groupings, ownership of productive resources, and jati) also determine the range of choices available to its members within which they can manoeuvre their political strategies. Then, the uneven distribution of these choices causes what Blau has called the unilateral exchange, resulting further in the differentiation of power.

The other point of focus is the political actor, the villager, who is viewed as rationally working for his own advancement by pursuing his self-interests and goals. He functions within the framework of his society, and is aware of the obligations and limitations imposed upon him, but still enjoys a range of alternatives within which he manoeuvres his relationships. His behaviour, in a given situation and field, is a function of how he perceives his own interests, the alternatives open to him, the resources and power at his command, and of those with whom he is interacting. Despite all the restrictive features of his structural position, his political relations are dyadic, contractual, voluntary, and revocable. They take the form of social exchange in which every interacting participant is trying to maximize his interests.

The emergence and nature of factions is a consequence of this change process. People tend to affiliate with others in order to better achieve their goals. The affiliation lasts while it remains profitable to both parties. Hence the relatively flexible nature of factional boundaries.

Leadership is factional in range and limited in effect. Political power is not the privilege of the "village elite". It is shared by every member of the community who participates actively or passively, positively or negatively — in the overall affairs of village.

It is along these lines that the political life in the village under study will be analyzed.

Notes

[1] The terms 'core' and 'support' elements in the study of an Indian village were first introduced by Bailey in a paper presented at the 16th Annual Meeting of the Association for Asian Studies, Washington, D.C., March, 1964. See Bailey [1964: 2].

[2] The same idea continues to reappear not only in Beals' own subsequent writings on the subject but also in those which he has jointly authored with Siegel. For example, in their later work they say: "Strains were present and recognized in both the community and the sacred literature, but there were established means of preventing the development of overt conflict around such points of strain" [Beals and Siege, 1966: 47].

[3] For an appraisal of these accounts, see Tinker [1963].

[4] One possible effect of these changes has been a decline in importance of sacred activities, thus reducing the area of cooperative enterprises. In Wangala, Epstein [1962: 131] tells us, many village ceremonies are no longer held because of local dissensions.

[5] Here we may recall an observation made by Marriott forty years ago. Contrasting Kishan Garhi society of about fifty-five years ago with that of the present he found that "....legal conflict and the formation of factions increased with alteration of local power groups, with complexity of social structure, with failure of caste councils, and with integration of local political structure into a wider grouping of powers" [Marriott, 1952: 332-333].

6   For a similar observation, see Nicholas [1963: 589].

7   A mention should be made here of the very significant contribution made along these lines by V.W. Turner. In his study of Ndembu village life, Turner [1957] on the one hand provides synchronic analysis of Ndembu village structure and, on the other, in the form of diachronic analysis and with the help of numerous "social dramas, impelled by all kinds of motives and private purposes, interact in may different ways" [330]. This general perspective in Social Anthropolgy has recently been gaining much ground. No longer is it limited to the "Manchester School" of British anthropology. Its widespread influence can be seen in a volume of *Political Anthropology* [Swartz, Turner and Tuden, 1966].

8   Attention was drawn to Chavannes in an article by John Knox [1963]. According to him, Chavannes, a Swiss emigrant settled in Knoxville, Tennessee, published the first periodical planned primarily for sociology. It was called *The Sociologist* and appeared between 1883-1885. His book *Studies in Sociology,* published later, contains most of the articles written for that journal.

9   Although this statement is too general to give useful predictions, it is essential as an initial point of orientation. As we shall see later in this section, the social context through the structural properties of a given collectivity as well as through its cultural ethos, imposes several limitations upon this general principle.

10 There are, of course, many other scholars who have mentioned that the Indian village is a meaningful sociological reality [e.g., Bailey, 1959: 92-97; Mayer, 1960: 132-147; Opler, 1956; Berreman, 1963: 1, 259; Marriott, 1955a].

11 A similar observation comes from Fention [1955] who, on the basis of comparative data from four different types of Indian society in America, concluded that "self-government inevitably flows from accustomed ways of political behaviour and shines through to modify whatever form of government is imposed on native peoples" [p. 330].

12 In this connection also see V.W. Turner [1966: 239]. Multiple relationships are those that "serve many interests", and are characterized by "total personality involvement in activities of all types, whether these may be defined as primarily domestic, jural, economic, political, or religious...(and) the consequences of interaction in one type tend to affect the premises of interaction in the immediately succeeding activities of another". Gluckman's concept of "multi-purposive relations", introduced by him in later work is also relevant here [Gluckman, 1965: 256-259].

[13] See, for example, Wood [1959: 381]. Wood, however, noted that the "mass" of village people will be found to be "leader-prone". But "...the leadership involved in this possible proneness of village majorities would appear to be that of persuasive, sympathetic, and well-educated non-villagers who come to stay with them" [373].

[14] See Blau [1964]. A unilateral exchange according to Blau is one where one of the parties is faced with no alternative but to continue securing help from the other.

[15] For a discussion of the issue see Foster [1960-1961], followed by comments from Lewis and Pitt-Rivers.

3

FIELD STUDIES IN CAKRA

This work is based on field studies conducted for about thirteen months between 1982 and 1983, in a village named Chakra in Jaunpur district of Uttar Pradesh, North India (referred in this work as Cakra). The investigation was carried out mainly by direct and participating observation, while the researcher was studying in Banaras Hindu University, Varanasi. No help of interpreters or assistants had been sought while living in the concerned village.

As this study is based on first-hand field work, all the findings depend on real data. And, the data used here were collected in different ways. For the correct understanding of the political situation in the village, it is necessary first to evaluate the data. Three important points are considered in the evaluation of the data: (i) the methods used to collect data, (ii) the nature of information, and (iii) the role which the researcher assumed as a field worker.

I. Evaluation of Data

One of the most accepted social survey techniques, i.e. participant-observation, was employed in this study. I tried to participate in all the relevant occasions of village life during the field work. As a part of the daily routine, interacting with others and participating in informal talks and events, and interviews with village people had been conducted.

Information was gathered by daily investigations and contact with people. The information which deals with political affairs was gained by talking with villagemen. I contacted and gained knowledge of village politics even from the women, even though the village is a highly sex-segregated society.

I tried to talk to members of all the jati groups. However, I preferred middle-aged villagemen who were key members of the two factions and their kinsmen. The other people who actively supported one faction or the other are supplemented by a companion for conversation.

I also spoke to many people from neighbouring villages and often visited these places and had also extensive contact with several government officials that included the village level worker in the Block, the Block Development Officer and his entourage, District Administrative Officers, Lekhpal, Irrigation department Officers, and Educational Institute Officers.

The census data of all households and mapping of the village was taken up in the early months of fieldwork. This was later supplemented by genealogies of important Rajput (Thakur) families, and the 'House Register' kept by the panchayat secretary.

The interview which constitutes questions on socio-economic matters was also prepared for all the heads of households. The questionnaire contained a number of questions relating to opinions on political affairs. Generally, more standardized interviews with a number of men conversant with village affairs, from investigated village and neighbouring villages were conducted. It was possible to collect several aspects of information about the disputes which occurred during my stay in the field.

The case history method has been used with a view to organizing the data, typically for drawing the political history of the village. For the purpose of focal discussion it deals with the case of panchayati raj election held in 1982.

Set in a variety of specific situations, the case study documents the various forms political behaviour in the village and also various political processes set in motion as a result of this behaviour. It is hoped that this case will substantiate the main theoretical arguments set out in chapter 2 and the observations made in the preceding pages.

The situation in the year 1982-83 is described in chapters 4 and 7 which were based upon direct observations and drawn from the accounts of villages. Of course, these accounts were not always uniform in content. In fact, people tended to interpret past events to suit their own interests and self images. However, on cross-checking with different segments of the village population, with different persons known to have been involved in a given event, and particularly with those who did not, apparently have vested interests in a given issue, nor whose involvement in a present event was likely to colour their interpretation of the past; it was often possible to establish a fairly objective version of earlier events.

Whenever possible, official records were checked to arrive at a final version. The tendency of some villagers to boast, referred to earlier, was only helpful in this. Their "confession" by and large seemed to conform to other accession. However, if with all this cross-checking no conclusive version of a certain event could be established, a mention to this effect has been made while describing the event.

A few words must be said about the selection of a particular case. As far as chapter 7 is concerned there was no problem of selection based on political implications, either in the actions or in their consequences.

But it is not so for chapter 6 which deals with historical material; it was neither feasible nor necessary. It was not feasible because no claim of including every event of political significance in the history of the village could possibly be made. This village never had, until 1950s an organized panchayat body which could have kept written records of disputes and decisions. Even if such records were available, they would still not conclude at the politically significant events which might have taken place in the past. Judging from the observations of the contemporary scene, the events that constitute political processes are far more numerous than are brought before the elders' councils, or inter-village arbitrations, or even the legal courts. There is yet another consideration. During the course of field work, many politically significant events of the past (disputes, arbitrations, community decisions, major alliances, etc.) were uncovered. But they were reported mostly in the form of gross facts, lacking the kind of data which is relevant in a study of this nature. They did not show, for example, the dynamics of personal involvement and the involvement of various structural units.

For these reasons, historical events are not described in this book. The case of panchayati raj election in 1982 presented in chapter 7 itself suggests the highly dynamic processes which characterized the village scene. The primary purpose is to provide the necessary background information for understanding in a better way the events of the field work period. Soon after starting the field work in 1982 it was observed, for example, that the village population was more or less sharply divided into two opposite factions, whose boundaries, for the time being at least, were also clearly marked because of the recently held panchayat election.

This selective procedure applied to historical events leaves an important question unanswered: To what extent is factionalism in village politics a recent phenomenon, caused by an increase in the external influences which result in a general break-down of the traditional systems of authority, control, and conflict-resolution? The question has been labelled "important" only because it has received so much attention in the recent literature on Indian villages, as indicated in chapter 2.

At a general level, the question has already been argued in the earlier pages. Here it might be added that this study has not undertaken the task of answering this question for the simple reason that it would only be a futile attempt. If factions are viewed, as continuously changing, dynamic phenomena resulting from the equally dynamic process of continuously shifting alliances which people make in order to achieve, we do not have the type of data which would provide the answer to the above question. The question arises only when factions are viewed not as a process but as structural categories, which they are not, as, this study ventures to demonstrate.

The most crucial liabilities, over which no one had control and which determined much of my subsequent role, were that the researcher was a Japanese student, a foreigner. The very first appearance of a student of sociology at the research site often provides the strongest, if not a most lasting, impression.

Besides the particular drawbacks of being a Japanese (*saheb*) that hampered my work, any field worker who seeks to collect information about politics in an arena organized mainly by faction is put in a difficult situation. I realized the importance of remaining neutral and discreet to extract the desired information and I sought to enlist the understanding of university friends.

It soon became clear that the political situation was a delicate one. Factionalism requires staunch loyalty (even if only temporary) to one's leader; hence, any divulgence of information is also treated as a personal matter. The only people with whom one speaks of such things candidly are the members of the same faction. Since I attempted to remain neutral, I was suspected by both of being loyal to the opposing side. This was highlighted by the villagers' open talk of their involvement in the local election that took place during my stay and was not greatly influenced by factional considerations.

Much of the information gathered about factional politics was from the extreme gossip, frequently quite malicious, that one side told about the other. It is, of course, difficult to assess the reliability of such data, and I often questioned whether I was learning anything at all of the true situation in the village ! A few features, however, saved me from abandoning hope altogether. There was usually some basic agreement between the version each faction gave of a certain situation. The major difference was their moral assessment of who was wrong. In addition, on rare occasions one faction would substantiate a particular interpretation given by the other side. Finally, the information given by people who were either known to be neutral or from outside the village, and hence uninvolved, was taken to be fairly reliable.

I had to be known as neutral and trustworthy because none would talk to me these on controversial affairs. I could not divulge any confidences. I was strongly committed to this approach and was eventually regarded as being either neutral or insignificant.

II.   Selection of the village

It was very difficult to select the village for a study; moreover, this task was even more complex for the researcher belonging to a foreign country.

Before the selection of village, several criteria for choosing a site were considered as follows:

1. There should be a population of at least one thousand persons to ensure the existence of a sufficiently large and active political arena to be reasonably studied in a year.
2. There should be a statutory panchayat; having contact with government development programmes that provide resources requiring distribution; and primarily relying on agriculture for subsistence (since this is true practically for all Indian villages).
3. There should be representation of one of the two major landowning and traditionally administrative jatis in the area of survey viz. the eastern part of U.P. They are either Rajputs or Bhumihars and are usually mutually exclusive in a given village.
4. The village should also record at least ten or more different jatis so that intra-jati as well as inter-jati conflicts might be observed.
5. The "people" (usually meaning the elected head of the village or any other influential men through whom initial contact is made) would have to welcome the researcher's intrusion and be able to provide some accommodation for the researcher.

Based on the above criteria, the researcher selected the village Cakra.

THE VILLAGE AND PEOPLE

I. Spatial and Temporal Aspects

Cakra (83° 02' E latitude and 25° 41' N longitude (Fig.1)[1] with a small multi-jati community is one of the 3397 villages which constitute the rural area of the Jaunpur district in eastern Uttar Predesh (abbreviated 'U.P.'). It is located about 40 Km north of Varanasi, the most sacred city of Hindu pilgrimage. To reach this village, one has to go about 34 Km by bus for more than two hours from Varanasi towards Azamgarh and Gorakhpur, on the Grand Trunk Road. After reaching a small bazaar (Bajrang Nagar), one has to walk a brick laid village road for 3 Km to reach Cakra. Many buses (state government buses) and private car services cover the distance to and fro Varanasi and Jaunpur. The bus service was started in the early-fifties. Before that, the villagers could get bullock-carts, rickshaws or private transport services.

Closeness to the large urban centre and the availability of frequent and inexpensive[2] transport have not, however, disintegrated the rural character of the village. In its social, economic and physical aspects, life in Cakra is like the villages of eastern U.P. or western Bihar. Rurality, in every sense of the term, is pronounced and rampant. It does not need social indices or indicators for its measure. From the point of view of administration, this village belongs to U.P., Jaunpur district, Kerakat tehsil (Fig. 2). Jaunpur town is at a distance of 30 Km northwest where the district headquarters and the district courts are situated. Kerakat with its tehsil office is about 8 Km west.

Village Cakra with its surrounding 84 villages is known as Dobhi

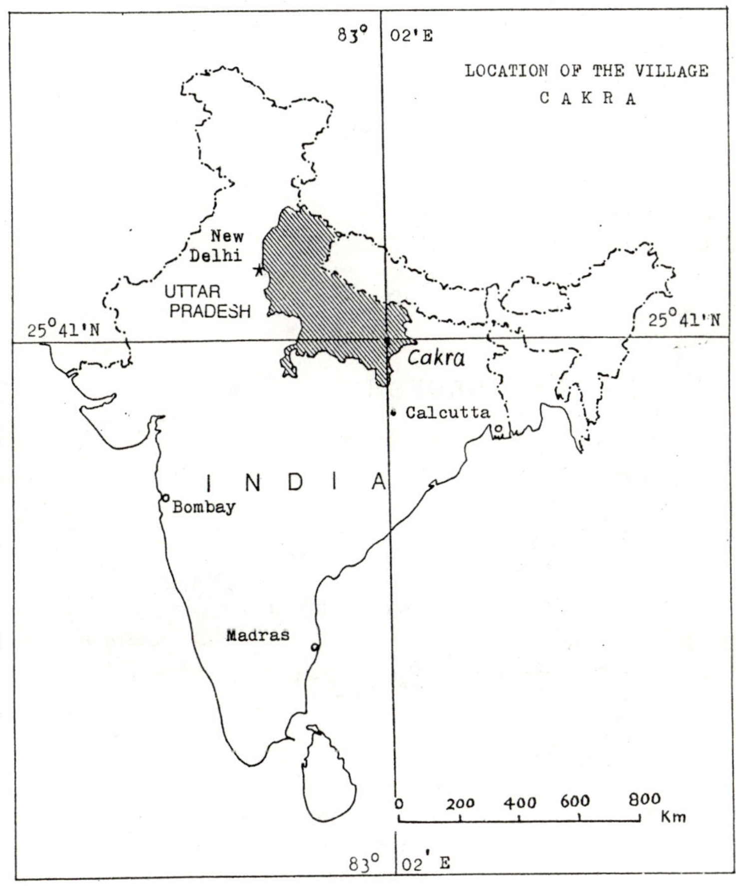

83° 02'E
LOCATION OF THE VILLAGE
C A K R A
New Delhi
UTTAR PRADESH
25°41'N
25°41'N
Cakra
Calcutta
I N D I A
Bombay
Madras
0   200   400   600   800
Km
83° 02'E

Figure 1.

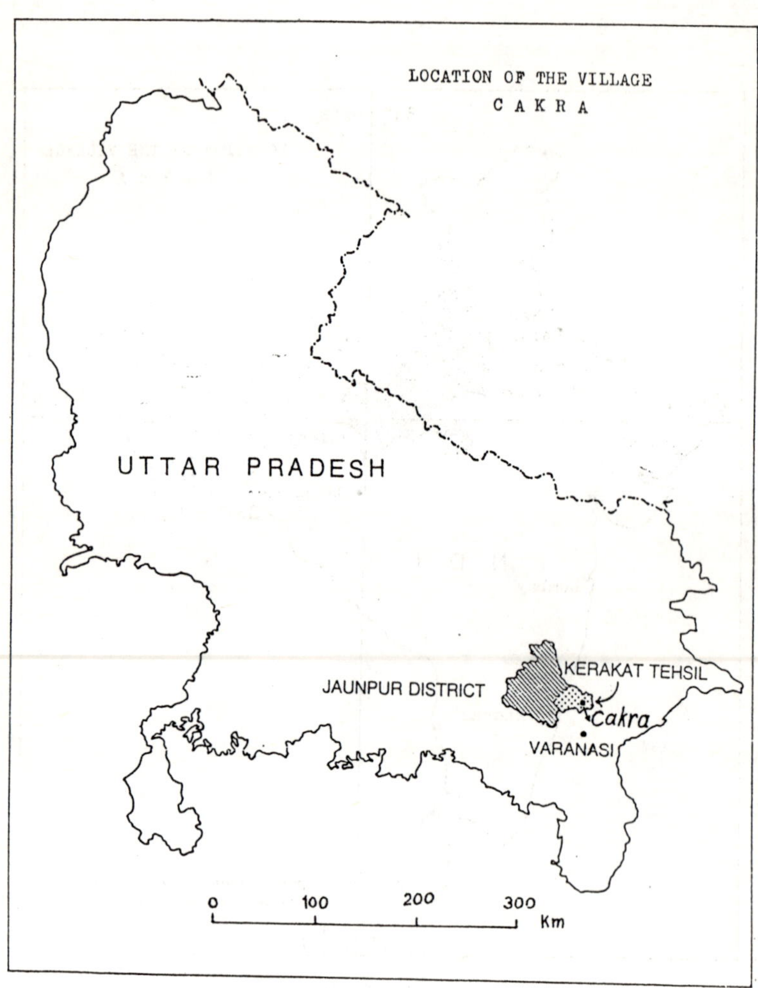

LOCATION OF THE VILLAGE
C A K R A
UTTAR PRADESH
KERAKAT TEHSIL
JAUNPUR DISTRICT
Cakra
VARANASI
0
100
200
300
Km

Figure 2 .

Pargana identified administratively with Dobhi Development Block (hereafter referred 'Block' or 'Dobhi Block'). The bazaar which has the block office and police station for this village is about 8 Km away in the southeast. A medium sized village, it occupies a long, narrow strip of land, stretching from north to south with an area of 55.44 hectares. The neighbouring village is about 3-4 Km away, and the jati groups in the village live separately.

A major part of this land (102 acres, i.e. 41.28 ha or about 74.45%) is under agricultural use, 35 acres (14.2 ha) are used for such community purposes as water ponds, roads and passages, irrigation channels, and pasture. The actual inhabited area occupies only about 27 acres (10.9 ha). As is common in this part of the country, the village has a nucleated pattern of residence: surrounded on all sides by farm lands. 27 acres of residential area, however, is not occupied by dwelling units alone. Streets, paths, drinking water wells, elementary school, and *Bhumaiya*[3] take their share too. Furthermore, a large part of this land, mostly in the periphery is used by individual households for storing their fuel, cowdung cakes, manure, farming equipment, etc. The rest provides living space to 187 households (Fig. 3) or to 1996 men, women, and children who share it with 138 bullocks, 108 cows, 207 water buffaloes, and uncounted dogs, cats, and rats. Animals play an important part in the household economy, and in many cases, are the main assets of the family. They are, therefore, treated with care and affection. In the cold nights of the winter, when a family cannot afford a separate shelter, animals, particularly the draft and milch animals, share the same living quarters with the members of the family.

Thus, for most people in village, living space is crowded, although a few well-to-do farmers own large and spacious houses. Still more significant is the fact that living in general is close and proximate. Houses stand against each other. In some cases they even overlap. Somebody's roof may hang out over somebody else's courtyard. A courtyard may itself be shared by several houses. This proximity also characterizes the distribution of work and storage areas, called the *ghers*,[4] where women and girls from different families make cowdung cakes. The women also go to the common well to fetch water for drinking and other household purposes. The village pond brings almost everyone to its shores to wash animals and to water them. People are constantly in each other's company. Regardless of how much a person tries to avoid his neighbours, he is likely to run into them occassionally. Because of the peculiar laws of inheritance and succession[5], the entire agricultural land is fragmented into many different and odd shaped pieces. A farmer may own as many as ten different plots of land located at ten different places. Therefore he has to crisscross narrow boundaries between several fields in order to reach his own small plot, which may be surrounded on all four sides by fields owned by four different persons.

All these spatial features are further reinforced by the temporal aspects of village life. The daily and yearly cycles of activities are so routinized that almost everyone carries out the same activity at about the same time. A sowing time for one is the sowing time for everybody. During the harvest season not one, but everyone, cuts crops. The canal irrigation system supplies water not to an individual farmer but to the entire village and that too for a limited period. Women, especially of lower jatis, carry meals to their working men in the fields at about the same hour. Their timings for milking the cattle, cooking meals, going to the well, working in the *gher*, and for almost all other daily activities are roughly the same. Marriages are generally held during certain months of the year, and repairs to the houses and building new ones are also carried out at a particular time of the year. One could also add to this list the numerous monthly and yearly festive days, when people perform uniform practices, carry out uniformly prescribed rituals, and eat uniformly prescribed foods.

As a result of these spatial and temporal features the villagers in general live an open and exposed life. A person is seldom alone. His fellow-beings, friends or foes are always around him. They watch his actions just as he watches theirs. Privacy is thus hard to maintain; it is not even attempted. Neither is its need nor its lack felt by the villagers. The reverse is, in fact, more true. People, especially men, are expected to live an open life. House doors are seldom closed before night fall. In fact, the men-folk generally do not stay inside their houses[6]. Those who can afford build separate men's houses, called *baithaks* preferably away from their homes. When they are not working on the fields or at their respective jobs, they sit in the *baithaks*. These *baithaks* usually have wide doors, sometimes more than one, to cover the entire front wall. When the owner is in his *baithaka*, he leaves the doors open, suggesting an open invitation to anyone who wants to come in. And people do come in, generally those who do not have their own *baithaks*. They come for a chat over the *hukkah*[7] or for a game of cards, or just to rest on a free afternoon. Even those who do not want to go to another's *baithak* do not often stay inside their houses. They simply pull out their *charpais*, chairs, and *hukkahs* and be in the company of their friends and neighbours, under the shade of a tree during the hot season, or in the open bright sun during the winter months. Staying inside the house most of the time is regarded as effeminate. The preferred thing is to stay out and in the company of other men.

The spatial proximity and the temporal congruence which characterize the situation make it necessary for the Cakra dwellers to make behavioural adaptations. These adaptations show mostly in the highly sensitive and keen perceptions of social situations which the people of Cakra have developed, as well as in the remarkably subtle and sophisticated use they make of the language and other symbols of communication. When people are constantly exposed to each other, or what they do and talk about is everybody's business, and when one's actions and interests at a given point of time are very similar to those of others, the result is a common frame of reference, common motivations, and perhaps competition (if the resources available to carry out a certain activity are limited). In a situation like this, these adaptations become necessary. The people of Cakra have learned well, for example, that words can be used to convey things, while in fact they do not carry literal meanings. They have acquired the skill, almost to the point of fine artistry, of conveying things without the use of language at all. When so much is common and shared knowledge, not much needs to be said anyway. Who is present at what place becomes a meaningful expression, as do numerous other symbolic gestures. The Cakra dwellers also realize that what appears on the surface is not necessarily the truth. They are able to make a distinction between the intended behaviour and its actual manifestation. This is the way they guide their own behaviour and judge that of others, too.

All this, however, is not uniform. The variation arises from the varying structural positions of interacting persons and from the varying situations and contexts of the interaction process. A pattern suitable in one situation or in one group becomes unsuitable in another. To understand the behaviour of Cakra dwellers, particularly the implied meaning of this behaviour, I may have to look into their motivations; but these motivations may, in turn, be contingent upon how a certain person is placed in relation to others and what the context of a certain situation calls for.

In the following section I will examine the structural arrangement of the village society. In doing so I would from time to time look at the present in the context of the past, and at Cakra in the context of the surrounding villages. Both temporal as well as spatial dimensions, although in a different sense, will further help to understand the structural organization of village society.

II. The Structural Arrangment

The two most important factors which characterize the social structure of Cakra and determine the position of its residents' perceptions, and inter-personal relations are jati and various levels of kinship organization. Age, sex, and the institution of land ownership are also important structural features but their importance is only secondary in nature, depending mostly on the first two factors.

1. Jati

All the villagers are Hindus, and they are divided in ten different jati groups, ranking from the Rajputs (called as Thakurs) at the top of the socio-economic hierarchy to the Chamars at the bottom. Table 1 gives the different jati groups with their population break-up.

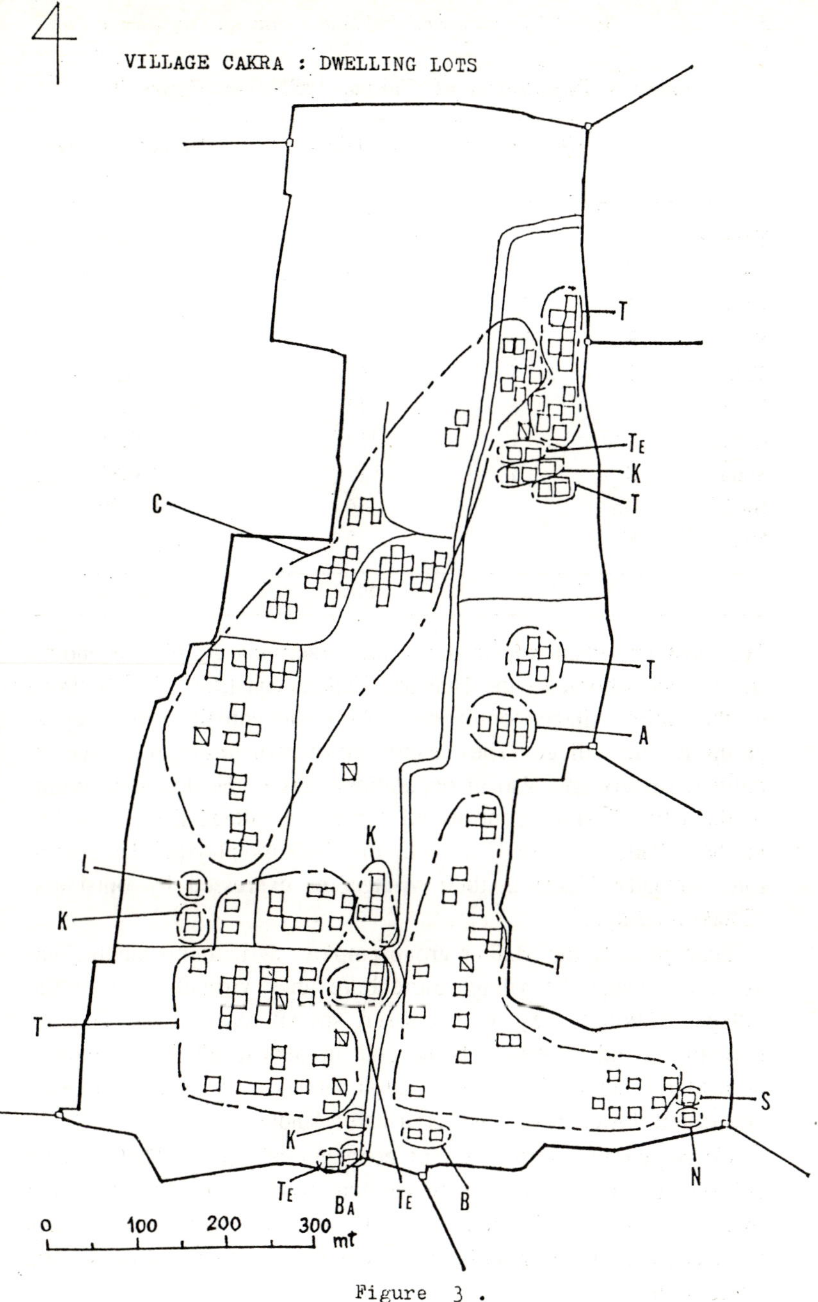

Figure 3 .

Table 1 Population of Cakra, 1982 (see figure 3)

		Households	Population	Percent & share (%)
Thakur	:T	74	948	47.49
Chamar	:C	67	609	30.51
Ahir	:A	15	154	7.72
Kahar	:K	13	108	5.41
Teli	:Te	8	64	3.21
Bhar	:B	6	56	2.81
Lohar	:L	1	19	0.95
Sonar	:S	1	17	0.85
Bari	:Ba	1	16	0.80
Nai	:N	1	5	0.25
		187	1996	100.00

The most important role in the village traditions, politics, economy and society is borne by the Thakurs. Thakurs constitute 47.49% (948) of the entire village population (1982) and constitute the largest group in the village. They exert an overwhelming influence in politics, society and also in population. This is the dominant group of the village, which controls all aspects of village life. Daily life in the village is carried on with the Thakurs playing the central role. Actually Cakra is their village; as expressed by outsiders: "Thakur-village."

Economically the Thakur group employs agricultural labour, and as they manage the village agriculture, they virtually control the village. Although they do not assert special reasons, the Thakurs normally avoid manual labour, and in almost all cases employ agricultural labour (This agricultural labour class belongs to discriminated lower class and is usually landless).

Consequently, in the peasant economy of Cakra, Thakur have enjoyed an unrivalled position of dominance. Regarding the land ownership of the jatis, more than 80% of the village land belongs to Thakurs and their agricultural activity forms the core of the village profession.

In the inter-village setting, it is known as Thakurs' area. Locally, Thakurs are the second dominant caste in the eastern U.P. after

Chamars and Ahirs [see Schwartzberg, 1978: 106, 108]. Thakurs are also called as the *Chaudharis* — the master — because traditionally they have owned most of the agricultural land in the region. Along with Jats, and to a lesser degree Ahirs and Gujars, Thakurs are the major land owners in most of northern India.

During the Aryan migration the Dobhi area was inhabited by aboriginal tribe, *Soiris*; their chief centres were Kerakat and Chandwak. By late 12th century the area came under the control of Raghubanshi Rajput clan of whom Hariharpur and Chandwak were chief clan centres. During Akbar's rule (1556-1605 AD) the region was one of the *parganas* of Sircar Jaunpur, called Khanpoor with headquarters in Chandwak. Subsequently the region, including district Jaunpur came under the rule of Benares state and so continued upto India's Independence in 1947 [see, Dinesh Singh, 1977: 78-79]. Thakurs were the pre-dominant and largest agricultural community, who had possessed 64% of landownership during Akbar's rule but by 1789-1790 their share had fallen to 55%, and by 1885 it declined to 39% [Dinesh Singh, 1977: 80-82]. Historically, they were the warriors who, moving in small tribe-like bands, conquered small areas, or opened up new unclaimed lands, and began cultivation. The growing population expanded in the surrounding new villages.[8] Many of the present day villages in the area are the result of this gradual expansion of the Thakurs [Singh, Singh, and Singh, 1976].

Cakra was founded in this manner when, about two hundred years ago, the ancestors of the majority of the present Thakur families — two brothers, named Ravindra Singh and Ashok Singh[9] — moved out of the nearby village of Kushrna to establish their own estate [Singh, Singh, and Singh 1976: 21-24]. Some other jatis in Cakra have also lived there from the very beginning, having moved in from the same parental village, while the others migrated subsequently from other nearby villages. Their arrival in the village depended upon the Thakurs' need for them. Once in the village, their sustenance too has depended upon the Thakurs and upon their land. Some of them became tenant farmers working for those who had land to rent, some worked as agricultural labourers, but most of them were tied to the Thakur families through the well-known *jajmani* system, under which they provided their jati services in return for a fixed share of the agricultural produce.

Until the first quarter of this century, the village was controlled by the *jajmani* system. It is a very significant structural change that the position of *jajmani* system in the village economy and life was reduced in the last fifty years.

Under the *jajmani* system, a Thakur family may give part of its produce to as many as eight families of eight different jatis; for example a Lohar to do the blacksmith's job; a Nai to work as the barber, etc. Not all the Thakurs keep *jajmani* ties with that many functionaries. It depends upon the need which in turn is determined by the size of land owned by a Thakur family.

The amount of foodgrains given to these functionaries also varies according to the size of land owned by a Thakur family and also from one functionary to another. Although the commitment on the part of the Thakur is in terms of fixed quantities for each crop, the quantity itself can fluctuate depending upon the relative success or failure of a given crop. A good harvest should enhance a farmer's generosity while a poor one will curtail it. The birth of a much cherished son in a Thakur family or a marriage in the household after a gap of several years would make a Thakur householder share his happiness with his functionaries by bestowing generous gifts. Thus to that extent the joys and sorrows of Thakurs become the joys and sorrows of the other jatis too.

But such dominance of Thakurs is not absolute, nor is it arbitrary. For one thing, in the ritual hierarchy they occupy only the second position from the top, the first being left for Brahmans in that order. The superior position of the Brahmans is well recognized. Even during the most casual interaction, their members are given due respect by Thakurs as well as by other members of the community. When seated on the same *charpai* they are invariably offered its upper side. They cannot smoke from a *hukkah* used by any other jatis. Most Thakur families keep separate *hukkahs* for Brahmans as a mark of deference. But, not a single Brahman lives in this village. The only occasions of such respect happen when the Brahmans of nearby villages visit Cakra.

As regards the other jatis too, the Thakurs' dominance is not wholly arbitrary. Within the *jajmani* relations there is an element of functional inter-relatedness and some degree of inter-dependence.

Each jati has an important economic function to perform, and thus enjoys its position in the village in its own right. In return for their specialized services, the members of a functional jati have certain claims which are honoured by everyone. This also gives them a type of bargaining power, and there have been occasions in Cakra when this power has been used, although in a subdued manner. In fact, to some extent jati still serves as a functional guild and protects the economic rights of its members.

For example, say, an Ahir has certain grievances against his Thakur patron, and, failing to obtain a satisfactory resolution, he decides to boycott him. If the rest of Ahirs in the village are convinced of the legitimacy of his grievance, they will support his move, in the sense that no other Ahir will be willing to work for the Thakur. As a result, the Thakur will have to either settle the grievance or function without the services of an Ahir. On the other hand, if he himself has a grievance against his Ahir, he would simply relieve him and hire somebody else. No other Ahir will work for him. The only recourse open to him is to approach the council of elders in the group of Ahirs which will deliberate on the issue and try to bring a compromise. If they find that the Thakur's grievance is genuine, they would reprimand their own jati member. If the grievance still persists, they may even decide to deprive him of his rights to serve the Thakur family and assign another member to do his job.

The dominant character of Thakurs is further limited by the fact that not all the members of given functionary jati[10] are bound by the *jajmani* relationship, particularly when there are more persons in a jati than needed by Thakurs. Even those who are so tied are not completely dependent upon the *jajmani* work. Over and above that, they are free to work for whosoever is willing to pay them. To their *jajmans* also they are committed to provide only certain specified services.

A Lohar, for example, is required under the *jajmani* obligation only to make and repair ploughs and other agricultural tools. To get a new plough made, or for any other work of carpentry — making furniture, doors, windows, etc. — he has to be paid a mutually agreed price. Moreover, many of these jatis have taken other subsidiary occupations which, although not their traditional jati callings, have almost become so by being carried on over several generations.

Members of several jatis including Ahir, Kahar, Bhar, Bari and Chamar have for several generations worked as tenant farmers besides carrying out their *jajmani* obligations.[11] And, finally, agricultural labour, as an occupation, has been open to any one, although it is only Chamars who engage in it. None of these tasks has anything to do with the *jajmani* ties; they are purely contractual and are executed between individuals in their personal capacities. Nor are these work relationships limited to the members of Cakra community alone. Any one is free to sell his skills or labour in the surrounding villages or town, if a demand exists. Thakurs, on their part, are free to acquire the needed help from outside the village.

Despite all these considerations, the Thakurs of Cakra still occupy the dominant position in the village. The facts that they are the largest group, and the earliest settlers in the village, dominant landowning group in the surrounding region who play the role of patrons for the members of almost all other jatis under the *jajmani* system, overshadow these other considerations.

As pointed out earlier in this section, this superiority of the Thakurs is recognized by everyone. The higher ritual status of Brahmans has its own limitations due to the fact that they all derive their sustenance from the Thakurs. The Brahmans thus have taken even the form of institutionalized behaviour. No Thakur, for example, would eat at a Brahman's place even if he (the Brahman) is giving a inter-community-wide feast. This avoidance is not for the fear of pollution; no one could be polluted at Brahman's hands. It rather arises from a Thakur's conviction that he is the giver, the supporter, the benefactor of a Brahman and could not, therefore, possibly eat at his place. On the contrary, he is obliged to send a cash gift every time there is a marriage or child-birth in the Brahman's family.

This benefactor's role of a Thakur is even more pronounced in his relations with the members of other jatis, whose ritual status is also lower than his. In times of scarcity, the most needy person gets economic support from the Thakur patron. And, such needs are not infrequent. A little cash or a few pounds of foodgrains might be needed at any time. A sick person in the family might have to be taken to the health centre located at the Block headquarters or big hospital in Varanasi and therefore a Thakur may have to be requested to lend some amount of money. Then, the privilege of cutting grass from around the agricultural fields in order to feed the milch cattle, which most people keep, can be granted only by the Thakurs. It is the Thakurs, again, who alone can grant small patches of land which a family, due to its growing size, might need to build another mud structure.

The facts, as noted earlier, that not all the members of a given jatis are bound by the *jajmani* ties, and that those who are so bound are still left with time and freedom to work independently of these ties, do not help to improve their position much vis-a-vis the Thakurs. Within or without the *jajmani* system it is the Thakurs who, because of their superior economic resources, are in most cases the paymasters. A person is, of course, free to work for someone outside the village, but if his services are needed within the village he is generally expected to meet this obligation. Similarly, within the *jajmani* system, a functionary is expected to give precedence to the work of his *jajman* over any other task he might be doing for cash. At the time of harvest, the Chamar family must help his *jajman*, regardless of how lucrative any other offer may be. The same rule applies to all such ties. The only way a person can get away from such obligations at a given time is to arrange a substitute for himself, unless he wants to completely sever the *jajmani* relationship. This latter recourse is open, traditionally to any one but not many people make use of it because of the economic security which *jajmani* bonds provide.

Yet another important indicator of the superior position of Thakur is the way some of the social norms characteristic of their own group have become binding on other jatis too. As will be seen in the following section, most of the male Thakurs in Cakra are descendants of the two settler brothers and thus agnates. In fact, this agnatic bond extends beyond Cakra and encompasses, together, 84 villages in the immediate area. Most of the Thakurs in these villages belong to the same *gotra*[12] and regard themselves as descendants of a single ancestor. They do not therefore, inter-marry. This agnatic bond, which exists mainly among the Thakurs of eastern U.P., has been extended, symbolically, to cover all the other jati groups.[13] Many of these jatis in these 84 villages are represented by several *gotras* and thus its members are otherwise eligible to inter-marry. But this has never been done in the entire history of the village. Eligible spouses have to be found beyond the Dobhi region; for example, the Brahmans of this region belong to two different *gotras* and came to the region from two different sources. According to their own jati norms they are quite eligible to inter-marry. Not only do they not do so within the region, which they would not do anyway because of the rule of village exogamy, but in their search for eligible spouses outside the village they avoid each other's *gotra*. They do not attribute this practice directly to the Thakurs but only to the "norm of the village", which in turn, has been patterned only after the practice among the Thakurs. Thakurs constitute, therefore, the major "reference group" in the region.[14]

Table 2. Occupational Structure of Male Adults (18 years and over) by jati (1982)

	Total male adults	High school or college students	Present main occupation				un-employed
			traditional in		new in		
			village	outside	village	outside	
Thakur	189	17	58	2	74	29	9
Chamar	106	3	48	6	22	23	4
Ahir	19	2	4	4	7	0	2
Kahar	23	3	6	0	10	4	0
Teli	16	1	1	2	7	3	2
Bhar	12	0	5	1	4	1	1
Lohar	4	0	1	0	2	1	0
Sonar	6	1	2	1	1	0	1
Bari	5	0	3	0	2	0	0
Nai	1	0	0	0	0	0	0
Total	381	27	129	16	129	61	19

2. *Jati and Occupation: Some Recent Changes*

Until a generation ago, a person's jati and his economic activity went hand in hand. He did what his jati, within the village context, prescribed as profession for him. Deviations did occur, as for example, Chamars largely left their traditional profession (as cobbler) and started cultivation of land as landless labourers of Thakurs. But these deviations, significant as they were, did not reflect any major departure from its traditional social and economic organization.

During the last four decades, however, many changes have taken place in the occupational pattern. Table 2 shows the occupational distribution of all the adult males (18 years and over) in Cakra by their jati.

In 1982, out of a total 381 male adults only 129 (or 33.8%) were engaged in their traditional occupation in the village. 16 others were engaged in their traditional trade, but in the bazaar or an urban setting. Even more significant is the fact that as many as 236 persons had completely moved out of their traditional occupations and 27 others were going to high school or the other higher institution. The other 19 persons had nothing to do, either because they were searching for a job or were having health problems.

Out of these 190, 129 were working within and around the village in such "new occupations" as tailoring, running a small grocery shop, agricultural labourers which all the Thakur land owners had acquired, or as milkmen (collecting milk from individual households and selling it in the nearby bazaar). The 61 men working outside the village showed a much greater diversity in their occupations, ranging from the unskilled or semi-skilled jobs of factory labourers, office bearers and truck drivers, to such white collar jobs as teacher, administrative clerk, bank officer, sanitary inspector, medical doctor and dispensary-incharge, textile engineer, etc. The army, air, and police force also had absorbed several people. And finally, quite a few of them had started their own business.

Both "pull" and "push" factors in the economy were operative in bringing these changes within a short period of less than thirty years. On the one hand, there was an overall expansion of the national economy and in educational facilities which created new and diverse opportunities and interests; on the other hand, over-crowding in several traditional occupations forced the extra man-power to find new outlets. The pressure on land too pushed many people out. This latter process was greatly accelerated when in 1954 the Land Reform Act was passed according to which any person who was cultivating a piece of land became entitled to claim its legal ownership after the payment of compensatory money through a long term easy instalment plan.

This triggered a mass eviction of the tenant farmers by the Thakur owners described in the next chapter. It was not an easy process. What is relevant here is that these evictions eventually displaced about 23 families belonging to the Ahir, Kahar, Bari, and Chamar jatis who had been tenant farmers for several generations. Many of these tenant farmers moved to the cities for new occupations, while others stayed on to find new ways within the village. As a result of this, Thakurs could get the landless agricultural labour very easily, at much less cost.

Despite this massive diversification in the occupational pattern of the village, the social and economic organizations and their essential features continued unaltered. Several factors support this observation. First the primary occupation of Thakur family, i.e., agriculture, was still maintained. It was only when a household had more adult males than it could absorb in the cultivation of land that the extra persons tended to seek outside occupation. Someone always stayed behind in such families to look after the land while others went to school and even to college in order to enter the urban job market. This was further borne out by the presence of 12 young Thakurs in their early twenties who, despite the fact that they had finished higher school education and could possibly get city jobs, were engaged wholly in agriculture since their fathers were growing old and they were the only other adults in the family to look after the land. They did not show any inclination to change their occupation.

The same was true about other functional jatis in the village. But now, groups who give their services to Thakurs do not wholly depend on the emoluments received for such services for their livelihood. Their livelihood, however, mainly depends on employment in *non-jajmani* type jobs.

Typically, one jati which performed important functions in the traditional village economy had completely ceased to do so. It is the Chamar group which maintain their livelihood by the landless agricultural labour who are overwhelmingly symbolic of subordination of Thakurs's control over the village. This group, at one time dealt with work which involved handling of hides and leathers. About 15 years ago, however, following a decision taken within the groups in this zone, their work involving hide and taking skin out of dead animals was abandoned. At present almost all members of this group are engaged as agricultural labour by the Thakurs.

Furthermore, except for the one third of such persons, almost everyone who had taken up an outside occupation was working within U.P. and other states. They either commuted each day to their work places, or lived there alone, having left their wives and children behind (if they were married), in which cases they frequently visit the village. In either cases, they were maintaining close ties with the community. Moreover, most of them, particularly among the Thakurs (who also had the larger number of outside workers), were not the heads of the households. They were mostly either younger brothers or sons of the heads, with whom they were living in an extended family. When off from their jobs, or on their frequent visits to the village, they would in a very inconspicuous manner engage themselves in the family occupation.

The only exception to the above were those who had not only moved away to such far away places as Bombay, Calcutta, Punjab, but mostly had also taken their families (wife and children) with them. This happened after the introduction of the Land Reform Act of 1954, growing pressure of household population, and increase in consumer prices even in the rural areas. Still, these families did not ever completely sever their ties with the village. This was particularly true of the 9 families, which were also consanguineous. The long distance and gap of several years and even memories of being forcibly evicted from their tenancies by the Thakurs, did not affect their sense of belonging to the village and to its region. For example, within one such Thakur family when three of their daughters attained marriageable age at about the same time, they all gathered together in Cakra in the summer of 1983.[15] Suitable grooms had to be searched within the region and the marriages were to be held in the village itself. All this took about three months but in this period many of the old ties were re-established and commitments were reinforced. Extensive repairs were done to the houses which had remained in disuse for all those years. Donations were given to the village panchayat towards its development fund to cover the past and future projects. Gifts were given to the family's Nai, Bari, Chamar, Kahar, Sonar and Lohar.

On the whole, thus, Cakra remains a traditional peasant community. The changes of the past four decades have, of course, linked many of its members with the wider economies. The onetime monolithic economic base is gradually being replaced by a greater diversity. But these changes do not seem so far to have made any discernible effect on the system of obligations and privileges prescribed by the village tradition and by its major structural unit the jati.

At the village level, jati continues to play a significant part in determining people's roles, status, associations and interpersonal relations. Normally, the manner of addressing each other, the seating arrangements at formal and informal gatherings, exchange of gifts at ceremonial occasions, the smoking and dining rules, and various other interaction situations establish paramount considerations to jati membership. The fact that a person has moved out of the traditional occupation and is engaged in a new, and perhaps prestigious one, affects his position only in relation to his fellow jati members; in the network of inter-jati relations and in the village-wide context it is the jati which counts.

Jati distinctions are further shown by the way residential units are territorially distributed and identified with a suffix — *an* like Ahiran. Although jati boundaries are not sharply drawn, members of a given jati still tend to cluster together.

3. Kinship Organization

Internally a jati group in Cakra is not a unified whole; nor are the ascribed privileges and obligations uniformly bestowed upon its members. Age and sex differences account for some differentiation within a jati, but the major factors are the linear segmentations and kinship ties which require a person to relate differentially with his or her jati member. This is particularly true of the landowning group of Thakurs, which is the largest in size and in which the levels of kinship organization are also elaborately defined.

Then, because of the ascribed economic privilege of landownership, economic differentiation among the Thakurs now is patterned after its kinship organization. Two interconnected factors which account for this latter phenomenon are: the agnatic relation among the Thakurs, and the nature of inheritance rights.

Before examining these factors, the historical setting of this area is explained: A written history of Jaunpur district in the Hindu period does not seem to exist. The district, however, assumed importance at the time of Feroz Shah (1351-1370). Afterwards till late 15th century the area was under the reign of Sharki Kings, followed by Mughal rule. During the time of Akbar (1556-1605) the district became an important administrative centre. We find a mention of Jaunpur, Kerakat (tehsil) and Chandwak (the block headquarters) in the *Ain-i-Akbari*. In 1775, this district was ceded to the East India Company by Asaf-ud-Daula. The revenue *pargana* of Chandwak or Dobhi was settled in 1790, and it was declared permanent in 1795.[16]

It is possible to get details of the original settlers of Dobhi taluka (local area) as follows: [cf. Cohn, 1979: 64-65].

> The Ragubanshi Rajputs of Dobhi taluk had an ancestor, Ganesh Rai, who had conquered the taluk in the late fifteenth or early sixteenth century. He had two sons, Iswardas and Ramdeo, each of whom inherited half of the taluk. Iswardas had four sons, and Ramdeo had eight sons. Therefore, each of Iswardas sons inherited one fourth of their father's estate or an eighth of the original land. Ramdeo's sons inherited an eighth of their father's estate or a sixteenth of the original land. Each of the members of the lineage traced his descent back to one of the twelve grandsons of the founder of the lineage. In the nineteenth century, the living representatives of each of the twelve grandsons formed a group known as *mahal*. Each member of the *mahal* had a share and was termed as *pattidar*. The size of his holding depended on the number of close agnatic kin he had.

A more detailed and authentic description of these agnatically related Raghubanshis, who in due course settled in several villages of the region (Dobhi), is found in published genealogical literature.[17] They all belong to one clan and are popularly known as "Dobhi Raghubanshi Thakurs" in the region.

This means that Thakurs of Dobhi are all descendants of Ganesh Rai's second son Iswardas who founded his chief clan centre at Hariharpur. All the lands in the village and the land throughout the taluka follow the descent line from Ganesh Rai. Ganesh Rai was Suryavanshi Rajput of Kasyap *gotra*.[18] According to the genealogical literature, Cakra village was inhabited by Jai Singh who was the third son of Iswardas' third son Thodar Singh.[19]

But, the Thakur population of Cakra village belongs to two distinct groups. One consists of 65 families belonging to the present male descendants of two brothers who were the sons of Jai Singh, and the joint heirs of the village land. The other group, having 9 families, consists of later migrants, but do not belong to the Kasyap *gotra* and have no ancestral rights in the village land. For the sake of identification, the first group may be called Jai-Thakurs and the second group the Alien-Thakurs. I shall first examine the internal organization and differentiation of the Jai-Thakurs. It is in this group that agnatic bonds between the members and the nature of inheritance rights are most relevant.

As far as the inheritance rights are concerned, like most Thakur villages in eastern U.P., Cakra is a "joint" village of the "ancestral *pattidari*" type.[20] This means that all the male successors of the earliest settlers form a co-sharing proprietary community. Together they are the sole owners of the entire village land — cultivated as well as uncultivated. However, the joint ownership since the beginning has been restricted only to the uncultivated land, mainly the grazing ground.[21] As far as the agricultural land is concerned, the "togetherness" has been maintained only in the collective payment of land revenue.[22] The land itself has all along been partitioned on the basis of ancestral rights. When the head of a family dies, all his male heirs get equal share in the family property.[23] This rule of inheritance has been carried out so thoroughly through the generations that even today one could tell simply by looking at the genealogical chart of the Jai-Thakurs how much land a particular family owns.[24]

However, there have been a few exceptions to this rule which have slightly altered the distribution of land along the male descent line. The major one occurred about a hundred years ago when one of the substantial owners in the village mortgaged about 15 acres (6.1 ha) of land to a money-lender in the urban area. Seeing no immediate prospects of getting this land released, his closest agnates in the village tried to claim it in return for the payment of the loan money. A court case followed which they lost because the money lender obtained legal immunity by cleverly registering the land in the name of a temple which he himself owned. Since then these 15 acres of village land have continued to be administered by the trustees of that temple in Varanasi, although it has always been leased to some of the Thakurs of Cakra.

4. The Jai-Thakurs

Additional exceptions to the inheritance scheme occurred when some the ancestors of the present Jai-Thakurs donated small pieces of land to one Ahir and a few Chamar families, as part of social aid and religious sacrifices. Until recently, while such land, called *dolidari* land, was in the possession of such jatis' families, it was treated as the property of the donors. With the implementation of the U.P. Land Reforms Act of 1950, these donors have been declared outright owners. Thus, the status of "landowners" which was traditionally the exclusive privilege of the Thakurs, has been extended to other groups too. But still, the amount of land involved was so small that the effect was negligible.

The Land Reforms Act of 1950 has had another upsetting effect. Until its enactment, quite a sizeable amount of land in Cakra was cultivated by tenant farmers, who, under the provisions of the Act were made eligible to become the owners. If the Act had been implemented properly, it would have materially changed the relation between a Thakur's position in the extended kin group of agnates and amount of land held by him. But by timely and effective intervention in the legal processes and by using several pressure tactics, most of the Thakur owners were successful in dodging the provision of the Act. Still, a few of them lost some bits here and there and, therefore, the relation between the genealogical chart and land ownership was slightly affected.

Despite these alterations, this relation still exists. The Jai-Thakurs still constitute the "cosharing proprietary community". The genealogical chart continues to tell the position a Jai-Thakur occupies in relation to his agnates. In any case, it is not the size of land, in absolute figures, which is important in determining a member's share of privileges and obligations, but the relative fraction of the co-proprietorship to which his structural position entitles him.

Now the source, extent and nature of agnatic relation are described. As pointed out earlier, all the land-owing Thakurs of Cakra are agnates, being descendants of the village settler Jai Singh and his three sons. This type of agnatic bond is not limited to the Thakurs of Cakra alone. It extends far beyond and rests on their belief that all persons born in a certain group are descendants of one man, i.e. Ganesh Rai, II. The land-owing Raghubanshi Thakurs of Dobhi belong to the Suryavanshi division of Rajputs. According to them, Suryavanshi (sun-descendants) was the name of the main agnatic group — one of three groups — the other two being Chandravanshi (moon decendants), and Agnivanshi (fire-descendants). The descendants of two main groups formed several different "vanshi" and are named after their personal and original names. How far this story is true is hard to say, as today the Rajput Thakurs of Suryavanashi and Chandravanshi divisions are scattered and mixed up in many parts of the North India.

The Jai-Thakurs of Cakra village treat the Dobhi Raghubanshis and also the other Raghubanshi Thakurs as their agnates and therefore avoid them in their selection of marital partners. Beyond this avoidance, not much affinity is felt for such a large and widely scattered group. However, in the mid-thirties an incident occurred which reflected the strength of these far-flung bonds. Some of the Raghubanshi Thakurs living in nearby Sultanpur district were involved in a bitter struggle with some other local people. A long court case followed which very soon left the Raghubanshis without money to carry on the struggle. They therefore sent their emissaries to other Raghubanshi areas appealing for funds. The Raghubanshi Thakurs of Dobhi recall this incident and their contribution to their "brethren" with a great sense of pride.

On a closer view, one finds that the agnatic ties of the Dobhi Raghubanshi Thakurs extend to 84 villages in the immediate area (formerly referred as *caurasi pargana,* quite close to the present). But Jai-Thakurs of Cakra village who belong to Iswardas group of Dobhi region are representative of half of the Thakurs in 84 villages of Dobhi.

Since the last two hundred years, these 84 villages have been settled at their present sites. Still the Thakurs living in these villages maintain the agnatic bonds. In fact, the villages themselves have been personified and are given the status of father, grandfather, brother, cousins, etc. For example, the Jai-Thakurs of Cakra village treat thirteen villages as brother village, all village residents belong to the five sons of Dodhar Singh. Visits and gifts are exchanged on ceremonial occasions. Whenever there is a serious conflict in a village or between villages, elderly representatives get together to try and resolve the issue.

Within the Cakra village the Jai-Thakurs are further classified along several varying degrees of lineage depth. The first major sub-group, what the villagers called the *pana,* is named after three settler-brothers: *Pana Kulan Singh* consisting of families of the male descendants of Kulan Singh, *Pana Naddu Singh* consisting of those of Naddu Singh and *Pana Dariyav Singh* consisting of those of Dariyav Singh. These three *panas* are further sub-divided into several *tolas,. kunbas,* and households.

A household is the basic hearth unit. Regardless of the size and nature of the family, nuclear or extended, when all the members share a commom kitchen they constitute a household.[25] Next to the household is a more inclusive unit: a *kunba,* which includes all those members who having four generations root, had a common ancestor. There are twelve such *kunbas* among the Jai-Thakurs. A still more inclusive unit within a *pana* is a *tola.* The principle is again the same; a common ancestor, but at a deeper level. Altogether, there are eight *tolas* among the Jai-Thakurs: four in *Pana Kulan Singh,* three in *Pana Naddu Singh,* and one in *Pana Dariyav Singh.*

Due to varying degrees of expansion in the various lineage branches, households, *kunba* and *tola* units, different patterns occur, sometimes overlapping. The differences in the degree of expansion also result in the enormous size differences between the three *panas.* While *Pana Kulan Singh,* multiplying rapidly with each successive generation, consists of 50 households today; *Pana Naddu Singh,* due to limited expansion, records 11 households; and *Pana Dariyav Singh* has only 4 households. Consequently these 50 households of *Pana Kulan Singh* together own one half of the total village land and are thus better off.

The distinction between the three *panas* has been maintained all along. Administratively, it was recognized by the British government by appointing separate *Amil* for each *pana*, whose job was to collect the land taxes from individual farmers and to deposit them with the State treasury. For this service to the State, they were given a fixed share in the land revenue. With passage of time the incumbents to these offices were appointed on the basis of heredity. Presently the *Amin* is a servant of government revenue department.

People are also expected to demonstrate a feeling of affinity and loyalty to their *pana* members. When Kulan Singh's ancestor mortgaged a part of his land to an outsider and when little hope was left for its recovery, it was his close agnates of the same *kunba* who felt obliged in the interest of *pana* prestige, and at a great expense to themselves, to first move the case in the court. The motivation here was to somehow keep the *pana's* share of ancestral land within the *pana*.

There is a pronounced display of *pana* distinction. Suppose, there is a marriage in the family of a person in *kunba* 'X' of *tola* 'Y'. Normally he would invite all the members — men, women and children — of all the households in his own *kunba* to come and eat at his place. Beyond that, within his *tola,* he would perhaps invite one person per household in each of the other two *kunbas* in the *tola*. If he is generous and has enough resources he might invite even one person per household.

Within a *kunba*, two brothers may not be on good terms with each other but when a gift has to be sent to a married sister (who due to the principle of village exogamy lives in a different village), regardless of how unfriendly the relation between the two brothers may be, they have to consult each other and share the cost. If a gift has already been sent by one without, for some reasons, consulting the other, the other is still obliged to meet his share of the cost.

In a village level meeting, when a decision has to be made on a matter of the whole village-wide concern, among the Jai-Thakurs presence of only a responsible representative from each *kunba*, generally the oldest male member, is regarded as necessary. A commitment made by this representative on behalf of the entire *kunba* would be regarded as binding on every member. Similarly a family's share of the contribution to any village level project is determined by its position in the lineage structure which also usually coincides with the size of its landholding vis-a-vis other families.

Within or without these various structural categories, another consideration which enters into people's relations with each other is a person's relative position in the inter-generational distribution. As one can understand from the genealogical study, the present adult male population of Jai-Thakurs represents four generations. Kinship terminology denoting generational differences is often used to address each other. But, in this situation, age becomes a secondary consideration. In fact, several persons on generation line 1 are much younger than those on other generation lines like 2, 3, and 4.

This is not to suggest that the age of a person is completely unimportant in determining his status in village society. Within a household and also within a *kunba* it is the oldest male member who commands the greatest respect. In the village affairs, it is he who represents the *kunba* and makes commitments on behalf of other members unless he decides to delegate this function to a younger member. Within these limits, however, age generally coincides with generational status too. But even otherwise, in the wider setting, an elderly person is recognized as such and is given due respect. It is only in the determination of relative privileges and obligations that one's structural position, and not age, is given primary consideration.

Many more examples could be cited to suggest the significance of these structural categories in the life of the village people. What is important to note is that they provide the initial framework which becomes a significant part of a Thakur's heritage when he is born into a certain family — a framework which determines his associates, his obligations, and his place in the overall structural arrangement. The bonds are strong and are felt in almost every aspect of a person's life. He is, of course, free to cross the boundaries of this framework to choose his associates and friends, as people quite frequently do. In view of the above description this crossing of the boundaries becomes of utmost importance, particularly when by so doing a person clearly violates some of the demands which his structural position characteristically makes on him, but more about this at a later stage.

Due to the variation in the size of land holdings, the economic position of Jai-Thakurs varies immensely. The range is between 2 and 30 bighas[26] of land owned by a household. This wide gap is reflected in numerous ways. On the one hand, there are farmers for whom agriculture is mainly a subsistence activity. They grow what they need. They can afford to keep only one bullock (while the minimum required for most agricultural operations is two), and therefore have to borrow the other from one of their kin, who might be in a similar situation. Their houses are small, built of mud bricks and furnished with the minimal items of conventional usage. Their life is one of constant toil. To augment their modest incomes, they often keep one or two water-buffaloes and sell the milk to the middle-men who take it to the city of Varanasi (34 Km south).

On the other hand, some of their agnates own so much land that they cannot possibly cultivate it by themselves. Prior to the enactment of the U.P. Land Reforms Act in 1950, a major part of their land was cultivated by tenant farmers on a share-crop basis. But with the abolition of tenancy cultivation they have hired more full-time labourers. They grow on their fields not only what they themselves need, but also what the market demands. To overcome the irregular and uncertain supply of water from canal irrigation, they have constructed deep wells in their fields and run them by motor power. They live in large two-three storyed houses made of fired bricks and cement, with equally impressive looking *baithaks* which are, in some cases, furnished with modern cushion sofas, tables, chairs and carpets. They keep milch cattle but not for augmenting their income by selling the milk. The milk is instead consumed at home. They also try and augment their incomes by managing the wholesale foodgrain in the market town to the north; having real estate in nearby bazaar; running a transport bus on an authorized route; operating a brick kiln; starting a small industry in the village to process milk products; turning a large part of their agricultural land into a more lucrative orchard; and even starting a poultry farm, an enterprise which in the traditionally vegetarian community of Thakurs is attractive. In all these activities, they mainly play the entrepreneurial and managerial roles, leaving the actual manual work to the hired people.

Between these two extremes live the majority of Cakra Thakurs who own moderate-size farms, a pair of bullocks and other conventional farming equipment, and make a reasonably good living from their land. Their houses are neither made of mud bricks nor are several storeyed structures. The milk their buffaloes and cows give is consumed by the members of their families but they do not hesitate to sell it to the middleman if a need for cash arises.

This disparity in the economic realm is an important factor in status differentiation among the Jai-Thakurs. Not only is this differentiation clearly visible in the style of life, it influences the nature of political relationship within the group of Jai-Thakurs. It permits some to favour others by lending some money in times of need or by slightly over-working their tractors to work somebody's tract of land. Moreover, it is only the economically well-off families which play, overtly or covertly, the leading roles in the factional politics of the village.

Despite this disparity in the economic realm, it is the agnatic bond among the Jai-Thakurs which seems to be emphasized more by them. The Jai-Thakurs do recognize the ranking based on wealth but tend to "play it down" and minimize it by various forms of social etiquette. Those with richness do not "behave rich". If they did they would only antagonize others. On the other hand, those with limited wealth do only show its lack. A sense of equality seems to characterize the inter-personal relations. It grows out of the cultural value that being agnates they all stand at the same footing in relation to each other. If someone has more wealth, it is because he was born into a certain *kunba,* not because he was inherently superior to others. He has, therefore, no right to show it off. Thus, modesty on the part of the rich and sense of pride on the part of the poor have the effect of equalizing the social disparity among the Jai-Thakurs.

The agnatic character of relationships among the Jai-Thakurs prevents any one of them from occupying a towering position in the village-wide setting. Influence, when it occurs, is an informal process, limited to small groups which in turn are based on reciprocity of interests. Beyond that, no one is in a position to tell others what they should do. As a matter of fact no one dare assume a village leadership role. It simply will not be recognized as such.

On the other hand, it is this group of Jai-Thakurs which serves as the main focus of village politics. Major political struggles are fought out in this group. Its members provide the core as well as the main support elements of the village factions. This is not to say that other groups are free from internal conflicts or political struggles. But these struggles either do not have village-level significance or they assume it only when they are tied up with the struggles within the group of Jai-Thakurs.

5. *The Alien-Thakurs*

The nine families comprising the group of Alien-Thakurs come from two different *gotra*. In one case, consisting today of 5 agnatic families, and belonging to Somavansh of Chandravanshi, and Atri *gotra,* their ancestor Shankar Singh came to Cakra about a hundred years ago from a village only 10 Km to the north.

Shankar Singh was reportedly a close friend of the ancestor of Daulat Singh who had mortgaged some acres of his land to a money lender in Varanasi. In fact, most of the villagers today believe that it was on Shankar Singh's instigation that Daulat Singh's ancestor mortgaged his land. What is, however, undisputed is the fact that as soon as that land was lost to the temple, the owner of that temple (the moneylender) appointed Shankar Singh to sell leasehold of that land. Since then, Shankar Singh and his successors have continued to manage the land. A large part of this land, almost one third, has all along been sub-leased to other families, mainly the remaining families of the Alien-Thakurs. The remainder of that land, still a fairly large holding by village standards, has been directly cultivated by the Atris against payment of fixed rent to the temple-trustees in Varanasi. Today the Atris, headed by an elderly man named Phool Singh, are among the better-off people in Cakra. In addition to this land in Cakra, they own a substantial amount of land under ancestral rights in their native village. Phool Singh has seven adult sons, only three of whom live in Cakra. The others either live in their native village to look after the ancestral land or in

Bombay, Calcutta, and Delhi employed in urban jobs.

Today, there are five Atri families in Cakra, because one of Phool Singh's sons, with his wife and children, maintains a separate household and cultivates his share of land independently.

Four other families in the major sub-group of Alien-Thakurs, belonging to Sulakhalain *gotra,* have ties with each other in an agnatic bond. Their ancestors also came to Cakra about a hundred years ago, but from a different lineage and under different circumstances. His native village was somewhere in the Muzaffarnagar district of north western U.P. where he is believed to have actively participated in the famous 1857 uprising against the British. When the uprising was suppressed by the British forces and reprisals took place he fled to Cakra where he received protection and security from an affinal relative among the Jai-Thakur ancestors of the three families in *Pana Kulan Singh.* Since then he and his successors have made Cakra as their home. From the very beginning they have cultivated a part of the temple-trust land as sub-lesees of the Atri family. Compared to the latter, they are not as well-off. Their houses are *kutcha* and their standard of living modest.

Since Atri families came to Cakra through initial contact with the *Pana Kulan Singh* and since their houses today are located in one part of this *pana,* they are regarded as members of *Pana Kulan Singh.*

On the whole, these nine families of Alien-Thakurs have a peculiar position in the Cakra village society. Being Thakurs, they share the superior status enjoyed by their jati members in the village and in its region. For example, they too are addressed as *Chaudharis.* Being primarily agriculturists they too play the role of patrons in the *jajmani* relation with many of functionary jatis. Economically, particularly the Atri families are much better-off than even many of Thakurs in Cakra. However, due to their alien status in the village and consequently due to the fact that they have no ancestral rights in the village land, they receive a differential treatment from the villagers. For all practical purposes they have been absorbed in the village society; their participation and contribution in village affairs is sought but in numerous subtle ways they are frequently reminded of their alien status. They are themselves conscious of it and resent it.

6. Structural Differentiation among the Non-Thakurs

When we look at the internal organization of the nine other jatis living in Cakra, we find that they not only differ considerably from the Thakurs but also among themselves. A household is still the basic structural unit with its internal differentiation along age and sex lines. But the household differs in its composition. While among the Thakurs, many families are of an extended nature, it is almost never so among the other jatis. Here, as soon as a son grows up and is married, he tends to establish a separate household. As a result, almost all the families in these jatis are of nuclear type.

The difference is even more marked beyond the household unit. The rigidly closed and highly elaborate system of differentiated structural organization along male descent which characterizes the landowning group of Thakur is absent among these other jatis. They are characterized instead by an element of fluidity in their internal organization. While most of these jatis too have agnatic bonds keeping the household units together, this is not always the only kind of structural relation between them.

Here it should be pointed out that these nine jatis fall in several categories in terms of internal organization. In the first place, there are jatis like Lohar, Sonar, Bari and Nai which are represented in Cakra by only one family each. Therefore, this discussion is not relevant in their case. Secondly, there are jatis like Teli and Bhar in which case either the relation between the households is agnatic or there is no relation at all. The six Bhar families are agnatically related to each other. The eight Teli families represent two mutually unrelated agnatic sub-groups. One of them, coming from eastern Bihar, and having five families, has been in Cakra since its founding. The ancestors of the remaining three families came to the village four generations ago from a place in Rajasthan.

It is in the third category of three jatis (Chamar, Ahir, and Kahar) that greater complexity is observed in the structural relations. Many of these jatis are quite large in size as compared to other non-Thakur jatis in Cakra. In the system of ritual hierarchy they occupy relatively intermediate or low positions. In fact, Chamars have traditionally been regarded as untouchables by the villagers with very low status accorded to the other two groups.[27] Perhaps there is no relation between the ritual status of a jati and its internal structural organization. What is noteworthy, however, is the fact that it is only in these three jatis in Cakra that I found family units related to each other not only through the system of extended male lineage but also through affinal ties. These affinal ties have not been established through intra-village marriages. This could not have been possible because of the principle of village exogamy practised in the region. Over a long period of time many of affinal relatives (son-in-laws, wife's brother, sister's son, etc.) moved to Cakra and settled in the village. Some of them have lived there for several generations, thus resulting in their own separate expanded lineages. As a result, I find in these jatis today several agnatic sub-groups inter-related with each other through affinal ties.

The agnatically related jatis, and also those other jatis having such relations could not be compared with a similar phenomenon among the Thakurs where the relations serve as the main basis for structural differentiation. Terms like *kunba, tola,* etc. have little relevance in the internal organization of the non-Thakurs. These jatis are too small in size to permit elaborately defined separate structural categories. But even more important than the size is the factor of landownership. It is not size alone which required the Thakurs to have these categories to differentiate among themselves. More than that it was the fact of co-proprietorship in the village land which made these categories relevant and significant.

Lack of landownership also seems to have affected the two other features identified earlier as characterizing the internal organization of the non-Thakurs and affinal ties between the households, and a greater preponderance of the nuclear family pattern. A share in the common proprietorship seems to serve as the greatest binding force among the Thakurs. It strengthens the familial bonds between them and also their ties to the village. Its absence in the other jatis makes these ties weaker. When land is there, the costs involved in separation between two brothers is greater. It is less expensive and more productive to keep the land-holding together. On the other hand there is not much to lose when two brothers in a landless family get separated. On the contrary the incentive for separation is greater, because the income by and large is personalized since it comes mainly from selling one's labour or one's traditional jati skills. Also, in such cases, if the village of one's affinal relative promises more opportunities for such income,[28] one is more likely to move out there. Again, there is not much to lose from such a move.

Because of all these features, the internal differentiation in these jati groups, to the extent this differentiation affects the political processes at the village level, does not present a clear-cut pattern. In such cases where a jati consists of separate and mutually unrelated agnatic sub-groups, as for example among the Ahirs, each of these sub-groups is regarded as a separate entity. In village affairs, they are represented separately. The same is true of the two mutually unrelated Teli families. These families also follow the *pana* division as it exists among the Thakurs. Their houses are located in three settlement clusters (see Fig. 3). Differentiation along the *pana* division among the Thakurs is followed by two other jatis: Kahar and Bari. Their houses, too, form two distinct clusters. In these jatis, the sub-groups have traditionally tended to be affiliated with one or the other *pana* division among the Thakurs. The hereditary nature of the *jajmani* ties seems to have perpetuated this division.

But in the groups such a Sonar and Lohar, no such divisions are discernible. *Jajmani* relations have been operative in these jatis too, tying their members to different sub-groups of Thakurs. But, unlike Ahirs and Telis, these relations have not caused divisions in these jatis along the *pana* lines. Faced with village affairs, an individual in these groups stands either as an individual or as a member of his jati; there is nothing in between. Most of the times, it is the jati as a collectivity which counts in these affairs. Representations and commitments in the community meetings are made at that level.

The discussion so far points to the various ways in which a person's position is ascribed in Cakra in many of its structural categories. Jati, intra-jati kinship organization, residential pattern, institution of landownership, occupational distribution, age distribution, *jajmani* system, and the inter-village network of agnatic bonds, all of these features work independently as well as in conjunction with one another to provide several frameworks within which a Cakra dweller operates. Each of these frameworks has a system of rules, governing the obligations, privileges, and the resulting inter-personal relations. These different sets of rules do not necessarily contradict themselves; in fact, often they support one another. Still, they have the effect of providing several alternative sources of legitimation which a person may invoke to rationalize his behaviour. The two sets of rules regulating the jati and *jajmani* systems, for example, are inter-dependent and mutually reinforcing. Without the support of one, the other would lose much of its significance. But in actual operation, at the level of personal behaviour, the two may, at times, make conflicting demands upon a person. In effect, they thus leave the person with a range of legitimate choices within which he has the freedom to choose. On such an occasion, it is up to him to decide whether he wants to meet the jati obligation or the obligation to the *jajman*, the patron. Many more similar choices present to identify his affinity with a person or faction as discussed in the following chapters.

This range of choices is considerably broadened when we take into account many other sets of rules which the village society has incorporated by being part of a wider universe and of the larger legal and administrative systems of the society.

7. *Cakra and the Outside World*

Especially by reason of being so close to the seat of the ruling authority, Cakra since its very inception has been subjected to various kinds of administrative procedures and rules, particularly as they applied to land management and land taxes. After the British annexed U.P. and its surrounding region early in the 19th century, these penetrations into village life have become more and more far-reaching. Extensive land surveys were undertaken soon after British annexation to determine the rights of ownership, the system of tenure and the mode of revenue payment. Although the traditional rules of inheritance according to the "ancestral-*pattidari*" system were honoured, this was the first time that an individual's right to his land was legally defined. Special functionaries called *Amins*, were appointed from among the villagers to collect land revenue. In fact, as Smith [1952: 47-48] has shown for this region, they became part of the new hierarchy which the British administration instituted for this purpose. Above them, successively, were the offices of *Sufedposh* and *Zeldar*, with increasingly larger jurisdiction in terms of the number of villages. The inter-village units thus constituted different such units as the Rughubanshi, the traditional inter-village unit based upon agnatic ties. This hierarchy of new functionaries was not actually a part of the formal, or official structure. At best it was only semi-official in nature, designed to create viable links between the administration and the peasantry. The remunerations of these functionaries were not uniform but varied according to the size of land revenue fixed for the village under the particular functionary's jurisdiction.

Many more hierarchies, formally official in nature, were gradually instituted, thus linking Cakra and other villages to the administrative-level order. These hierarchies concerned the maintenance of law and order (police department), interpretation of laws and imparting of justice (civil, criminal and revenue courts), maintenance of land records and collection of land revenue (under the revenue department), etc. With passage of time the British government became more firmly rooted in the country, many more administrative hierarchies were added to look after agriculture, irrigation, health and sanitation, education, co-operation, etc. Each one of these hierarchical setups, with its own system of rules, regulations and procedures, made separate inroads into the village society and gradually became part of its structural organization. The city of Jaunpur, being the district headquarters and the place where all the courts and administrative offices were located, also became a part of an average Cakra dweller's operative framework. It was from there that he saw the new rules and the functionaries descending from time to time to impinge upon his life. In times of doubt and conflict, he, in turn, began to look towards the city and various new mechanisms which it provided. The city thus furnished new sources of legitimation for this behaviour and considerably broadened the range of choices available to him.

Early in the 20th century, the British government also made several half-hearted attempts to introduce different institutions of local self-government in the countryside. Some forms of panchayats were instituted at the village level, with official status and limitations but well-defined responsibilities. However, the most viable and enduring of these institutions in this area was the District Board with elected local representatives from the entire district. This Board, with administrative offices in Jaunpur, had limited advisory functions in almost all the areas of administration which concerned the rural population. None of Cakra's citizens was ever elected to this Board, but most of them, particularly the Thakurs, took an active interest in the periodic elections of its members and in its over-all functioning. They saw it as an avenue through which to channel influence upto, and favours down from the various branches of district administration.

The first half of the present century, moreover, witnessed several new developments in the outside world which affected the percep-tions of Cakra dwellers. The two world wars and the economic depression of the intervening period were events of global signifi-cance, as a consequence of which the residents of Cakra, for the first time, began to see the link, however weak, between their own destiny and that of the rest of the world. The names of major battle grounds in the European, the Middle-Eastern and Asian regions became part of the common vocabulary because it was there where some of the residents of Cakra or their relatives from the immediate region were engaged in fighting. Instead of using the generalized term *Vilayati*, which they had always used to denote any person of the white race, people now began to differentiate between the English, French, German, American, etc.

While all this was happening, two parallel movements of great significance were taking place in the country itself. Both of them were mass movements in nature and thus encompassed the rural populace. Cakra being so close to the city of Varanasi, was par-ticularly exposed to them. One of them was the nationalistic political movement led by the Indian National Congress which eventually led to the country's Independence from British rule. A few of the Cakra residents became paying members of the party and took part in its local organization. The other development was the nativistic and revitalization movements[29] which took various forms throughout the country. In northern India, it emerged in the form of the Arya Samaj movement led by Swami Dayanand Saraswati and his fol-lowers. This movement aimed to revitalize the philosophy and the way of life of the ancient Vedic period as explained in his book the *Satyartha Prakash.* In effect, it aimed to liberalize the rigid inter-jati relations and to simplify the marriage practices and other life-cycle rituals. Education was seen as a key tool for social reform by the members of this movement. As a result, a whole series of educational institutions called Dayanand Anglo Vernacular Schools or Colleges were opened in the Punjab, Rajasthan, U.P., and Delhi, mostly with the effort and financial help of the local people. The residents of Cakra, along with those of several neighbouring villages, supported the founding of a similar institution in a village lying 5 Km to the north.

The combined effect of these two movements, i.e. the nationalistic political movement of the Congress and the nativistic-revitalization movement of the Arya Samaj, was to raise a new level of collective consciousness among the Cakra villagers and to provide them with a new set of values. Equality, regardless of jatis, class, creed and sex, abolition of untouchability and numerous other handicaps with which the people of lower jatis had been living, land reforms, provision of special privileges for under-privileged groups, were the slogans repeatedly used by the Congress. They could not help penetrating the value system of the village people. In particular, they raised new hopes and aspirations in the minds of the lower jati people. But in Cakra, these people did not have to fight, at least in the beginning, for these new privileges. It seemed that the entire village population was caught up in the surge of new civil and political   consciousness.

On August 15, 1947 the day of Independence from Britain, the villagers, led by a few politically active Thakurs, gathered at the village well. Under the national flag and with much fanfare and slogan shouting, a representative of the Chamar jati (an untouchable) was publicly invited and allowed to draw water from the well. This was a revolutionary step in the history of the village meant to symbolize the beginning of the new era in social feeling.

After the Independence, many developments began to take place which had a direct bearing on the traditional structural organization of the Cakra society. Untouchability was constitutionally abolished. Any practice of discrimination on the basis of caste or creed became a legal offence. In addition, the government provided special privileges for members of the lower groups (such as Scheduled Castes) in the areas of education, job training, recruitment, and political representation, by providing extra incentives and by reserving a certain percentage of seats (around 30% in 1989) for them in these areas.

In terms of land ownership, various states passed Land Reforms Acts which were to curtail the privileges of the landed gentry and make land distribution more egalitarian. In U.P., an Act was passed in 1950, a brief reference to which has already been made in this chapter. This Act aimed at abolishing completely the tenancy form of cultivation and to grant ownership rights to all those persons, tenants or otherwise, who were found to be cultivating a piece of land in the agricultural year 1953-54. By a subsequent amendment, the Act fixed a ceiling of 30 acres (about 12 ha) of land which a family of five persons could own. Possession of land above that ceiling was to be taken away (against a long term payment of compensation) to be redistributed among the landless people.

Another significant development in the post-Independence period was the introduction of Community Development Programme in 1952 which sought on the one hand to co-ordinate administratively, the efforts of all the developmental agencies and, on the other to provide the necessary incentives, resources and technical knowledge to the village people in order to promote community-wide self-help programmes.

To overcome some of the inherent weaknesses of this programme and to elicit better participation from the village people, a new development took place in the late fifties. A three-tier system of local-self government, popularly known in India as the system of democratic decentralization, was instituted. This new institution is called the Panchyayati Raj.

The details of the problems in the process of community development programme, and their explanations are described in the next chapter.

In an ever-increasing way the village has thus been exposed to many of the forces from the outside world. It is no more now an isolated community. Contacts with surrounding villages are not limited to the traditional agnatic and familial bonds. Through numerous links, its members are tied to the over-all legal and administrative structure of the country. To some extent, their values too have been influenced by the currents of change in the world outside.

The net effect of all these links with the outside world and of all the forces of change has been to provide several additional frameworks in which the Cakra dweller can operate and from which he can draw sanctions. His range of choices is still determined by the structural position he occupies in village society, but this structural position is defined not only in terms of the traditional rules of the village but also in terms of the various linkages with the outside world. But neither these external linkages nor the currents of change in the structural organization and in the system of values are sources of political conflict and of factional behaviour in the village. Their importance lies only in changing the context of behaviour and in providing additional sets of rules by which to legitimize one's behaviour.

In the next chapter, aspects related to the governmental policy of rural development, Community Development Programme, and will be discussed for understanding the political life in Cakra village.

Notes

1   A pseudonym, originally "Chakra".

2   In 1982, a one way bus fare to Varanasi was only Rs. 5.

3   A sacred place for worshipping the village deity, *Bhu* means land, and *maiya* means the mother. It is a small temple like structure about 3'×3'×3' built on a raised platform under a *pipal* tree. It was built at the time of founding the village.

4   A place like this is called a *gher* in the local language. Those who can afford build brick or mud walls around their *ghers,* but most of the people either grow bushes as boundaries, or simply leave them unbounded.

5   I have talked about this in a subsequent section of this chapter.

6   The *baithak,* in a way, symbolizes the separation of the men's world from that of the women. This separation is greatly emphasized in Cakra, as in most of northern India. Seldom, if ever, are women allowed to enter the *baithaks.* Moreover, it is only men who are normally expected to live an open life, women keep a great deal of privacy in their living. Politics belongs to the man's world.

7   A pipe, which rests on a large earthen or metal base filled with water, and which has a long extended stem. The base is generally fitted with a revolving device, so that while it stays steady at one place, the stem

can rotate to reach several people.

8 The following observation reportedly made by John Lawrence about Delhi region is pertinent here: "It would seem that the present groups of villages are usually gradual growth of expansion from a central village originally founded in the midst of a wide undefined area; the cultivation extended, first around the original foundation, and then, in time, around the off shoot villagers; it became necessary to define the boundaries and separate the rights of each as so many separate estates" [Quoted by Baden Powell, 1892: Vol. II, 688].

9 These and all other personal names used in this study are fictitious.

10 The term "functionary jatis" is used in this study to denote those jati groups whose members provide their traditional jati services to the Thakurs under the *jajmani* system.

11 In fact, Brahmans, for the most part, have long since given up their traditional jati calling. It is on very rare ceremonial occasions that a few of their members are called upon to play the highly specialized sacred roles.

12 A clan or *sib* is exogamous sub-group within the endogamous group of a jati.

13 For a detailed description of this phenomenon in this very region, see M. Sharma [1979] and Shrinath Singh [1976].

14 This inconsistency between the ritual status of the Brahmans and secular status of the landowning dominant caste has been noted by many other scholars of the Indian village. In the central Indian village of Ramkheri, Mayer [1958a:424] found that it was the Rajput customs, and not the Brahman customs, which were the objects of emulation. The same was true in Khalapur [Hitchcock, 1956], Sirkanda [Berreman, 1963], Rampur [Lewis, 1958], and Mohana [Majumdar, 1958]. Also see in this connection the observations of Beidelman [1959:18-19], Pocock [1955:70-71], and Singer [1964:101]. Even Srinivas, whose original conception of the process of Sanskritization provided insightful lead to many subsequent researchers, has in recent years modified his position and has recognized that it is not the Brahmans alone who provided models for emulation, "... the other models are mediated by the locally dominant caste, and the concept of dominant caste supplements in some ways the concept of Sanskritization" [1966:8].

15 This coincided with the field work in the village.

16 See Srinath Singh [1979:33].

17 These descriptions are based on the account of Cohn [1979:64-65].

18 Gauri Shankar Singh [1982].

19 Gauri Shankar Singh [1982].

[20] These terms are borrowed from the classificatory scheme presented by Baden-Powel in many of his voluminous writings on the Indian village and its land system [1892, 1894, 1896, 1899].

[21] The statutory Panchayat instituted at the village level in 1952 is now responsible for the maintenance and superitendence of this land.

[22] For this purpose, the British government had appointed, from among villagers, special functionaries, called *Amil*, whose job was to collect the land taxes from individual farmers and to deposit them with the State Treasury. For this service to the State, they were given a fixed share in the land revenue. With passage of time these offices became hereditary and highly prestigious.

Under the provisions of the recent land laws, this office of *Amil* has been abolished in U.P. The payment of land taxes is no more the collective responsibility of the village; each individual owner pays his taxes directly through the government appointed person, called *Amin*.

[23] The sons do not have always to wait for their father's death before getting their shares separated. There have been cases when ageing fathers partitioned the land among their sons during their life-time.

[24] This has been mainly because traditionally there has been a strong taboo against selling one's ancestral property. When a sale became unavoidable, mostly due to economic scarcity, the owner would normally mortgage it to his closest agnate. Only when this agnate was unable or unwilling to make the deal, would the owner mortgage his land to others. In either case, the owner or the members of his succeeding generations were entitled to claim the land back against repayment of the loan money. If the owner died without a male heir and the land was mortgaged to an outsider, his closest agnate, who would have otherwise inherited the property, could claim its ownership in return for the payment of the loan money. The legal system recognizes such claims.

[25] The terms "household" and "family" are used interchangeably in this study.

[26] Two standard bighas is equal to one acre, and 2.471 acres equal to one hectare.

[27] For a study of caste ranking in this region, using statistical tests of significance, see [Freed, 1963b]; [Dinesh Singh, 1977:136-137]; [Singh, Singh and Singh, 1976:27-31]. For the treatment of attributional theory of caste ranking in relation to man-land ratio, see [Singh, Rana, 1975:20-46 and 1977:67-97].

[28] Cakra promised these opportunities which has been borne out by the fact that it only attracted outsiders. Never in the history of the village has any person moved out to seek a living in a village of his affinal relatives.

Outmigration from Cakra is a recent phenomenon.

[29] For a general discussion on these concepts, see Wallance [1956].

5

PANCHAYATI RAJ

The term "Panchayati Raj" has come into vogue recently. Previously the terms used were "village panchayat", "district board" or "sub-district board" which were self-governing bodies at the village or regional level. Rural self-governing bodies play a vital role in rural administration particularly in the field of social services and rural reconstruction. They are the link between the people and the machinery at the state level. In fact, the powers entrusted to them really make a state democratic or un-democratic.

I. History of Panchayati Raj

In India the system of village panchayat is very old though it was very different as compared to the modern system which is based on formal elections. The history of village panchayats in India since the early Vedic period could be traced; also the causes which led to their decay during the British period have also been discussed. During the British period attempts were made under the Government of India Act, 1919 and local self-government became a provincial subject. While some provinces passed the Village Panchayat Acts in 1919; some provinces followed later. For example, there was the Bengal Village Self-Government Act, 1919, Madras Village Panchayat Act, 1920, Bombay Village Panchayat Act, 1920, Central Provinces Village Panchayat Act, 1920, the U.P. Village Panchayat Act, 1920, etc. But the panchayats formed under these acts were not democratic bodies and their members were mostly nominated by the government. As a result these panchayats did not make much headway and these acts remained only on paper without any significant effect. It is only after Independence that some real progress has been made.

The regional self-governing bodies were formed during the British period on the lines of self-governing bodies in Britain, but their growth and development was also very slow. The local bodies in order to improve civic life were first created for the urban areas. The legislative enactments passed between the years 1842 and 1862 provided the base for setting up of the municipal institutions in towns only. The origin of the District Boards as the local self-governing bodies may be traced to the consultative committees which assisted the district officer in the management of funds devoted to local schools, roads and dispensaries [Madan, 1969: 170]. The committees were formed as a result of Lord Mayo's Resolution of 1870. These district committees were nominated by the government including half of the members as non-officials. In Lord Ripon's time, his Resolution of 1882 on local self-government led to the passing of a series of provincial acts. Only Madras and Assam followed up the suggestion of setting up sub-district boards, while other provinces concentrated powers in district boards. Regarding their success, the Royal Commission on Decentralisation 1909, remarked: "The scant success of the efforts hitherto made to introduce a system of rural self-government is largely due to the fact that we have not built them from the bottom. The foundation of any stable edifice which shall associate the people with administration must be the village, one in which the people are known to one another, and have interests with coverage on well-organized objects." The Commission along with the retention of district boards recommended the formation of sub-district boards in each taluka and tehsil and village panchayats at the village level. The Montague-Cheimsford Report recommended grant of complete control to local bodies. The village panchayat acts passed on the basis of these reports are already discussed, and the district board acts were also amended in order to reduce the power of interference by government directly in the administration of the boards.

The district boards continued to function until India's Independence with some variations in their powers. These district boards might have served the purpose for which they were created, i.e., educating the people in self-government; but they had neither the tradition nor resources to take up the development work which was started after Independence. They were also handicapped by having too large a charge to receive their detailed attention. The chairperson and members of the district board were not in a position to give any considerable portion of their time to the affairs of such a vast area. The very size of its charge compelled delegation of a very large area of authority and discretion to its own officers; the effect was to replace state officers from larger cadres by officers of limited experience in restricted fields. Due to poor revenues of the district boards the tendency had been for the state to take over many of their functions. Finally, due to the large number of village panchayats in a district it was neither convenient nor practicable to link the village panchayats directly to the district board.

1. The Concept of Democratic Decentralization

The question of democratic decentralization became the most crucial point of discussion after Independence. A provision was made in the Indian Constitution for the establishment of panchayats in the villages. Even before the framing of the Constitution, village panchayat acts were passed in some of the states. They were given larger number of functions in order to have full and free development of the rural institutions. The government sponsored its community development programme to promote the development of rural areas. However, it was soon realized that the success of the programme largely depended upon popular initiative and public cooperation. The Planning Commission clearly recognized that unless there is comprehensive planning from below which takes into account the needs of the entire community and every family partakes in the community development movement, the living standard of the people cannot be raised. And, these aims cannot be achieved unless there are agencies at the village level and above which represent the community as a whole, can assume responsibility and initiative for developing the resources of the village and can bring all the people into a common programme to be carried out with the assistance of the government. It was, therefore, emphasized in the First Five-Year Plan and re-emphasized in the Second Five-Year

Plan, that the administration of the country has to provide for the establishment and development at the village level and above of, appropriate agencies which derive their authority from the people only. The First Five-Year Plan pointed out: "The Constitution has provided for democratic institutions at the Centre and in the States, but so long as local self-governing institutions are not conceived as parts of the same organic institutional and administrative framework, the structure of democratic government will remain incomplete. Local self-governing bodies have to play a vital role in the fields of development. It may also be necessary to work out suitable arrangements for linking local and self-governing bodies at different levels with one another, for instance, village panchayats with district or sub-divisional local boards" [1952: 130].

The Second Five-Year Plan pointed out, that in the First Five-Year Plan it was suggested that the general direction of policy should be to encourage local bodies in the development programme and assist them in assuming responsibilities for a large portion of administration and social services within their area as may be possible. The subject requires careful and objective study in the light of conditions prevailing in different parts of the country and experience during the First Five-Year Plan. Therefore, a special investigation under the auspices of the National Development Council has been recommended [1957].

The National Development Council in its eighth meeting decided that a special investigation into such a reorganization of the district administration should be carried out by the team which had already been constituted by the committee on plan projects to study and report on the community projects and national extension service (N.E.S.) with a view to enhancing economy and efficiency.

II. Reformation of Panchayati Raj

1. The Study of National Development Council

The team pointed out that admittedly, one of the least successful aspects of the community development and national extension service work is its attempt to evoke popular initiative. I have found that few of the local bodies at a level higher than the village panchayat have shown any enthusiasm or interest in the work; and even the panchayats have not come into the field to any appreciable extent. An attempt has been made to harness local initiative through the formation of ad-hoc bodies mostly with nominated personnel and invariably advisory in character. These bodies have so far given no indication of durable strength nor the leadership necessary to provide the motive force for continuing the improvement of economic and social conditions in rural area. Therefore there was need to discover and create a representative and democratic institution. Neither the district boards nor the block advisory committees or district planning committees could take up this work. All these bodies were to be replaced by a single representative and vigorous democratic institution to take charge of all aspects of development work in the rural areas. Such a body had to be statutory, elective, comprehensive and in possession of adequate resources. They defined this process as democratic decentralization.

Democratic   Decentralization

Democracy has to function though a certain executive machinery but the democratic government operating over large areas through its executive machinery cannot adequately appreciate local needs and circumstances. It is therefore necessary that there should be a devolution of power and a decentralization of machinery and that such powers be exercised and such machinery be controlled and directed by popular representatives of the government. Delegation of powers cannot be equated with decentralisation. Decentralization is a process, whereby the government divests itself completely of certain duties and responsibilities and devolves them on to some other authority. Delegation of powers is taking place to progressively lower levels of executive machinery. Decentralization of responsibility and power, on the other hand has not taken place below the state level in recent years. Such decentralization has become urgent and can be effected by a devolution of powers to a body which, when created, would have to take the entire charge of all development work within its jurisdiction. If this body was to function with any vigour, initiative and success, the government will have to pass on to it all of its own functions in these fields within this body's jurisdiction, reserving to itself the functions of guidance, supervision and higher planning and where necessary providing extra finance.

Panchayat Samiti

The lack of efficiency of many of the present rural self-governing bodies has been due to too large a jurisdiction, too few powers and, scant finances accompanied by an absence of close relationship with the village panchayats and of guidance by the government or by the political parties. The jurisdiction of the proposed local body should be neither so large as to defeat the very purpose for which it is created nor so small as to mititate against efficiency and economy. Therefore, one might think that the most efficient and useful arrangement in this regard is to have an elected self-governing institution whose jurisdiction would coincide with a development block. The panchayat samiti (committee) should be constituted by indirect election from the village panchayats. A certain number of seats equal to 10% of elected seats be filled up by the representatives of the directors of cooperatives in that area. It should have a life of five years.

The functions of the panchayat samiti should cover the development of agriculture in all its aspects, improvement of cattle, promotion of local industries, public health, welfare work, administration of primary schools and collection and maintenance of statistics. It should also act as an agent of the state government in executing special schemes of development entrusted to it. Other functions should be transferred to them only when they have started functioning as efficient democratic institutions. The state government should give adequate grants-in-aid to them conditionally or unconditionally or on a matching basis with due regard to economically backward areas. All central and state funds spent in a block area should invariably to assigned to the panchayat samiti to be spent by it directly or indirectly except when the samiti recommends direct grant to an institution.

Village Panchayat

The constitution of the village panchayat should be purely on an elective basis with a provision for the cooption of two women members and one member each from the scheduled castes and scheduled tribes. No other groups need be given special representation. A close link should be maintained between the Gram Sewak and the village panchayat or panchayats by making him the development secretary of the committee of the village panchayats within its jurisdiction. The main source of income of the panchayats will be property or house tax, tax on market and vehicles, octroi or terminal tax, conservancy tax, water and lighting rate, income from cattle ponds, grants from the panchayat samiti and fees charged for the registration of animals sold, etc. In addition, the panchayats should be entitled to receive from the panchayat samiti a share upto 3/4th of the net land revenue assigned to the latter. The compulsory duties of the village panchayats should include among others provision of water supply, sanitation, lighting, maintenance of roads, land management, collection and maintenance of records and other statistics of the panchayat samiti in executing any scheme entrusted to it.[1]

Zila Parishad

To ensure necessary coordination between the panchayat samitis, a zila parishad should be constituted consisting of the presidents of these samitis, M.L.A.s (Member of the State Legislative Assembly) and M.P.s (Member of Parliament) representing the area and the district level officers. The Collector will be its chairperson and one of his officers will act as secretary. Functions of the parishad may include examination and approval of the budgets of the panchayat samitis, where funds are allotted by the government for the district as a whole for their distribution between the various blocks, coordination and consolidation of the block plans, supervision of the activities of the panchayat samitis, etc. States which consider it advisable to devolve power on a local institution powered by the state on the same lines as the panchayat samitis, though on a correspondingly larger scale than the panchayat samitis, may constitute such bodies to carry out work as agents of the district body.

The team further pointed out that if this experiment of democratic decentralisation was to yield maximum results, it was necessary that all the three tiers of scheme, vis., village panchayat, panchayat samiti and zila parishad should be started at the same time, and operated simultaneously in the whole district.[2]

The recommendations of the study team in favour of a system of democratic decentralization were considered by the National Development Council in January, 1958. The Council emphasized that the foundation of any democratic structure needs to be in the village. The two institutions which made effective village democracy possible were the village panchayat and the village cooperative. The first step in any area should, therefore, be to establish the network of institutions needed at the village level. Democratic instituitions at the district, block and village levels should be viewed as part of one connected structure of development administration within the district. The Council, therefore, affirmed the objective of introducing democratic instituitions at the district and block levels and suggested that each state work out the structure which suited its conditions best [Third Five-Year Plan, 1961: 333].

2. *Progress of Panchayati Raj*

Legislation for the introduction of Panchayati Raj, was enacted in twelve states by the end of 1962, and in the remaining states later. The Fifth Five-Year Plan observes: "Panchayati Raj now extends to all the states excepting Meghalaya and Nagaland. In Jammu and Kashmir, Kerala, Manipur and Tripura only gram panchayats were functioning. In Bihar panchayat samitis have been established in seven districts and all three tiers in five districts ... The pattern of organization is not uniform in all the states. While West Bengal had four tiers, Karnataka and Orissa have two tiers, Jammu and Kashmir and Kerala one tier and the rest of the states have three-tier system... During the Fourth Five-Year Plan, some significant developments took place with respect to enactment and implementation of Panchayati Raj Acts in different states. For instance, zila parishads were abolished in Orissa, Karnataka and Haryana states... The governments of Andhra Pradesh, Rajasthan, Maharashatra, Madhya Pradesh and Gujarat have got the working of Panchyati Raj examined by high powered committees and their reports are under consideration of the state governments. . . The bulk of the budget of panchayati raj bodies consists of grants provided by the state governments for certain specified schemes initiated at the state level. In the states like Tamil Nadu, Andhra Pradesh and Rajasthan, the trend is encouraging as considerable funds are placed at the disposal of panchayat samitis and the quantum has increased from year to year. States like Gujarat, Orissa and Maharashtra are also routing considerable funds through panchayat samitis, but the amount has shown a decrease from year to year.

The position in other states cannot be said to be satisfactory. At present the only inclusive source of revenue to the panchayats is cess or surcharge on the land revenue. In this regard the states of Tamil Nadu, Madhya Pradesh, Kerala and Haryana account for 89% of the total effects. It is recognized that rural development should include agricultural development in its widest sense so as to embrace, besides crop production, all its allied activities.

Integrated rural development would be possible only through co-operation and participation of people. This could be secured by strengthening the panchayati raj institutions at various levels. It would be necessary in this context to review the size and availability of (i) gram panchayats; (ii) whether the panchayat samiti or zila parishad could be the best agencies for carrying out these program-mes, and (iii) what specific programmes the panchayat samiti or zila parishad, could or should administer" [1974: 85-87].

3. *Ashok Mehta Committee (1977)*

The Government of India appointed the Ashok Mehta Commit-tee in December, 1977 to study panchayati raj institutions and recommend measures to make them an efficient instrument of development. The Committee submitted its report in August, 1978. The Committee pointed out that the disassociation of the growing and complex programme of development with panchayati raj institutions which were considered inadequate, the inability of the bureaucracy to execute the programme through elected bodies, the lack of political will to foster institutions, several internal deficien-cies in the functioning of panchayati raj institutions and above all, the lack of clarity about the concept of itself have weakened the entire system.[3]

The establishment of democratic bodies below the state-level was an imperative from the political and social-developmental perspective. They recommended that to achieve a balance between the technological requirements and possibilities for a meaningful participation by the people in development, a number of villages should be grouped to constitute Mandal Panchayats. Such Mandal panchayats should cover a population of 15,000 to 20,000 to forge the necessary linkages with schemes for development of focal points and growth centres. While they preferred the two-tiers system, a district level zila parishad and a Mandal panchayat for the time being, the other two tiers, i.e. panchayat samitis and village panchayats could continue to function.

As regards finances, the Committee pointed out that the norm "no taxation, only representation" should be discouraged. It suggested that all panchayati raj institutions should have compulsory powers of taxation. The Committee also recommended complete transfer of land revenue to panchayati raj institutions over a period of five years. To protect the interests of the weaker sections, the Committee recommended their representations in all panchayati raj institutions on the basis of their population. The reservation system should be supplemented by the formation of social justice committees whose chairperson would be only from scheduled castes/ scheduled tribes. It also recommended a regular social audit by district-level agency as well as by a committee of legislators (comprising mostly MLAs/MLCs) belonging to scheduled castes/ scheduled tribes to review the working of the programmes and funds meant for these weaker groups.

However the recommendations of this Committee were still under the consideration of various state governments [Bhargava, 1979a, 1979b; Jain, 1981].

Here I give in brief the pattern being followed in U.P. which will give some idea as to how it has been implemented in practice.

III. Panchayati Raj in U.P.

In the beginning, the state of U.P. did not agree with the three-tier system recommended by the study team and the idea was to strengthen the district level bodies. As a result, the Antarim Zila Parishads Act was passed in 1958 to replace the existing district boards and district planning committees by Antarim Zila Parishads. However, after making this interim arrangement, the state government gave the most earnest consideration to the final set up of district councils, and ultimately decided to have the three-tier system as recommended by the study team. As a result, the Uttar Pradesh Kshetriya Samitis and Zila Parishad Adhiniyam was passed in 1961 which was amended in 1963 [Shiviah, Rao, Murty, Malkiajuniah, 1976; Zaheer and Gupta, 1970].

The main provisions of this Act are [Government of Uttar Pradesh, 1961, 1963]:

1. *Zila Parishad*

Under section 18 of the above Act, the Zila Parishad was to consist of (i) Pramukhs of all Kshetriya Samitis established in the district, (ii) As many persons, as may be specified to be chosen by each Kshetriya Samiti out of its members in the manner prescribed, (iii) Presidents of all municipal boards in the district, (iv) Four representatives of the co-operatives namely the Managing Director of the Co-operative Bank, a representative of the District Co-operative Bank, a representative of the District Co-operative Foundation, a representative of the Co-operative Societies as the State Government may, having regard to the usefulness of their activity in the district specify for each district and representative of the Cane Unions in the district, (v) members not exceeding three as may be specified to be chosen by the state government from among persons engaged in cultural, literary, or professional activities, (vi) all the M.P.s and the M.L.A.s whose constituencies include any part of the district and all members of the Council of States and the State Legislative Council who have their residence in the district. Some women and scheduled caste and scheduled tribe members shall be co-opted as members of the zila parishad; in the case of scheduled castes and scheduled tribes in proportion to their population.

Under Section 19, each Zila Parishad shall have an Adhyaksha (President) and Up-adhyaksha (Vice-President) who shall be elected by secret ballot by the members of the Zila Parishad. The Adhyaksha must be a resident of that district though he may not be a member of the Zila Parishad but he must not be an M.L.A., M.P. or President of Municipal Board. He would have attained the age of 30 years. The term of office of the Zila Parishad shall be five years which may be extended to six years. The term of office of an Adhyaksha shall be five years while that of an Up-adhyaksha one year.

The functions of the Zila Parishad (Section 33) include among others, supervision of activities of Gaon Panchayats and Kshetriya Samitis of the district, to act as the main channel of correspondence between the state government on the one hand and Kshetriya Samitis and Gaon Panchayats on the other, certain functions in the field of agriculture, animal husbandry, village and cottage industries, medical and public health, education and cultural activities, public works, relief works, planning and statistics and such other functions as may be prescribed.

As regards finances, the Zila Parishad under the Act (Section 119) can impose tax on property and any other tax which has been recommended for the Zila Parishad by the study team. Besides these taxes fees and tolls can be charged for the use or occupation of an immovable property vested in or entrusted to Zila Parishad (Section 142). Moreover they can charge licence fee, school fee, fees for the use of libraries and sarais, fees at fairs, markets, agricultural shows etc. (Section 145).

2. *Kshetriya Samiti*

Under Section 6, Kshetriya Samiti comprises (i) All Pradhans of constituent Gaon Sabhas, (ii) Chairperson of each town area committee and President of each notified area committee lying within the Vikas-khand (development block), (iii) Two of five representatives of such co-operatives as have their registered offices within the khand, (iv) All M.P.s and the M.L.A.s whose constituencies include any part of the khand, (v) All members of the Council of States and State Legislative Council who have their residence in the khand. In addition, there will be certain co-opted members which will include two persons interested in planning and development, some women, to make their number five, and scheduled castes and scheduled tribes members to make their number as eight.

Every Kshetriya Samiti shall have a Pramukh, one senior Up-pramukh and one junior Up-pramukh to be elected by the members by secret ballot. The term of office of a Pramukh or Up-pramukh shall be the same as that of the Kshetriya Samiti, i.e., five years.

Under Section 32, the functions of the Kshetriya Samiti shall include development of (i) agriculture, co-operatives and minor irrigation, (ii) animal husbandry, (iii) cottage industries, (iv) medical and public health, (v) education, social education and cultural activities, (vi) harijan welfare, (vii) planning and statistics, (viii) executing the schemes of government and of the Zila Parishad that might be entrusted to it, (ix) supervision over Gaon Sabhas, and (x) public works. The staff to be employed by the Kshetriya Samiti will be the same as now employed by the state government in the block. The finances of the Kshetriya Samitis include any tax allowed by the state government. The fees and tolls as already discussed may be levied either by the Zila Parishad or the Kshetriya Samiti.

The functions of the village panchayat under this Act were almost the same as under the U.P. Panchayati Raj Act, 1947 with a few exceptions. For example the land management committee which was previously an independent institution, would now be a part of the village panchayat and the latter would appoint from among its members a Bhumi Prabandhak Committee. Some of the supervisory functions over panchayat which were previously performed by the state government shall now be performed by the Zila Parishads or Kshetriya Samitis. The Act was enforced in July, 1963.

IV. Village Panchayats

1. The History of Panchayats

The history of village panchayats since the early Vedic period till the British rule has already been traced, and also the causes of disintegration of the village panchayats during the British period. Montague Chelmsford Report (1918) made recommendations for provincial autonomy and under the Government of India Act 1919 the local self government became a provincial subject. After this, attempts were made to revive the old village panchayats and in pursuance of this policy of the central government various provinces passed Village Panchayat Acts in 1919, some provinces followed later. But as these panchayats were not democratic they did not make much headway, and these acts only remained paper laws without any significance.

After the Independence and the declaration of the Indian Republic (1950), a radical change has occurred in the government approach towards village panchayats. This is apparent even from the Indian Constitution. It lays down as a directive principle of state policy that the state shall take steps to organize village panchayats and endow them with such powers and authority as may be necessary to enable them to function as units of self-government. Even before the Constituent Assembly's above decision to popularize village panchayats, the Congress governments in various states tried to revive this institution of panchayat by revising their earlier enactments. U.P. was the first state to give a lead in this matter. The first comprehensive Village Panchayati Raj Act was passed in 1947, which became a model for other states. By 1953 almost all the states had created separate departments for panchayats, whose functions were to administer State Panchayat Raj Act, to arrange the organization of panchayats through their field staff and to supervise their work. The panchayat secretaries were appointed to look after the work of panchayats.

The functions of panchayats were conceived widely enough to permit them to comprehend most of the civic and economic activities of a village community along with judicial functions. In practice, however, few panchayats discharged all the functions entrusted to them and the activities of many of them suffered from local factions, lack of resources, and want of proper guidance. Though they helped in social awakening, they did not achieve much success in raising the level of village life and did not become an instrument of village reconstruction and development which they were intended to be.

The National Planning Commission in their First Five-Year Plan rightly observed: "Although there are exceptions, the panchayat as an institution has not yet become the instrument of village reconstruction and development which it was intended to be" [1952: 133]. At the same time it also added: "unless a village agency can assume responsibility and initiative for developing the resources of the villages, it will be difficult to make marked impression on rural life, for only a village organization representing the community as a whole can provide the necessary leadership. As the agencies of the state government cannot easily approach each individual villager separately, progress depends largely on the existence of an active organization in the village which can bring the people into common programmes to be carried with the assistance of the administration" [1952: 133].

It is recommended that for the proper performance of civic functions the village panchayats should be associated with an active process of development in which they should be given effective part. For carrying out economic development programmes envisaged under the Five-Year Plan they should assume responsibility for the following with suitable legislation, if necessary to enable them to do so:

1. Framing programmes of production for the village;
2. Framing budgets of requirements for supply and finance needed for carrying out the programme;
3. Acting as the channel through which, governments' assistance other than assistance which is given through agencies like co-operatives, reaches the village;
4. Securing minimal standards of cultivation to be observed in the village with a view to increasing production;
5. Bringing waste-land under cultivation;
6. Arranging for the cultivation of land not cultivated or managed by the owners;
7. Organizing voluntary labour for community works;
8. Making arrangement for co-operative management of land and other resources in the village according to the terms of the prevailing land management legislation; and
9. Assisting the implementation of land reform measures in the village [1952: 133].

The process of election may not bring in a sufficient number of persons with qualities most needed in village reconstruction; such as, good farmers engaged in improving agricultural practices, enthusiastic workers of the co-operative movement and persons whose main interest lies in constructive social work, etc., a small number of additional members belonging to the above classes may be appointed by state government on an adhoc basis. This village agency should gradually draw up production plans for the village as a whole on the basis of programmes accepted by individual farmers and local co-operatives and this should become an effective base for planning on a national scale in the field of agriculture and rural development.

Regarding finance various states allotted a percentage of land revenue to the panchayats for various activities to be undertaken by them which varied for 3 to 15%. Grants to panchayats were also to be given for specific activities, i.e., for public works, for opening libraries, etc. Later on the resources of village panchayats were reviewed by the Local Finance Inquiry Committee, which recommended that 15% of the land revenue should be given to the village panchayats. The Planning Commission in the First Five-Year Plan endorsed this view but at the same time pointed out that as this step may affect the state plans which have taken into account the full land revenue in their resources, the state government may impose a suitable surcharge with reference to the land revenue and hand over the proceeds of this surcharge to the village panchayats.

Regarding training of officials and members of village panchayats it was provided in the State Panchayati Raj Act that it would be responsibility of the state government to make such arrangements. The commission pointed out that though the village is the basic unit of community organization yet for particular purposes, like employment of paid staff for the panchayats and the co-operative societies, arrangements for supplies and credit or for providing various amenities in the rural areas, a larger unit may be chosen.

2. Congress Village Panchayat Committee Report

As a result of the above measures, the progress has been quite good in the establishment of village panchayats in various states. It was estimated that by March 1954, 50% of the villages were already covered by village panchayats. The All India Congress Working Committee, which reviewed their progress in May 1954, appointed a committee known as the Congress Village Panchayat Committee with Dr. K.N. Katju as its chairperson to review the progress made so far and to consider the question of their proper development from various aspects. The committee made the following important recommendations:

1. The panchayat system provides a strong basis for the establishment of healthy democratic tradition in India, therefore,

its development should be encouraged by the state.

2. Great importance should be attached to the need for unanimity in the elections of village panchayats and to encourage this unanimity, greater authority and power should be delegated to those panchayats which elect their panchas unanimously.

3. The election of panchayats should be on the basis of adult franchise. All adults of the village should constitute a Gaon Sabha. The village panchayat should be elected by this Gaon Sabha and will be in the nature of its executive. The strength of the village panchayat will depend upon the population of the village. It should generally be in multiples of five. There should be reservation of seats for the scheduled castes and scheduled tribes in proportion to their population.

4. There should be generally one panchayat for a population of about 1500 to 2000.

5. It would be helpful to have some sort of supervisory body to regulate and coordinate the activities of panchayats and these supervisory bodies should preferably be at the sub-divisional level, though their existence at the district or other convenient levels is not ruled out. Such bodies should not be nominated but should be indirectly elected by the Sarpanchs.

6. The panchayats should have a variety of functions such as municipal, social, economic, judicial, etc. Municipal functions should include sanitation, village roads, construction and maintenance of community buildings, drainage, provision for drinking water, street lightings, etc. In addition to certain compulsory municipal functions, there may also be some discretionary functions which the state government may entrust to them.

7. The composition and functions of the judicial or Adalati Panchayats should be separate from the village panchayats. Each judicial panchayat should serve a few villages covering a population of about 5000-6000 in a radius of say 4-5 Km Each Goan Sabha should elect along with their village panchayat representatives a panel of five members to work on the judicial panchayats. On this basis the judicial panchayat should have 25 to 30 such members and a bench of five out of this total, should be constituted by a system of rotation. The cases should

be heard in the villages where they occurred and the whole legal procedure should be completed in one sitting in order to avoid unnecessary delays. Lawyers should not be allowed to appear in these judicial panchayats. In the judicial panel of five members elected by the Gaon Sabhas there should be at least one from scheduled castes/scheduled tribes and one woman.

8. The community project officers, the N.E.S. block officers and the village level workers should actively help in the evolution and growth of village panchayats so that the latter may be able to shoulder the ever-growing responsibility for the implementation of the National Plan in their area.

9. Special provision should be made for the training of workers so as to enable them to discharge their functions properly.

10. Panchayats should be increasingly assigned the task of revenue collection and 15 to 25% of the revenue collection should be allotted to them for their day to day functioning. They should be empowered to levy a labour tax, though efforts should be made by them to get voluntary contributions in the form of *shramadan*. When a panchayat has successfully worked for some time, it may be permitted to impose any of such taxes, as tax on landholdings, vehicle tax, profession tax, tax on tea shops, etc., and also allowed to collect revenue from management of bazaars, mela (festival) grounds, etc. Under the existing circumstances state aid is absolutely essential to enable them to carry out their functions properly.

11. Functions and organization of the co-operatives and the village panchayats must be kept separate for various reasons, e.g., the scope of co-operatives is much wider besides their being optional bodies. The panchayats, however, must mobilize public opinion for the growth of a co-operative movement.

3. Local Self-Government Ministers' Conference

At the same time when the above Committee was making its deliberations, a conference of Local Self-Government Ministers was held in Simla in June 1954, with Raj Kumari Amrit Kaur, the Union Health Minister, as its chairperson. The conference decided to form two sub-committees, one to discuss problems of village panchayats and the other to discuss problems of municipal and local boards. The sub committee on Village Panchayats made certain recommendations just on the same lines as were made by the Congress Village Panchayat Committee, though in greater details about the performance of judicial functions by the Adalati panchayats.

The Conference approved a proposal for setting up a council of Local Self Government Ministers with Central Minister of Health as chairperson, and the first meeting of the Council was held in Simla in June 1955, which reviewed the progress made in the earlier year and also made several recommendations.

Later the Planning Commission reviewed the progress made by the village panchayats during the First Five-Year Plan and suggested certain measures for their development during the Second Five-Year Plan. First it pointed out that the preparation of the First Five-Year Plan in the states suffered from an important defect in so far as it was done mainly at state headquarters and later on attempts were made to break it up into district plans. But as in the programmes of local development works, local communities had to propose schemes which they could undertake through their own labour with the support of the government, it was now recognized that unless there was comprehensive village planning which took into account the needs of the entire community, the weaker sections of rural population like tenant cultivators, landless workers and artisans may not benefit sufficiently from assistance provided by the government. Secondly, as the N.E.S. movement aimed at reaching every family in the village, this aim could not be fulfilled unless there was an agency in the village that represented the community as a whole, and could assume responsibility and initiative for developing the resources of the village and provide the necessary leadership.

Both these considerations were to be taken into account in the preparation of the Second Five-Year Plan and the state governments were requested to arrange for the preparation of plans for the Second Five-Year Plan period for individual villages and groups of villages at the level of tehsils, talukas, development blocks, etc. This would help to relate the plans to local needs and conditions and also secure public participation, voluntary efforts and contributions.

The Planning Commission also realized that district administration envisaged in the N.E.S. and community development programmes would remain incomplete unless village institutions were placed on solid footing and were entrusted with a good deal of responsibility for carrying out local programmes. Their development on right lines was significant for several reasons. Under the impact of new developments including the growth of population, land reforms, urbanization, spread of education, increase in production and improvement in communication, the village society was in a state of rapid transition. In emphasizing the interest of the community as a whole and in particular the needs of those sections which were at present handicapped in various ways, village panchayats along with co-operatives could play an important part in bringing about a just and integrated social structure in rural areas and in developing a new pattern of rural leadership.

Keeping these considerations in view the Commission pointed out that it was the general aim to establish a statutory panchayat in every village. During the First Five-Year Plan the number of village panchayats increased from 83,087 to 117,593 and it was proposed in increase this number to 244,564 by 1960-61. The Commission also pointed out the need to review the village boundaries so as to evolve good, efficient and working village units with live panchayats. Leaving aside villages in the hilly tracts where grouping was difficult, the question of combining existing villages into units with a population of about 1000 deserved consideration. In 1969, the village panchayats existed in all states and most union territories [Fourth Five-Year Plan, 1970: 228]. The number of village panchayats which was 214,967 in 1968-69 rose to 221,270 in 1971-72 covering 98% of the rural population [Fifth Five-Year Paln, 1974: 86].

The functions relating to village production programmes and the development of village land and resources were re-examined by the Planning Commission in the Second Five-Year Plan. In the light of recommendations made during the First Plan, it was stated that the functions of panchayats might broadly be grouped under two heads, viz. administrative and judicial. Administrative functions might further be divided into four categories: (i) civic, (ii) development, (iii) land management, and (iv) land reforms. Civic and development functions enumerated by the Commission are almost the same as already stated. Land management and land reform functions included functions on the lines along which it was proposed to reorganize the agrarian structure during the Second Five-Year Plan. The land management functions included: (i) regulation of the use of common land, (ii) adoption of standaards of good management, and (iii) maintenance of land records. Land reform functions included: (i) determination of land to be allotted to owners and tenants, (ii) determination of surplus land on the application of ceilings, and (iii) redistribution of surplus land.

The judicial functions included: (i) administration of civil and criminal justice, (ii) enforcement of minimum wages for agricultural workers, and (iii) simple disputes pertaining to land. The common pattern in states for facilitating the exercise of these functions should be to establish separate judicial panchayats and their territorial jurisdiction should extend as rule to a number of villages.

As the process of election did not always throw up a sufficient number of persons with qualities most needed in village reconstruction (such as good farmers, co-operative workers or social workers) it was desirable to empower village panchayats to co-opt a limited number of persons. The method of nomination of additional members suggested in the First Five-Year Plan, was found defective.

Regarding their financial position, the Commission pointed out that as the village panchayats develop, they would soon face the problem of finance. It was desirable that all states should assign a proportion of the land revenue to the panchayats for local development. These grants should be made in two parts: a basic proportion, say 15 to 20% of the land revenue with an additional grant extending to say 15% of the land revenue on the condition that the panchayat raises an equal additional amount by taxation or voluntary contributions. Panchayats should also be assisted in developing sources of recurring income. For example, assistance may be given for the payment of salaries to panchayat secretaries, and the staff for the panchayats should be suitably trained.

V. Gram Panchayats in U.P.

As the gram (village) panchayats is a state subject, to apprise the reader, their actual working, legislation and functioning in one of the important states, i.e. U.P. is described here. The U.P. Panchayati

Raj Act was passed in 1947. It was subsequently amended in 1950, twice in 1952 and then in 1955 to remove the difficulties which were found in the proper development of these panchayats. The first election of panchayats was held in 1949 and the second in 1955. The features of the U.P. Panchayati Raj Act, 1947 as amended up to 1957 are given below. [Government of Uttar Pradesh: 1947, 1952, 1955, 1957; Zaheer and Gupta, 1970].

1. Constitution of the Gram Panchayat

There should be a Gram Sabha for every village or group of villages (Section 3).[4] All adults above the age of 21 living within the area of that Gram Sabha are to be its members except persons of unsound mind (Section 5). The Gram Sabha is to elect from amongst its members an executive body called the Gram Panchayat and also a Pradhan and Up-Pradhan. The terms of office of the Pradhan and panchayat members are to be five years, while that of Up-Pradhan one year only. The term of the Pradhan may be extended to six years by the state government under certain circumstances. The seats for scheduled castes and scheduled tribes in the Gram Panchayat are to be reserved till today, according to their population in that area. The election is to be hold on joint electorate basis.

To assist the panchayat in its function, a Secretary is to be appointed by the Director of Panchayats for every Gram Panchayat or for a group of Gram Panchayats. His salary may partly be met from the funds of the Gram Sabha and partly by the government.

2. Functions of Gram Panchayats

According to Section 15 of the Act, it is the duty of every Gram Panchayat, so far as its funds allow, to make reasonable provision within its jurisdiction for (i) construction, repair, maintenance, cleaning and lighting of public streets, (ii) medical relief, (iii) sanitation, (iv) upkeep and protection of buildings belonging to the Gram Sabha, (v) registering births, deaths and marriages, (vi) removal of encroachments on public streets and public places in their area, (vii) regulation of melas, markets and *hats* within its area, (viii) establishing and maintaining primary schools, (ix) construction, repair and maintenance of public wells, tanks and ponds, (x) assisting the development of agriculture, commerce and industry,

(xi) maternity and child welfare, and (xii) fulfilling other obligations imposed by any other law on a Gram Sabha.

Besides these obligatory functions, there are certain discretionary functions for the Gram Panchayat under Section 16 of this Act. These are: (i) planting and maintaining trees on the sides of public streets and in other public places, (ii) improving breeding and medical treatment of cattle, (iii) organizing a village volunteer force for watch and ward, assisting them in the discharge of their functions, (iv) development of co-operatives, (v) arrangement for recreational facilities, i.e., establishment and maintenance of a library, *akhara* or club, public radio sets and gramophones, promotion of harmony between different communities, etc.

3. Sources of Revenue (Section 32)

There is to be a common fund for each Gram Sabha, which is to be utilized for carrying out duties or obligations imposed upon it. The fund is to consist of (i) proceeds of any tax imposed under the Panchayati Raj Act, (ii) all sums handed over by the state government to the Gram Sabha, (iii) all sums ordered by a court to be placed to the credit of a Gram fund, (iv) sale proceeds of all dust, dirt, dung or refuse including the dead bodies of animals, (v) sums contributed to the Gram fund by any district board or local authority, and (vi) sums received by way of loan or gift.

Under Section 37 a Gram Sabha may levy the following taxes and fees subject to rules made or restrictions imposed by the state government: (i) a tax on land not exceeding one anna in a rupee on the amount of land revenue payable thereof, (ii) a professional tax on a person carrying trade or calling or any other profession upto a maximum of Rs. 6 per annum, (iii) tax on animals or vehicles plied for hire, (iv) fees on registration of animals sold in melas, (v) fees for the use of slaughter houses, and (vi) a tax on buildings owned by persons who do not pay any of the aforesaid taxes, etc.

4. The Nyaya Panchayat

The state government shall divide a district into circles, each circle comprising as many areas subject to the jurisdiction of Gram Sabha as may be expedient and shall establish Nyaya Panchayats for each such circle (Section 43). The prescribed authority shall appoint five persons of prescribed qualifications out of the village panchayat members elected at the election of village panchayat by the Gram Sabha. They will be the panchas of the Nyaya Panchayat and shall cease to be the members of Gram Sabha. The panchas so appointed shall elect from amongst themselves two persons, who may be able to record proceedings, one as the Sarpanch and other as the Sahayak Sarpanch. All these panchas shall be members for five years which may be extended to six years by the state government.

The Sarpanch shall form benches consisting of five panchas each for the disposal of cases and enquiries coming before the Nyaya Panchayat. The bench shall choose one of its members as chairperson and at least three will form the quorum (Section 77A).

As regards criminal cases the Nyaya Panchayats can try some specific criminal cases coming under certain sections of the Indian Penal Code, 1860 (Section 52). The Sarpanch can ask any person to execute a bond of Rs. 100 if any breach of peace is apprehended. The matter will then be tried by a bench. No panchayat can inflict a substantive sentence of imprisonment, nor can it impose a fine of more than Rs. 100. The panchayat may release offenders on probation (Section 62). As regard civil cases the Nyaya Panchayat may take cognizance of civil cases subject to certain restrictions imposed by this acts and whose value does not exceed Rs.100, in respect of money due under a contract for the recovery of movable property, for wrongfully injuring a movable property, or for damages caused by cattle trespass.

Before any civil or criminal case is instituted by the complainant, he shall have to pay the prescribed fee. The case shall be heard by a bench. No legal practitioner is allowed to appear before the Nyaya Panchayat. The superior court, i.e. the Sub-Divisional Magistrate, the *Munsif* or the Sub-Divisional Officer have complete powers over the Nyaya Panchayats, and can transfer cases from one panchayat to the other or recall the case to their court in their respective spheres i.e., criminal, civil or revenue. The Superior Court can revise the decisions of the Nyaya Panchayat, but there is no appeal against any order of the Nyaya Panchayat (Section 89).

VI. Review of Working of Panchayati Raj in U.P.

According to the General Administration Reports issued annually by the U.P. government and the reports of the Local Self-Government Department of the U.P. government some of the achievements of the panchayats are given below.

1. Gram Panchayat

It will be observed that particular attention was paid by the panchayats to the improvement of rural communication, public health, sanitation, providing medical aid and educational facilities. Importance of *Panchayat-ghars* in rural life was specially realized for making a living centre of community life. They were generally so constructed as to house a village school, a seed store, a library and reading room. Construction of Gandhi *chabutras* with the twin object of perpetuating the revered memory of the Father of the Nation, enhancing community life by arranging *bhajans, kirtans* and a variety of entertainment and other programmes, helped in radiating cultural activities.

The panchayats helped considerably in furthering various development activities in community project area and N.E.S. blocks. They extended whole-hearted cooperation to other departments. To step up agricultural production, half-field demonstrations were organized in large numbers and a considerable number of plots sown by the dibbling method. Efforts were also directed toward making crop competitions a success. Increased irrigation facilities were provided by constructing wells, tanks, *nalas* (drains) and *gullies*.

With a view to improving the breed of livestock in villages, panchayats maintain community stud bulls of good breed in every Gram Sabha. Suitable arrangements for pisciculture in the ponds of the villages were also made by some of the panchayats. Besides this, Gram Sabhas render considerable assistance to animal husbandry department in connection with celebration of Gopashtmi work and the organization of cattle exhibitions.

Keen interest is also evidenced in organizing co-operative societies. They established 2,906 co-operative societies upto September 30, 1955. These have been successful in arousing public enthusiasm and securing voluntary labour *(sharamadan)*. *Sharamadan* weeks are observed in which generally roads or *gullies* are constructed or repaired, tanks are dug or deepened, drains are dug or repaired, etc. They took initiative in organizing such activities as community recreation centres, libraries, purchase of radio sets, youth *mahila* (women) samitis, *vikas mandals* and melas, etc.

Land revenue is also collected by the panchayats where it is entrusted to them by the collector. The panchayats also helped in the preparation of the village plans to be included in the Five-Year plans and annual village production plans. But this appears to be doubtful as the Programme Evaluation Organization (P.E.O.) in one of its reports points out, "It is claimed by some States, notably Uttar Pradesh, Bihar and Maharashtra, that the Panchayats have been associated with the drawing up of development plans for the villages. In the few panchayats covered by this study, however, such association even if it were there, must have been superficial, for it has not led to any noteworthy effort for agricultural improvement in the villages, nor created any particular conciousness about the village plan among the villagers".[5] The P.E.O. found similaar conditions with regard to the management of common land: "In Punjab and Uttar Pradesh where panchayats were given the management of village common land, no panchayat took the initiative either in reclaiming any part of the land or augmenting its productive capacity."

2. Nyaya Panchayat

The Nyaya Panchayats have done useful work in the 1950s. They decided cases with the least possible delay and without much expenditure by the panchas elected by the people themselves. The settling of disputes through mutual compromise in a large number of cases is a clear indication of the fact that the panchayat adalats enjoy the confidence of the people. For example in 1953-54 out of a total number of 525,318 cases coming up before these adalats, 422,622 were either disposed off or transferred to other courts. Of these, 1,49,754 cases were disposed off through mutual compromise, and 3,980 cases which were beyond the jurisdiction of Nyaya Panchayats were disposed off with the consent of the parties. Revision was filed in 13,557 (i.e. 3%) cases of panchayati adalats, and were allowed in only 6,030 (i.e. 1.3%). Similar results have been recorded in other years.

In spite of their remarkable achievements, it has been alleged that the establishment of Nyaya Panchayats has led to increase in litigation and there has been no such panchayats at the door of the villagers. But it may be pointed out that the increase in litigation in rural areas is not only due to these Nyaya Panchayats but also due to redressal of all their grievances, which was not possible in the past.

The Ashok Mehta Committee (1977) observes that the working of Nyaya Panchayats has shown mixed results; in most cases they remained inactive. The committee favoured association of a qualified judge to preside over a bench of elected Nyaya Panchas [1978: 5]. The evaluation of the role performed by Nyaya Panchayats after 1950, will be discussed in the next chapter.

Notes

[1]   The working of panchayats have been discussed in detail later on.

[2]   Report of the Study Team for Community Projects and National Extension Service [1957: 128].

[3]   Recommendation of Ashok Mehta Committee on Panchayati Raj Institutions [1978: Vol.2, 3].

[4]   U.P. Panchayati Raj Act 1947.

[5]   The Fifth Evaluation Report on Working of Community Development and National Extension Service Blocks [1958: 131].

6

HISTORICAL OUTLINE OF VILLAGE POLITICS

I. The Nature and Level of Political Action

Life in Cakra as elsewhere has many aspects consisting of several layers of social reality. The different aspects and layers are inter-related. Particularly in an undifferentiated structural organization like Cakra, political relationships are not always independent of what goes on in the social, economic and ritual aspects of life. Also, what appears on the surface, may only be a reflection of what goes on underneath. Nevertheless, for analytical purposes, it is necessary to isolate one aspect of life and one layer of social reality from the others. Moreover, while in this study the author is primarily concerned with those actions and processes which are political in nature and which generally do not take place at the surface level, it needs to be pointed out that these by themselves constitute about a fraction of the totality. On the surface level, for example, one gets an entirely different picture; a picture of a remarkable ease and casualness with which people go about the daily business of their lives. It would be a rare visitor from the outside world who would fail to be impressed by this seeming tranquility.

In order, therefore, to provide a proper perspective as well as a contrast to the main body of the data, let me take a brief look at what may be called a day in the life of Cakra village. In the following paragraphs, glimpses are presented, which represent what goes on, typically, at the surface level in Cakra.

(1) Ram Nath Singh (R.N.Singh), a 'Thakur', has just come back from sugarcane fields. Today it was his turn to receive his supply of canal water. Starting at 4 a.m. his turn lasted eight hours. He had to be in the fields all this time to channel the water and to make sure it was evenly distributed over his fields. He would be now tired and hungry, although he had a meal four hours ago which his wife had brought to the fields. Taking his shirt off he sits on a *charpai* in front of his house to relax before taking a bath. Soon after Hari Prasad Singh (H.P. Singh) 'Thakur' passed on the street. He is riding a bicycle with a sack in its rear carrier. The sack is full of new millet seed which H.P.Singh brought from a co-operative store in the town market. In reply to R.N. Singh's greeting, he gets off the bicycle; and opening the sack, he takes out a handfull of grain. He looks at it intently, chews a few grains, and asks H.P. Singh about the price. He also asks if the co-operative store had received a supply of fertilizers. H.P. Singh tells him it had not. They talk about the inefficiency of the government supply system until R.N. Singh's daughter appears on the door step and reminds him of the bath as the food is ready.

(2) In his airy *baithak* Santram Singh 'Thakur' is making a rope out of hemp which he grew on the borders of his fields. There are several other people from the village in the *baithak*, some sitting while others are lying on *charpais*. They are all taking about the High School examination results which appeared in daily Hindi newspaper. They have learnt that Santram Singh's son has failed in the examination. The son is present there refilling the *hukkah* for his father and the others. They are discussing the advisability of letting the son live in the city of Jaunpur next year where he can attend a private school and concentrate on his studies. In that case Santram Singh would have to hire more full time workers to look after the farm.

(3) Bhola Khatik, a 'Lohar', is working on an axle for the cart he just finished making for Surendra Singh 'Thakur'. It was a big project and he has been working on it for several weeks, whenever he had time from other day to day commitments. Today his young son is helping him. It does not happen often because the son seldom works as a carpenter. There is not enough carpentry work in the village to keep two persons in the same family fully engaged. The

son instead works mainly as a mason. It pays good money, at least Rs. 15 a day. Yesterday he finished adding a new room to the house of a Thakur. Tomorrow he starts on a new job in a village 30 Km away. It is a big job and will last at least a month. He will have to live in that village all this time. They are talking about the things he should carry with him.

(4) Phoolwati, the young daughter of Parvat Nai, is applying with her hands a fresh plaster of mud to the outer wall of their house. It is a job which has to be done before the monsoon rains start. Her hands and arms are covered with mud; her face and clothes are smeared too. A few yards away Chanda, the daughter of Om Prakash Jogi, is making cowdung cakes in their *gher.* Chanda has recently returned to the village after first two-months' stay at her husband's house. The changes which this first visit to new house have brought to her are quite visible in her looks, her clothes, and most prominently in the new pieces of jewellery which she is wearing. Both Chanda and Phoolwati are giggling while talking to each other. Perhaps Chanda is discussing her husband. All of a sudden, she bursts out in laughter and throws a ball of cowdung at Phoolwati. Phoolwati screams and in turn throws a handful of mud at her.

The above glimpses show what goes on in the village at the surface level. These are the kind of situations which keep the villagers busy most of the time. Everything seems to be moving in a slow and set pattern. Everyone seems to be engaged in daily chores. If the hoe is broken, it has to be repaired, particularly if the owner cannot afford a new one at the moment. Who else but the family Lohar will do the repair job? New seeds and fertilizers have to be purchased. This called for a visit to the town market. When one's turn comes, the fields have to be irrigated, which may mean eight hours of continuous work in the fields. When that happens, the wife has to bring the food. Cowdung cakes need to be made every day, otherwise the dung would get dry and hard. The walls of *kutcha* house need a new coat of mud plaster every year and it has to be done before the rains start. If the son continues to fail in the examination, something has to be done about that too. And, in this way, an endless stream of daily routine goes on which seems to change only with the change in the seasons and with major events in one's life cycle.

This is what an outside visitor sees on his casual visit to the village.

But underneath routine activities on the surface, there are other aspects of life in Cakra which begin to reveal themselves to the visitor after he has spent some time in the community. It is a major revelation because the picture that emerges is very different. Nothing seems to follow set patterns at that level. It is a dynamic world full of constantly moving forces. Even some of the surface level activities assume new meanings in the light of what goes on underneath. Why is it, for example that H.P. Singh on his way back from the market town stopped only at R.N. Singh's place ? Did he not pass a few other Thakurs sitting in front of Sanjay Singh's house, who apparently did not even notice him? Who were those people sitting or lying in Santram Singh's *baithak,* smoking his *hukkah,* and showing so much interest in his son's educational problems? Perhaps these are all minor issues, but often they become significant in view of what else goes on at that level.

One thing which became clear soon after the field work started in the village was that most of the conscious political maneuvering through which the villagers sought to advance, or at least maintain, their positions took place at the sub-surface level. It was at this level that political alignments were made. Factions, too, to the extent to which they were based on these alignments, were sub-surface level phenomena. It should not, however, mean that everything which went on at this level was political in nature. Nor should it mean that all political actions took place only at this level. As regards the non-political activities, most of the borrowing and lending between the villagers, in cash or in kind, was found to be undertaken in privacy and confidence. At attempt was made to keep such transactions out of public knowledge. Extra marital liaisons, by their very nature, called for secrecy. The same was true of love affairs between village boys and girls, which, due to the principle of village exogamy, were strongly tabooed. Nevertheless such relations did take place and remained only at the sub-surface level. All these activities were of non-political nature, unless they were dragged into the political arena by the contending parties.

On the other hand, political actions, or at least aspects of these, took place on the surface level too. For example, much surreptitious maneuvering went on before a village-wide decision on an important issue was due, but when the actual decision was made it was usually made in public where people were expected to declare their stand on the given issue. Hostilities between families were usually matured and nursed in an underhand manner but often erupted and took the form of open confrontation.

In this way, political behaviour has consisted of both public and private aspects. One more observation regarding this distinction is relevant. The sub-surface level activities, political or non-political, did not necessarily remain secret. Sooner or later they became part of the commonly shared knowledge in the village. Everyone came to know, for example, who had borrowed money from whom or what new extra- or pre-marital liaison had been effected. In the political field, people were not only found to be aware of behind the scene maneuvering on the part of so and so, but, most of the time, they could also foretell the nature of that maneuvering. This gave a strange flavour to village politics. When Mathura Singh, for example planned his tactics and strategies, he did so in view of what he thought the tactics and strategies of Taj Singh would be. Moreover, he also seemed to know that whatever strategy he himself might use, Vikram Singh had perhaps already anticipated it. In a way, thus, it looked like a skilled game of chess. For different chessmen on the board there are separate rules of movement. Yet the two players plan their strategy with a fairly high degree of anticipation of each other's moves. The difference lies in the fact that while there are only two players interacting in the game of chess, there were many more in the political arena of Cakra, and, that, while a chess player can make only one move at a time, the political actor in Cakra has no such limits. These moves are made till a more complicated and interesting game emerges.

By and large, there seemed to be a widely shared tacit recognition that clandestine maneouvering in the political arena was a legitimate form of action. In other words, it was not only a part of the behaviour pattern but had also been incorporated in the belief system. So much so that even if a person was found to be acting with honesty and with no underhand maneouvering, others were likely to suspect some long range personal interest involved in this action.[1] Another indication of this tacit recognition was often seen in public meetings. If a person in a meeting felt that his pre-planned strategy was not likely to be effective, he was free to walk away from the meeting place with his allies in order to confer and plan a new move, while the rest of the people patiently waited. It was regarded as a perfectly legitimate action.

But if the sub-surface level activities were so much a part of the villager's shared knowledge, what then was the difference between them and the surface level activities? The two were distinct primarily because the villagers themselves were found to be making such distinction. Despite the fact that everyone seemed to know what went on at the sub-surface level, in their overt behaviour, they seemed to pretend not to know it. This applied to both political and non-political activities. Very seldom would people talk about them in public. In fact, there was even a certain amount of informal sanction against public discussion of such things. One reason for such avoidance of open confrontation lay, perhaps, in the widely shared fear that once someone's secret dealings were brought into the open, no one else would then escape similar exposure.

However, the villagers were found to make a major and crucially important exception to this rule. Once an event had run its course and became a matter of the past they did not hesitate to talk about it. In fact, they did so quite freely, often with an explicit intention of asserting or proving one's own rightness over the other. Mixed with it, quite often, was an element of boasting and crowing about their past deeds. With a certain smile on his lips and a certain twinkle in his eyes, a person would recall a past encounter with one of his opponents and say; "You see! He thought he would outsmart me. I played such tricks on him that he will never forget the lesson." Or; "I would have really 'smashed' him that time. Everything was planned out, if only those bastards (referring to some other persons) had given me full support." It should, however, be readily admitted that the above observation is in the form of a broad generalization. People differed from each other in age, in disposition, and in overall personality make-up, which affected differently the projection of their self-images. Also the position one occupied in the various structural categories and in relation to a given event made a difference. Nevertheless, the important fact is that people did talk about past events. From the point of view of research it was very helpful, although not a completely unmixed blessing.

II. From Pre-Independence to 1960s

After 1950, there have been remarkable changes in political trends in northern India village due to the introduction of Panchayati Raj. Traditional villages society which was built on trust and harmony collapsed with the introduction of election by vote, and this in turn brought about distrust and strife which developed into fights.[2]

In the first half of this century, i.e., before Independence, the rural political conditions were such that the British had introduced their setup of administration and judiciary, taking away the traditional administrative and judicial functions of the traditional panchayat. Thus the panchayat came to lose its dignity and authority. The traditional panchayat structure continued in one aspect in that its core was the upper jati groups. The reflection and carrying out the intent of the upper groups was its objective and the village was controlled by this group.

The Thakurs as the dominant caste in Cakra had monopolized the old traditional panchayat. They decided and arranged all matters relating to daily life in the village. The post of *Mukhiya*, the head of the traditional panchayat, was also monopolized by a Thakur. The person who had the post of *Mukhiya* of Cakra immediately before Independence was R.V. Singh. He was one of the leaders of the Thakurs in this area. He had also functioned as the *Mukhiya* of Cakra and of several other villages in the neighbourhood. Not only did he belong to a family which possessed large land but also had a background of being economically well-off and so he built himself into a strong position in the village. He was also earnest in the activities that he pushed through. While he carried out the interests of the community to which he belonged, he had a grasp of the entire village. Further he had the support of the Thakurs. Besides this he was supported by the lower and middle jati groups, who served and helped him. This was learnt through talks with the old people of the village.

Of course, there were quarrels before Independence also, but, conditions did not exist where a faction — going beyond the jati framework — brought about confusing political situations within the village with its severe tensions.

After India's Independence the introduction of Panchayati Raj by the Indian government was a revolution, and it brought about large political changes within the villages. Thus irrespective of status or vertical economic level, all the people could take a direct part in village politics by means of their vote. In this system, the importance of elections was no more tied up with the basic factors of the village internal society. If the candidate has even one extra vote, he wins. And so it comes about that economic power that comes through landowner and agricultural labour relationship, as also religious and social discipline, bears no direct relationship with the election results. One vote from any body is one full vote, and so only the parent body which supports a candidate becomes important. Hence the pursuit is to gain every supporting vote, and the opposition among the supporters of the various candidates comes up as a problem.

The first election for Pradhan and Gram Panchayat members was held on December 16, 1955. The political conditions within the village were comparatively stable upto that time. There was no hectic electioneering in Cakra and R.V. Singh was elected without voting. Not only that, all the members of the traditional panchayat and those Thakurs nominated by R.V. Singh were appointed as members of Gram Panchayat without voting. The internal political power of the village was in the grip of the Thakurs, and thus they came to continue their control.

In the 1960's, however, there was a great change in the social and economic factors in Cakra. In the neighbouring village, the state government Irrigation department installed a heavy electrical irrigation motor and pump. After its installation, water was brought by the tube to Cakra and this initiated the change mentioned above. The installation of this pump brought about strife over water. Each one tried to get more water and more quickly into his own field without regard to the sequence and timing of the use of the water tube.[3]

The dispute over water among land owning Thakurs brought about a crack in the unity of the dominant caste which had been maintained upto that time. Now it was the pursuit of the interests of the individual and families.

In the strife among the Thakurs, the agricultural labour also became involved (as it was the duty of these labourers to watch the functioning of the water tube). This in turn brought about a large amount of opposition and strife, resulting in tension in the village daily. Finally deaths occured due to fights with fire-arms.

The Gram Panchayat should deal with the judiciary and arbitration cases within the village. But the Pradhan himself and the Panchayat members were involved in these disputes. And hence, it was hardly possible to expect them to solve these problems. The Nyaya Panchayats stood paralysed in their functions as courts and members fought tooth and nail to establish their case. Thus, it could be said that the Thakurs were engaged in law suits day in and day out.

Among the large number of disputes over water, a small group of villagers was formed to cooperate and help each other. This group had two Thakurs as leaders. This was the beginning of the formation of 'faction' in the village. This faction was formed with the objective of getting together for the fight over water, defeat the opposing party and to get as much water as possible. The split within the Thakur group, and the weakness of the Panchayati Raj gave an opportunity to factions to indulge in this activity. The Pradhan R.V. Singh and the Gram Panchayat member D.K. Singh took up leadership and with them as nucleus two factions came into being splitting the village into two groups.

Although the fights were between individuals and families, the place of direct clash and fighting was always the faction. The opposition amongst individuals and families for water spread to the factions supporting their respective members and the fight broadens into opposition among factions. These tendencies in the faction were basically a strife within the Thakur group. Members of the other jati groups did not subjectively form a part of this structure of strife.

In the water disputes by factions, even though the disputing persons might belong to the same faction, there were cases where disputes arose concerning the position of the field and the water tube and because of this, the unity of the faction was weakened. Thus, it would be seen that all members who made up the faction, did not form one unit with the aim of achieving an important common objective. Priority was given to the current water disputes to the interest and advantage of the participating members. Indeed, the faction was built up so that fight could be carried out in conjunction with other like-minded members.

The water disputes which brought about violent changes in social and political matters in Cakra, came to an end in the second half of the 1960s when the large landowners installed irrigation motor pumps one by one, for their own use. Simultaneously the faction activities waned, leading to natural extinction. This happened specially with the leadership of one of the two factions, and D.K. Singh died due to illness.

In this way, jealousy, hate, criticism, and attack came to the surface in the life of the village in 1960s as a result of opposition and strife as compared to the earlier period. The 1960s brought about an injury in the hearts of the people and matters proceeded in the direction where the village solidarity and unity was lost. Thus seeds of opposition and disputes were germinated. After this period a new epoch of change came into being in the village.

III. Period of 1971-1981

By 1971, in the entire state of U.P., Pradhan and Gram Panchayat elections had taken place. In Cakra, R.V. Singh who was the Pradhan, retired from this post having reached his seventieth year. Even before independence R.V. Singh had functioned as the *Mukhiya* and Pradhan for many years. This, in consequence, brought about a generational change in the political arena of the village.

Due to the previous faction and opposition mainly arising from water disputes, an air of tension prevailed throughout the village. But in such an atmosphere, a movement was initiated among the elders in the Thakur group that the new Pradhan should be elected not through opposition, but by a pattern of consolidation. They wanted that there should not be a recurrence of tension and opposition.

S.J. Singh, the eldest son of a Gram Panchayat member, who had worked as a lecturer in the State Agricultural University and had later returned to the village, was recommended and supported by R.V. Singh and other village elders. He was elected Pradhan without voting.

S.J. Singh was young (37-years old,) who had knowledge of agricultural technology and management, refined in education and culture and moreover knew English. He was popular, and was considered to be a person who could be trusted. There were other candidates of the same generation as S.J. Singh, but in education and culture S.J. Singh was better than others. Further, he was not living in the village at the time of the water disputes' of the 1960s and he was not personally involved in those disputes (though as a member of his household he was involved). As an individual he had no personal or family level enemy and this was one of the reasons why he was elected as Pradhan. Along with the election for the new Pradhan, candidates for Gram Panchayat were also confirmed after adjustment among the Thakurs. These were men who would give a helping hand to S.J.Singh. The selection of S.J. Singh as Pradhan was a measure taken by the Thakurs toward political stability. On the surface this step did not invite any criticism, or opposition. This perhaps shows that even in a village society where strife and opposition are rife, there is a consistent base movement seeking stability. It can also be said that the change was carried out smoothly because it was a change over from elderly leaders to leaders of a younger generation.[4]

Other groups like the Chamars, showed no concern for the elections and did not take any part in them. At the time of the 1971 elections, the Chamars did not give them much importance. The Chamars and other lower jati groups thought that it was natural that the Pradhan should be a Thakur. Hence, there was no resistance or opposition and they naturally accepted a decision made within the Thakur group. The campaign for improving the status of the Chamars and their economic betterment became active in the 1970s. At the same time this group began to take part in political activity.

The functioning of the Panchayat of Cakra started again after the revival of the Pradhan and the Panchayat members. With the appointment of the young S.J. Singh as the Pradhan, self-government and administrative functions of village and the liasion with the outside organizations became strong (e.g. other Pradhans, the B.D.O., etc.). He also actively collected the needed information.

The Pradhan who is the head of the village is the local person responsible for administration, self-government and the judiciary.

He is the chairperson of the Gram Sabha and the Gram Panchayat. He maintains liaison with the B.D.O.'s office, listens to the complaints and demands of the villagers and also carries out all work relating to public affairs within the village.

Let me present some examples of the work implemented by him during the 12 years, till the next elections.

Introduction of Government Subsidy Development Programme

Towards this programme, monetary aid of the central and state governments for each administrative village is distributed through the B.D.O. Since the amount to be distributed is decided by the B.D.O., it depends much on political backing and power of persuasion of Pradhans.

Further, the development programme stipulates particular villages as receivers of government's monetary aid. In this process also, the factor mentioned above applies. In Cakra, the aid for installation of irrigation motor pump and the Gobar Gas Plant (gas produced with cowdung) was put together (bank loan with guaranteed low interest by the government). More than half of the Thakurs of the village installed Gobar Gas Plants in their houses. This was the highest rate of installation among the villages of this Block. This happened because the Pradhan explained the use of Gobar Gas Plants to the people and persuaded each family to purchase Gobar Gas Plants.

Aid to Discriminated Lower Jati Groups

As a government policy to help the weaker sections of society, the central and state governments implemented a number of development programmes.

Due to the efforts of the Pradhan, a number of efforts were made for the Chamars namely digging of wells, occupational training, guidance, purchase of equipment of public address (mike, speaker), leasing of public land, etc. From the 1970s onwards, the government policies were vigorously implemented. S.J. Singh made concentrated efforts and helped groups other than the Thakur also.

New Build Up of Public Facilities in the Village

The bazaar along the Trunk Road is about 3 Km away from Cakra.

The allotment of money was obtained from the Government for this small road and the surface was redone with bricks. An elementary school for small children was opened in the village. Although modest and simple construction was made, teachers were employed and an effort was made to spread education. Now this school has become a fine institution where children of all jati groups get education.

Guidance in Agricultural Technology, and the Spread of Such Technology.

S.J. Singh, formerly a lecturer in the State Agricultural University, with a lot of knowledge in the field of agricultural management took keen interest in introducing new technology and effective management methods. New methods introduced by the Pradhan were a success. The village people came to understand the big advantages of the new systems and every one tried to introduce them. Hence new technology and new methods of management were popularized.

This kind of work could not be accomplished by every Prahdan. It could be said that it was mostly the individual action, individual expression and the political acumen of S.J. Singh which brought about such a success. In the life of the village therefore S.J. Singh took many steps and implemented almost all projects. Therefore the general evaluation of S.J. Singh as Pradhan was high and he began to display a new dimension advancing from the position of a village leader to a regional leader.[5]

During this period serious trouble like the water dispute did not arise. But there were disputes on land, inheritance, families, and among neighbours. In these cases the Gram Panchayat and the Nyaya Panchayat were bypassed and the cases were taken to the courts. Hence the panchayat could not have an opportunity to carry out its judicial functions. There were no cases of factions being formed and attempts to divide the village into opposing groups. Compared to the 1960s these 10 years were with fewer disputes. One reason for this was the declaration of Emergency by the Central government when strong political measures were taken, and the society as a whole was tense and few cases of strife and opposition erupted in the village.

In the 1970s special mention needs to be made of the economic betterment of the Thakurs and the participation in politics of the discriminated lower jati groups. The introduction of the motor pump, improvement in agricultural technology and effective management, altogether increased the harvest, and in consequence improved the economic condition of the Thakurs. These profits were mainly used for dowry of marriageable girls, building of houses, house renovations, rebuilding with bricks, etc.

The campaign aimed at improvement in the position of the Chamars first of all made them give up their traditional work with leather and emphasized their socially weak position. In practical terms, however, they demanded a rise in the wages received for employment by the Thakurs. Further they disputed and resisted the various ways in which they had been oppressed and persecuted by the Thakurs. For the first time a Chamar filed a law suit against a Thakur.[6]

Further, most of the Chamar young men began to go out for employment in Calcutta, Bombay and Punjab. This further strengthened the Chamar group's involvement in political activities.

With the appointment of S.J. Singh as Pradhan, "the village Cakra has come to possess a Pradhan who is very active and cooperative; who takes a positive attitude towards development programmes and the village is getting to be well equipped". Such was the evaluation of the B.D.O., which he freely expressed. All the good results were achieved by S.J. Singh but, of course, there was also some opposition to all this success.

In the 1970s village facilities and the economic power so increased and developed that Cakra came to be fairly stabilized. This stability, however, was the cause of future opposition and meant a stage in Cakra village for new strife.

Notes

[1]   There were occasional exceptions to this. A person over time would establish for himself a reputation of being honest and would be recognized as such by others.

[2]   See Sharma, Miriam [1979: 222, 225].

3 Sharma, Miriam also quoted similar types of water disputes in 1960s [1979: 185-200].

4 Leaders within a village are called as '*bara admi*' (big man).

5 Regional leaders are called as '*neta*'.

6 There are six court cases, filed by Chamars against Thakurs.

ELECTION OF PRADHAN, 1982

In April 1982, the state government of U.P. announced that Panchayati Raj elections will be held in June. The Block to which Cakra belonged would have its elections on June 4. The election for the Pradhan and Gram Panchayat members would be held during the hottest part of the year when the harvest is over and agricultural operations are at a low level.

With the announcement of the elections, Cakra changed into a field of strife, tension and opposition.

I. Election and Mode of Voting

An overview of the election and methods of voting of the Pradhan of Cakra and the Gram Panchayat is described here. The entire village is one zone for the election of the Pradhan, one post in this case. In case of the Gram Pachayat elections, the village is divided into three sections: I, II, III. The allocated 11 members are divided among the three sectors in the proportion of 4 : 4 : 3. The division of a zone into sectors and allotment of proportion of members is done through a draft proposal by the Gram secretary on approval by the B.D.O. Fig. 4 shows the division into sectors and the areas where the various jati groups live. As a constitutional right all men and women above 21 years have voting rights for this election. The number of voters in the various sectors and the distribution as per jati groups are shown in Table 3.

Each candidate has to file his application with the Election Management Committee set up at the office of the B.D.O. Afterwards each candidate is given his election symbol (for example, Table, Pen, Bicycle, Chair, etc.). The election campaign is carried on by each candidate using his own symbol. This method is special to India where there is so much illiteracy. Hence the voters are not made to remember the names of candidates but they have to use cross stamp for the various symbols in the ballot paper. On the election day, the voters go to a school where the election booths are set up. Here they receive the ballot paper on which the various symbols of the candidates are printed. The voter stamps (cross mark) on the symbol of the candidate whom he favours. This voting method is applicable in all elections.

Table 3. Number of Voters by jati in each Sector, 1982
        (See Fig. 4)

	Sector I	Sector II	Sector III	Total
Thakur/Rajput	199	285	78	562
Chamar	202	17	122	341
Ah.r			68	68
Kahar	18		41	59
Bhar		32		32
Teli	9	3	15	27
Lohar			13	13
Sonar		9		9
Bari		6		6
Nai		2		2
Total	428	354	337	1119

II. Trend in Putting up Candidates

In village politics, the election of the Pradhan is considered to be more important than the Gram Panchayat election. This is so because the Pradhan would put up candidates who would support him for the Gram Panchayat membership. Then electrioneering is carried out together for the post of Pradhan and Gram Panchayat members. Hence it can be said that the concern of most villagers is for the election of the Pradhan.

When the elections are formally announced, the main point is who will put up the candidates. In the last elections the resignation of the old Pradhan led to the selection of S.J. Singh without voting. In Cakra, regular elections for Panchayati Raj were being held for the first time.

1. *Candidature of S.J. Singh*

The first move was made by the present Pradhan, S.J. Singh. He had accomplished much, as already mentioned in the last 12 years of his tenure, and acted "not only as the village leader, but also as a regional leader".

Immediately after the public announcement of the elections, S.J. Singh aimed at re-election and accordingly started his activity. The first step was to obtain the support of the Thakurs. The Gram Panchayat members who could stand as opposing candidates (regular members of Gram Panchayat men recognized in the village as leaders, i.e. *bara admi,* or people equivalent to this category), usually campaigned and looked for their own support. The method adopted was to call together all the members of the Panchayat (excepting members who were Chamars) and tell them of all the activities for the past 12 years enumerating their success. It was acknowledged that all this was possible due to the cooperation of the members. He finally said that "I would like to endeavour to work towards the progress and development of this village as Pradhan again".

The present Pradhan S.J. Singh has his own supporter and he was also the main supporter for panchayat members who were recognized as local leaders. It was in this capacity that he aimed for re-election. It means that his comparatively stable base was established as he was able to build up his support within the Thakur group.[1]

In fact, it was almost sure that S.J. Singh would be re-elected since he had the support of the Gram Panchayat members and so attention of most of the Thakurs was attracted towards the activity of other groups and the election of new Gram Panchayat members. By "activity of other groups" is meant the voting tendencies of the middle and lower jatis. Among them, particular attention was drawn to the voting tendencies of the Chamars, who were the second largest

VILLAGE CAKRA : SECTORAL DIVISIONS OF DWELLING LOTS

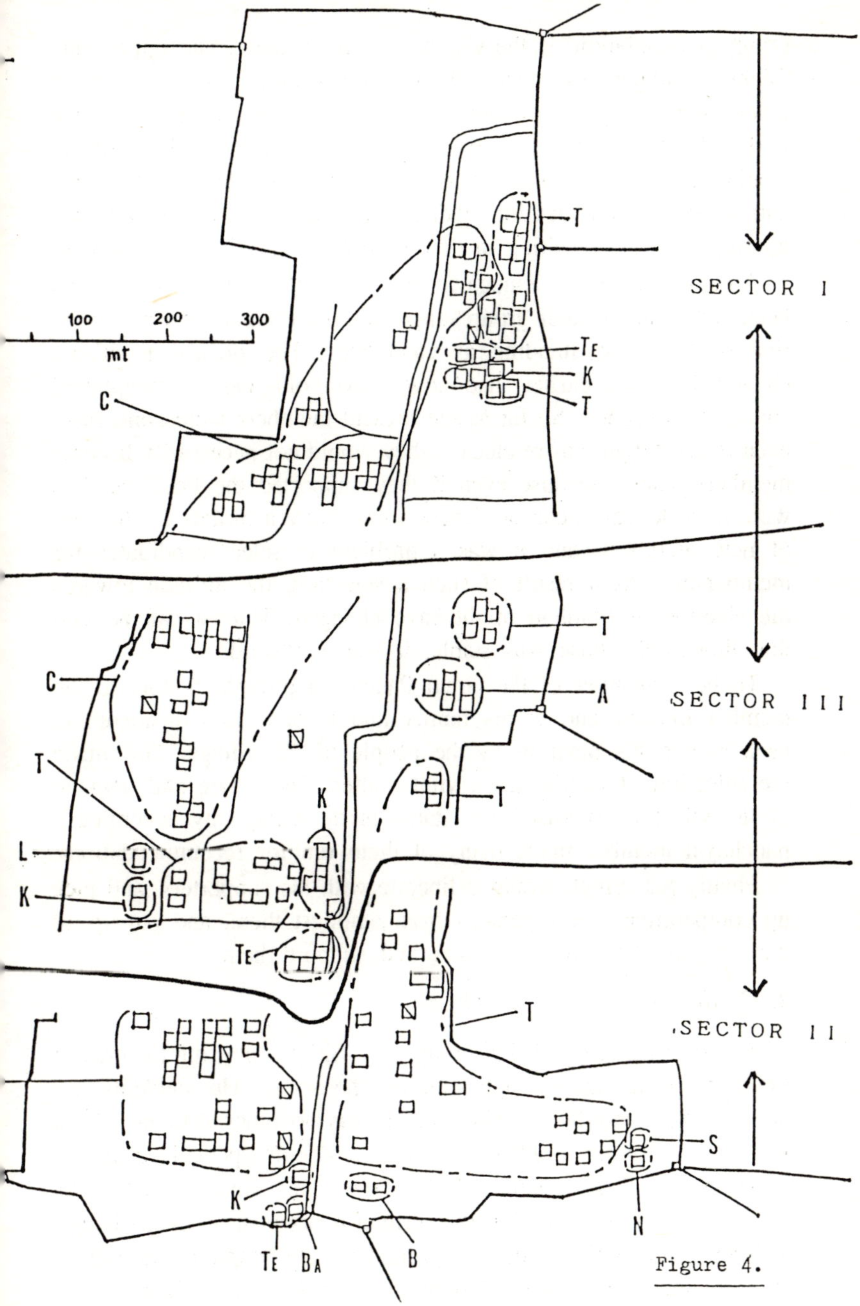

Figure 4.

group in population. If the Chamars were to unite, and oppose the Thakur candidate by means of their votes, and if they put up an independent candidate of their own, it would come as a rude shock to the Thakurs. In fact, the Thakurs did not imagine that the Chamars would oppose them. They were however aware that the Chamars had stood as candidates for Pradhan elections in a number of neighbouring villages, resulting in new political trends in these villages.

Among the Gram Panchayat members, there were some who belonged to the Thakur group supporting the Pradhan and possessed fine qualities for standing as candidates. The present members, elected 12 years earlier, had now grown old and a generational change was needed. So far as the present members were concerned, even if S.J. Singh was re-elected, they would not necessarily become members again. Because even if they supported the Pradhan, they were in a delicate position. There were many aspirants to the post of new members, and it was a problem to select candidates for membership. As a result of such a selection, the attitude towards the election of Pradhan might have changed. Thus it can be said that though the base was stable, it was not solid.

To be a member of the Gram Panchayat brought honour to the member himself and to his family and it was also considered to be a rise in his position by the people of the village. This made the selection of candidates a vital matter. The desire and demand of the villagers to raise their status in the village by becoming a panchayat member made many of them run for recommendations.

Finally S.J. Singh would deliberate with his supporters, and pick up comparatively new persons from amongst them, and put up all the 11 candidates for 3 Sectors and support them.

2. Candidature of S.N. Singh

A person from the Thakur group, S.N. Singh, opposing the present Pradhan for re-election appeared on the scene. He suddenly announced his candidature. This person was no other than the eldest son of the former Pradhan. He was a doctor specialized in the traditional medical system of India (Ayurveda). He practised in the tehsil office grounds and in the morning hours in front of his house. This made his house a meeting ground for the people of the village and became one of the information centres of the village.

The reason why S.N. Singh decided to run for election, as he put it, was that "the present Pradhan does not work for the good of the entire village but works for the benefit of a small minority." Further he stated that "the panchayati raj works for the benefit of its own members, but ignores the life of the villagers as a whole. Especially, nothing is being done for the welfare of the weaker members of the society, i.e. the lower jati groups". He, thus, criticized the current administration and politics as unjust.

The candidature of S.N. Singh stood on the policy of criticizing the present Pradhan and in pulling him down from this seat. Just as new candidates oppose the re-election of old candidates, all the actions of S.J. Singh in his 12 years tenure as Pradhan were now negated and criticized.

Of course, it is a fact that S.N. Singh had the desire to take up the position and status of Pradhan and by this appointment the status of his family and social status would increase. Further, S.N. Singh had also desired to succeed his father and continue the position.

S.N. Singh's criticism of the current Pradhan did not stop there but extended to the Gram Panchayat members also. As already mentioned, this was because these members were elected by virtue of their support for the Pradhan, and because they now stood for the re-election of the present Pradhan.

Those who now supported S.N. Singh were the Thakurs who usually gathered at his house. Their common opinions opposed the current Pradhan, and not the Gram Panchayat members (or those who could not be appointed as Gram Panchayat members). In other words, these were men who had the same opinions and interests and who concentrated there in the presence of their leader, S.N. Singh. Their action had its root in their individual faith and loyalty to S.N. Singh and his family, together with criticism of persons in opposition. This way they showed their stand against the present Pradhan.

Secondly S.N. Singh was supported by the middle and lower jati groups. It became clear particularly that the Chamar group would support S.N. Singh. The Chamars who are second to the Thakurs, in terms of population, supported those who opposed the re-election of the current members. This came as a big surprise. Further, in case of the Ahir group, there was an internal split. Hence half the

Ahirs, and all the middle and lower jati groups came into step with the Chamars reacting as to why most of the jati groups supported S.N. Singh, perhaps because he was a doctor who had the opportunity to meet other jati groups in the course of his daily work. But this kind of political support, going beyond the strict form of the jati group is not formed through the kind of meeting mentioned above. In this case it took place because, the support-giving side and the support-receiving side both had the same interests and objectives.

Thus assured of support, S.N. Singh decided to stand for the election. Further he put up candidates for the Gram Panchayat from among his supporters. He decided to put up candidates in each Sector: full 4 members in Sector I (3 Chamars and 1 Thakur), and full 3 members in Sector III (2 Chamars and 1 Ahir). However, the main body of voters in Sector II were Thakurs and S.N. Singh supporters were few and hence he could not put up all the 4 prescribed members in Sector II, but put up only 2 members (both Thakurs).[2]

III. Tendencies in the Middle and Lower Jati Groups

The middle and lower groups proclaimed their support for S.N. Singh as Pradhan, opposing the re-election of the present Pradhan.

The various jati groups after consultations among themselves, aligned against the dominant caste, Thakurs (more than 80%), who supported the current Pradhan and decided to put up opposition candidates. The Thakurs had an internal split, which led to the appearance of two candidates in opposition to each other. The middle and lower jati groups came to support the minority Thakur group candidate.

There is an overlap with the reason stated for S.N. Singh's candidature, as to why the middle and lower jati groups decided to support S.N. Singh. Again, why was S.J. Singh not able to earn the support of groups other than the Thakurs? To understand this, let us look into the tendencies in the middle and lower jati groups.

1. Tendencies in the Chamar Group

The group which was most significant in the internal politics of the village was the Chamars. Although the Chamars were the weaker members in the village society, yet they could play an important role in the Pradhan elections due to their second largest numerical strength in the village. This potential had given them a way to raise their status in the political facet and expansion of their influence. Economically, the Chamars resisted the Thakurs, but raising their status was very difficult.

Groups with a large population have an advantage in politics as in all elections; all is fair with each person getting one vote. Here the personal possession or specialities have no influence whatsoever, but each vote has equal value. Election or non-election is decided by the number of votes obtained. Such an election was a weapon in the hands of Chamar group in their betterment and political counter-attacks.

But if the Chamars supported a candidate, it would be a serious threat to the Thakurs. As shown in Table 3, even if they were to top the number of votes obtained, it was not possible to obtain the top position. Even if the Chamar candidate obtained the support of the middle and lower groups the result would be the same. Hence the problem would arise only when there is a split within the Thakur group and they set up multiple candidates and one of them is supported by the Thakurs. With split in the Thakur group, they cease to be the controlling group from the point of view of population (number of voters). Chamars could come up with understanding and tie with other groups — becoming the core of a terrific political shock and would become a group grasping the vital casting vote.

The example taken for this study, deals with exactly this kind of political situation with a vertical tie within the village. Due to a split among the Thakurs, the Chamars had a tieup with the minority candidate among the two Thakur candidates. The Chamars had a tie with the Thakurs' minor groups and opposed the majority candidate of the Thakurs. In the case of the Pradhan's election, both the candidates were Thakurs, but the core of the basic support of these two were different.

The Chamars were economically and socially oppressed, and

were groaning under a vertical pressure. They had left their old profession of working with the hides and skins and were making efforts to raise their status by imitating the living style of the Thakurs.[3] The only contact between the Chamars and the Panchayati Raj, now was a *Mukhiya* given a non-elective post as per policy of the Government of India — a member of the Gram Panchayat.

This member took part in regional and national meetings and also took part in political party movements[4]. But within the village he neither had influence nor took part in village politics or in-group activity, and this situation continued.

The target of the state government, through the B.D.O., who executed their development programmes was the Chamars, because of their specially weak group status. In Cakra also, as already mentioned, such development programmes were being implemented.

These programmes were obtained as a result of negotiations between the Pradhan and the B.D.O., and hence the Chamars had no say in the matter and they could not put forward their demands. The position was that they "received what was allotted".

The present Pradhan S.J. Singh brought a lot of projects for the middle and lower groups of Cakra in comparison with the surrounding villages. In spite of this it was a source of dissatisfaction and criticism from the Chamars, who were of the opinion that; (i) More money could have been approved for them, but the Pradhan was filling his own pockets; (ii) More projects should be started for them — but this was not done. The Pradhan was to be blamed for this; (iii) The Pradhan never asked for their opinion, but only consulted his own companions — the Thakurs.

As much as the Pradhan was active, the Chamars criticized him to the same extent. It is clear that the Chamars awaited the appearance of a Pradhan who would be intimate with the Chamars: one who would listen to their opinion, and take positive steps to promote development schemes for them.

When S.J. Singh was elected in 1971, the Chamars did not particularly oppose him, but were rather agreeable to him. But during the 12 years of his tenure, they clearly came to take up a position in opposition to him.

Further in some of the villages surrounding Cakra, Pradhans of

Chamar group had already taken up this post, and were politically and administratively active towards the interests of their own groups implementing many development programmes. This kind of political changes in the neighbouring villages (where Thakurs in spite of the dominant caste had been defeated by Chamars) influenced the Chamars of Cakra, and hence they were deeply concerned with the coming election.

So far, the decision for the attitude to be taken towards elections was taken as a group with the core opinion of the *Mukhiya*. This time also the same pattern was followed, the support to be given as party which was decided by a meeting of the Chamar group and all voters both male and female were to follow their directions.

The two candidates approached the Chamars in different ways for their support, S.J. Singh approached the Chamars through the Gram Panchayat members, i.e. the Chamars working in the houses of Gram Panchayat members were approached[5]. The Thakurs and S.J. Singh who did not ever step into the areas where the Chamars lived, had only this indirect method of approaching and communicating with the labour class. While, S.N. Singh regularly met with Chamars in his capacity as a doctor and had often gone into the Chamar-areas for examining his patients, he had easy entry to the Chamar-areas and asked directly for their support.

The propaganda against S.N. Singh began with criticism by the officials then in position. However, he made a public pledge about the projects he would implement, if he were elected as Prahdan. He further appealed to the Chamars reminding them of the ways he had been helping them as a doctor, and emphasized that he was a Thakur who could understand the Chamars' standpoint and problems.

.The Chamar group who were already opposed to the present Pradhan, welcomed the appearance of new opposing candidate which was possible only because of the split within the Thakur group. Because the new candidate usually met with the Chamars, the talks for supporting S.N. Singh proceeded easily and smoothly, finally ending in the decision to support him.

Between the Chamars and S.N. Singh, a verbal policy agreement was made. In this agreement promises were made that Chamars would be nominated to stand for the Gram Panchayat elections and that when S.N. Singh is elected as Pradhan, the maximum possible projects would be implemented for the Chamars.

This way the Chamar group came to support S.N. Singh in the Pradhan elections and oppose the candidate supported by the majority of the Thakurs and also set up and backed their own candidates for the Panchayat elections.

In that electioneering campaign, the strife between the candidates to make them leaders brought about the formation of 'faction'.[6] Where there were tie ups following an understanding among people beyond the framework of jati groups, strife arose later.

2. *Tendencies in the other Middle and Lower Groups*

In Cakra, besides the Thakurs and Chamars who made up the majority of the population, there were eight other middle and lower jati groups, and they were in a minority. Hence the persons with voting rights in this category were small in number and naturally their influence in the election did not amount to much.[7] In the current election, however, the eight middle and lower jati groups, except a few of them, joined S.N. Singh who had obtained the support of Chamars and the Thakur minority groups.

The third largest group in the village, namely the Ahirs, split into two small groups due to support pattern in the Pradhan elections.[8] This split came about because the Ahirs who lived in an area very close to S.J. Singh's house, debated as to whether they should support S.J. Singh as they were acquainted with him or whether they should support the new candidate. At this time there was a dispute between a number of Ahir families represented by the current Pradhan, regarding land owned by them and land needed for the village elementary school. A law suit was continuing, this was one of the important reasons. Those who were opposing S.J. Singh had a strong feeling that they should support S.N. Singh, and so there was an internal split. The Ahirs who supported S.N. Singh, put up one candidate for the Gram Panchayat election later on.

The middle and lower jati groups were under the control of the Thakurs in one way or the other, though not to the extent of the landless agricultural labour to which group the Chamars belonged. When a group mainly rendered a service to the Thakurs, and their source of income were the Thakurs, it had resulted in an important connection with them. Politically also they were controlled by the Thakurs just as the Chamars through the Panchayati Raj.

Economically the Chamars monopolized the work of agricultural labour among the middle and lower class groups. The middle and lower class groups also began to lose their service jobs rendered to the Thakurs as new culture and technology were flowing in. Further male labour leaving the village for jobs available outside was largest among these groups.

In the development programmes at national and state level, there is a tendency to make a social and economic network with the uppermost or the lowest jati groups.[9] This means that the jati groups sandwiched in between, would find it difficult for the development programmes, projects and financing of state funds to reach them. It was because of this that the middle and lower jati groups had a deep dissatisfaction that the various projects implemented by the government and the B.D.O. by-passed them, and that only the uppermost and a few lowest groups benefitted.

These groups pushed up by the lowest positioned Chamars, and pulled down by the Thakurs at the top, henceforth had to go to distant urban cities for livelihood. Therefore, they were dissatisfied and became critics of the administration which presented a cold front to them. The object of their criticism was, of course, the Pradhan and the members of the panchayat. And so it was that S.N. Singh approached these middle and lower groups who opposed the present Pradhan and also obtained their support for the elections.

The middle and lower groups, of course, desired a change in place of the present Pradhan S.J. Singh and the present panchayat members who did nothing for them. Hence they decided to elect a person, who could appreciate their problems and try to solve them even to a small extent.

The Chamars supported S.N. Singh, the candidate of the Thakur minority group after the split among the Thakurs. This move was received well by the other groups and brought a situation where these groups took the opportunity to act similarly at equal status (for the time being).

Support to S.N. Singh was decided because of the situational occurrence, opinion and intentions with an aim to give a big shock to the Thakur majority.

IV. Tension and Opposition among Factions

Two factions were formed with the two Thakur candidates as the leaders. Member of different jatis came together with their objectives and interests to form factions. The main objective was to work as a wide political fighting group in the Pradhan elections. The two factions brought into being on the occasion of the elections led to terrific tensions in the village. It changed Cakra into a village of opposition and strife.

1. Formation of Factions

The electioneering started in earnest with the candidature of two Thakurs. This in turn meant intensifying strife of factions with their two leaders *(agua)* as the candidates for the election.

The activity of the faction was to work towards the election of their candidate, to increase their benefits thereby, defeat the opposition candidate, and give a shock to the opposing faction. The cardinal objective of the faction was not only to pursue its benefits but also to defeat the opposing faction.

The details of the structure of two factions showing the number of voters for each faction in each Sector are given in Tables 4 and 5.

Table 4.   Structure of Two Factions by jati (in%)

J Faction		N Faction	
Thakur	92.8	Thakur	18.4
Ahir	7.2	Chamar	56.9
		Kahar	9.9
		Bhar	5.3
		Teli	4.5
		Lohar	2.2
		Sonar	1.5
		Bari	1.0
		Nai	0.3
Total	100.00		100.0

Table 5. Number of Voters of each Sector Pertaining To Two Factions

	Sector I		Sector II		Sector III	
	J	N	J	N	J	N
Thakur	138	61	254	31	60	18
Chamar		202		17		122
Ahir					35	33
Kahar		18				41
Bhar				32		
Teli		9		3		15
Lohar						13
Sonar				9		
Bari				6		
Nai				2		
	138	290	254	100	95	242
Total	428		354		337	

S.J. Singh's faction (hereafter called J-faction) aimed at re-election of the present Pradhan, and it received over 80% support of the Thakurs, the core of this support being the present members of the Gram Panchayat. They also had the support of half the Ahir group.

On the other hand the faction which recognized the son of the former Pradhan S.N. Singh (hereafter called N-faction) as their leader, had the support of the middle and lower jati groups (but only half the Ahirs' vote) and less than one-fifth of the Thakur group.

Both the factions also put up their candidates for the Gram Panchayat membership. J-faction put up all 11 candidates, but N-faction put up 2 candidates in Section II, i.e. half the number of candidates but in the other Sectors they put up members for all the seats available.

In this election, the candidates of both sides were from the usual Thakur group and also those known as *bara admi* or *neta*, both were active leaders in village society and politics. From the fact that they are candidates, they automatically assumed leadership of faction (in other words *agua*) and they formed the core of leadership for the electioneering. Candidates for the election and faction leaders were not one and the same person. One who had large political influence could not become a candidate by himself but it could be assumed that they were controlled by factional leaders (this kind of a situation existed in a neighbouring village where Chamars were active in village politics).

Members of the Thakur group decided as to which faction they should join, according to the integrity, reliability, and advantages to be received from the leader (in this example, the candidate for election) and also as per animosity and opposition with the other faction.

Adults (with voting rights) belonging to the Thakur group did not individually decide as to which faction they had to support. The basic unit of the village society, namely each household or family formed a unit in voting and it was the elder of the family who made the decision and others in the family followed this lead (But when there was a split in the family similar consolidated decision was not possible). The relationship between the faction leaders and the heads of the respective families was the most significant factor in the decision to support candidates. The relationship not only involved integrity and reliability but also opposition.

The relationship between one family and other family; person and person; whether good or bad, promoted the support and cooperation within the faction; as also a structure of animosity and opposition. These relationships went to make up the faction, and also the adherence between the leader and the members. The householder with all his myriad problems, decided on the voting attitudes based on the normal social relationships and as how best to obtain maximum benefits for his family.

N-faction firmly supported the candidature of S.N. Singh. Further their main objective was the defeat of the opposition candidate. This brought about the splitting the Thakur group. The one who joined the faction showed a strong link with the leader, although they constituted only 20% of the Thakurs and some small groups, and they clearly exhibited an intense animosity towards J-faction.

Different from the Thakurs, the support of the middle and lower groups towards their candidate had its origin in their criticism and dissatisfaction towards the present Pradhan who carried out the administration within the village. To prevent the defeat of S.N. Singh on whom they placed greater trust, and to raise their status as a group and to increase their political influence, they decided to support N-faction.

The faction which was playing its part within the jati groups and between the various groups, acted beyond the discipline and rank of the village society, by giving their cooperation to members of other jati groups.

A special characteristic of the faction is the coordinated action brought about through combination of members of different jati groups with the objective of common benefits, though normally they would be at loggerheads.

The dilemma of horizontal tie and union among the Thakur groups which were the dominant caste was now disclosed and diffused. Individuals and family unions went beyond their jati frames to form combinations as members of the faction. On the other hand in the middle and lower groups, greater cohesion came about within the group because of their resistance to the faction whose base anchor was the Thakurs, thus further increasing their homogeneity.

In the power struggle within the village, for the post of Pradhan, the members of the faction acted in mutual cooperation to achieve a common goal. In encouraging mutual cooperation, it was significant that there was an interchange between voting and exercise of voting.

The members with loyalty towards their leader, offered their votes in his support and the leader in return promised to exercise his power to help. By electing the leader of the faction that one supported, the authority of the Pradhan was exercised for increasing one's own benefits. This was an important reason for supporting a faction.

The cohesion within the faction was rather high, and with the internal unity the opposing faction was resisted. The rules of behaviour to be obeyed according to the jati in daily life were strictly followed only in the matter of eating and drinking. Other matters were greatly relaxed amongst the members of the same faction. For example, sitting on the same *charpai,* changes in the mode of speaking Hindi (changing over form imperative to ordinary parlance). If they were members of the same faction, the behaviour of jati had been removed. Moreover, the *Mukhiya* of the Chamars, who commanded the largest number of voters, acted as one of the core members, and to that extent their political authority increased.

To push through the objective of having one's candidate elected, the vertical status relationship of jati was suspended and the factions activity developed and pushed through. The unity within the faction signified cooperation and mutual help within it. It also included a collective defence against attacks from the opposing faction. The members of a faction did not directly disclose their alliance, but it was clear as who was on which side. There was a necessity to consolidate and strengthen the unity within the faction as weaning away of members or bargain of members by the other faction was to b. resisted. The make up of faction and its special features have been discussed so far. I will now turn to election trends in both factions.

2. Electioneering Trends

The trends of the faction in the Pradhan election consisted broadly of: (i) strengthening of unity within the faction, and (ii) attacking other factions. In pursuing objectives (i) and (ii) opposition and strife start, resulting in conditions of tension.

Trends (i) and (ii) are not separate items, but are closely connected and operated together. Internal unity signifies cooperation, assistance, and defence as its objectives within the same faction. This is done so that there is no alienation or revolt among its members. This activity signifies ensuring of votes for a faction.

(i) Strengthening of unity within the faction

At first, leaders of both the faction doled out money to try and strengthen their internal unity. Soon after the filing of nominations the younger brother of S.N. Singh went to the Thakur supporters, and distributed Rs. 50 cash to the heads of the families. To the main members of the middle and lower jati groups, he gave Rs. 200. Against this, J-faction candidates distributed Rs. 30 each to the Thakur families.

The difference in the amounts was because the main support for the J-faction was stable. But N-faction was in the fray for the first time and moreover it only had the support of the minority Thakur group. Unity was channelized through concrete means, i.e. money.

At the same time the leaders gave as much assistance as possible at the request of members of their side. Since they were members of a regional leader's side, they pushed their purpose through their leader's influence, and also took this opportunity to pursue their demands. The candidates made full efforts to obtain votes, and went to the extent of attending to minor items of request which were normally unthinkable. During the elections, members were getting their miscellaneous problems solved such as advocating the mediation of the tehsil office or Lekhpal; using the influence of lawyers; arranging good offices for appointment; taking up the burden of others debts, etc. S.N. Singh of N-faction took a positive action in respect of the demands of Chamars, and it was an incident worthy of attention. In fact, after the elections, members of J-faction teased S.N. Singh calling him a "Chamar-Pradhan" because of this reason.

The Pradhan is the head of the village administration. As such, administrative policies were brought up in the elections. The policies put up and backed up by the candidates were:

(a) Borrowing of government funds at low interests,
(b) Provision of educational and welfare facilities,
(c) More good offices for appointments,
(d) Implementation of schemes to ensure reasonable living conditions for the poorest class.

A public promise was made by the candidates, by way of a policy statement, of the increased benefits to the members. These statements implied that "the announced policies will be implemented after getting elected". So far as the faction members were concerned, it implied: "If this faction is supported, and if our candidates are elected, you will enjoy maximum benefits".

This meant that only those who supported the candidature of the Pradhan had been promised benefits. The political circles and administration which promised this would surely implement the same after the elections. In this case, as actual example it signified the possibility of a vital political change. That was whether Thakur-centred politics would continue or whether there would be a Chamar-centred politics.

Internal faction unity was achieved not by loyalty to the leader or benefit to self and achievement of objectives, but by an important factor, i.e. giving a shock to the members of the opposing faction. To elect the candidate supported by one and to defeat the opposing candidate had the same interests. For members who come together in different circumstances and with different reasons, defeating the opposing faction became an important event. Specially in the case of the middle and lower jati groups, the members of which had their base in the N-faction; this kind of opposition was an effective factor for unity. Therefore the attack on the opposition faction became severe, and so opposition and strife became rampant.

(ii) Attacking the opposition faction

Attacking the opposition faction was carried out in various ways and with full force of the faction. The obtain votes in the elections the main attack was to break the loyalty and to get the support of the members of the opposing faction while pulling them to one's own side.

Money was distributed to the members of the opposing faction and promises made to them for greater benefits after the elections and in this way to obtain motivated change in their support and loyalty. Both factions however were warned to desist from this practice of dislodging support, and hence such activity was carried out secretly. Members of one faction had a system of vigilance on each other so that there was no contact with the opposing faction.

Such an important network was set up during election period. All the happenings and behaviour within the village were carefully watched, and if there was an opening, a plan would be put into operation. If the person concerned was known or intimate with the leader or members of the opposing faction (especially if there was a case of money lent, or land leased), his loyalties would be dislodged at a personal level.

Such activity of transforming loyalty was mostly carried out for transfer of members from Thakur majority of J-faction to minority group of N-faction. The majority J-faction opposed this by the slogan "a jati group should form one united group". They brought out this theory to the forefront to bring pressure on the Thakur's N-faciton.

The second mode of attack was implementation of public act of enmity and opposition against the leader and members of the opposing faction. The act of enmity involved criticism, censure, and above which was estrangement between members of the opposing factions, rumours were floated with evil intent, and when they met face to face they would insult each other. The opposition members were severally attacked, the opposing members' failures were exposed and they were slandered and such clashes and fights were repeated daily.

The main object of the attack was the leader among the candidates, but others were also attacked and often all members of the faction were dragged into the fight.

Since the Thakurs of N-faction had a tie with Chamars, who were the lowest rank in society, they were severely criticized and taunted "though Thakurs they hold hands with Chamars and hence should be ostracized from the jati"; and "they are brothers of Chamars".

This kind of attack was frequently and suddenly carried out on the face when opposing groups met on roads. If one could shout out more words than the opponent, he considered it his victory. To attack a member of the opposition faction like this was not only damaging to him but it also meant a united confrontation of the enemy.

Then there was a further escalation of the attack. The third attack was the faction participating in the trifling quarrels between families in daily life, in law suits, and in personal quarrels. Among these quarrels of individual faction members, the entire faction would support its members on an organized basis.

Outwardly, the village seemed to be "peaceful with no quarrels". But normally when people live together, quarrels would occur. As already mentioned, there were a lot of disputes regarding land and water rights and even in the same family there was continuing opposition and land strife. Normally such opposition and strife would be considered to be a problem needing to be dealt with by the concerned persons. But participation of others (of course of the same jati) took place when the quarrels had been large for other's participation or when others chose to join in. But when factions were in the fray at the time of electioneering, conditions changed largely. Even in trifling individual or family quarrels, if the opposite side belonged to the opposing faction, the incident blew up to large proportions. To the place where arguments or quarrels were taking place, members of the faction went to support and take sides with their faction members.

The fight of an individual faction member became the fight of the total faction group. As already indicated when members of both factions were engaged in repeated arguments and fight, particular reasons could not be found as the cause of the arguments and quarrels. The cause could be anything, from the use of the village well, past loan, sequence of the use of irrigation water tube, to the grazing of cattle, etc. from which a fight could start and spread to larger fights.

The second and third attacks were direct attacks, but it was mainly a fight among Thakurs of the two factions.

The fourth attack was action of the Chamars in relation to the Thakurs of J-faction. This concerned the labour class to stay away from work without permission and collective demand for increase in wages.

The period in which elections were held was after the harvest when agricultural work became slack, and when there was not much work in hand. At this time cattle were looked after and the farms maintained. The Chamars tended to stay away from work without permission. Even if they turned up for work they would often be half a day late.

These Chamars gave the maximum possible resistance to the Thakurs. When they resorted to such actions, it meant that the members of the family had to take up the work normally performed by the Chamars. As a symbol of their status, the Thakurs evaded manual labour, and to do the work formerly done by the Chamars, was extremely humiliating to them.

The source of supply of agricultural labour and the population itself was limited. If the Thakurs, for example, arbitrarily dismissed the Chamars working in their houses, it was difficult for them to replace such agricultural labour from within the village. In other words, such dismissal was not possible. The Chamars attack of staying away from work, also had the effect of denying time to the Thakurs during the period of election campaign and had serious consequences in the election.

The remuneration of the agricultural labour was usually decided at the time of initial employment and these terms were mostly reviewed at the time of new planting. The demand for higher wages during the election period happened also to be the period just before the planting. As such, the demand was not abnormal, instead note-worthy in this case was the collective demand there.

Up to now, each employer discussed, or rather arbitrarily fixed the wages of the person he employed, but now the Chamars held out a collective and indiscriminate demand to increase the wages. This was a new posture of opposition to the employers against whom there was a collective, strong, and united demand.

When the dominant caste who controlled the village suffered from an internal split, the Chamars decided to implement their intention to improve their status and economic conditions. The Thakurs of N-faction who were political-partners of the Chamars, came to an agreement with them to ensure their own support. This action further consolidated the unity within the N-faction and brought pressure on the J-faction.

Finally the fifth attack. This was a dramatic attack in the form of a direct attack on the opponent, i.e. collective assault on the opposing group.

Incidents of this sort had not taken place in the past in Cakra, but in the present election they were frequent. In this case, a person sleeping alone in the fields or returning home by himself at night was threatened so that he would change his loyalties. If he did not agree, violent action such as slapping and kicking was also resorted to. Personal attacks were carried out and immediately before the election such attacks got intensified. In a single night 3 to 4 persons were attacked, and this continued for 3 to 4 days.

The object of these attacks were the leaders (*bara admi*) — candidates for the Gram Panchayat and others in the faction who wielded political influence. A Chamar *Mukhiya* was seriously wounded; this incident could not be said to be extraordinary. Such personal attacks were not a rare occurrence in North Indian villages; in fact, several incidents occurred in surrounding villages. There was an escalation of animosity within the village, generating extreme tension. Factions began to feel the touch and go situation. Now since no restraint was possible, the people of the village also got involved in the action.

The dominant caste, which had so far stabilized the situation within the village was now internally split. And since they were busy fighting the elections, they lost the function of maintaining political stability within the village. Because of this, there was a break in the law and order situation and indiscipline prevailed and, the fourth method (as mentioned in this section) of attack was adopted finally ending in personal attacks.

Spades, axes, things made of horn, bicycle chains were used as weapons. When there were fights and quarrels, the supporters ran to the site with their weapons. In this way strife between the factions by way of electioneering intensified and brought about very tense conditions.

So far the issues described are: (i) the internal combination and strengthening of the faction, and (ii) the attack on the opponent faction, i.e. the trend of the two factions during electioneering. There were political strifes within all jatis, and between the jati groups brought about by the political small groups, the faction going beyond the framework of the jati. People while having common objects aimed at common benefit; while members belonging to different jatis were people with differing intentions, who had come together in the faction to cooperate. Hence such a faction exerted vital influence not only in the political structure of the village but also in the social living conditions.

Let me examine a few concrete examples of opposition and strife of the factions:

(a) One day during electioneering, Kashi Nath Singh, a Thakur, belonging to J-faction, went to Shamsher Singh of N-faction to collect an advance loan he had given to S. Singh about six months ago for purchase of manure. But S. Singh refused to pay. He said so far there had been no demand for repayment even once and he could not countenance a sudden demand. Thus, S. Singh had a loud argument in front of the house. The subject of argument was not only money, but also the support given in the coming elections.

This incident started at 7 a.m. in the morning and the news of this quarrel spread and there was a gathering of members of both factions, and it became a big fight among 10-15 persons. Many persons who gathered came with weapons and thus created a very tense situation. Then the group fight developed among the persons gathered without any relation to the original cause of fight.

Here is a case of a quarrel over a trifle developing into an inter-faction fight. This shows how incidents developed into severe opposition and animosity at election time.

The group clash continued for many hours, and the leaders of both the factions appeared and pacified the members and then dispersed.

(b) A Chamar, Sita Ram who was a landless agricultural labourer belonging to N-faction was working at the house of Thakur Yogendra Singh belonging to J-faction. Sita Ram's contract was to work in the fields, to look after the cattle, and miscellaneous work at the house. The monthly wage was Rs. 50 per month with lunch, clothes to wear, and a small proportion of the harvest. He was working under severe labour conditions with no leave and had to work from morning till night.

About 10 days before the elections, Sita Ram stayed away from his work without permission. On the day, all the other Chamars who worked at the houses of Thakurs belonging to J-faction also stayed away from work (to repeat only those Chamars who worked in the Thakurs' houses belonging to J-faction). This was a collective display of unity among the Chamars to the employer Thakurs. Since Sita Ram did not carry out his duties, Y. Singh had to carry out much of these duties himself as there were few male workers in the family and the family was small. The circumstances in the houses of other Thakurs, where the Chamars stayed away, were also the same. The next day Sita Ram went to Y. Singh's house and joined work saying that he stayed away from work as he was not well. The same excuse was trotted out by the absenting Chamars at the other Thakurs' houses also. This kind of unpermitted leave for one-day or half-day was taken within the space of two or three days. This was collective action implemented by the Chamars, a kind of incident not known before.

(c) Candidate 'E' of J-faction who was a cousin of S.J. Singh (Pradhan candidate of J-faction) was involved in a law suit for making improper use of irrigation water tube at election time. The person who filed this law suit against him was a candidate from N-faction.

The State Irrigation Department had installed a large type of motor pump for lifting water from a well. Through a brick lined water-passage, water was supplied to Cakra. These water tubes made a criss-cross grid in the village. But as time passed, Thakurs installed motor pumps one-by-one in their own houses, and the water tubes had become less important. Further, the ones who could use the water tube were the owners of the pumps, but they could use it only for their own farms when water was needed. Water from another owner of a pump could not be used.

'E', however, wanted to use water in abundance for his field and hence he brought water from another person's pump, and used the water tube for this purpose without any proper permission. This un-lawful method had been adopted for a number of years and the people had overlooked this matter and did not rebuke the offender.

Against this unlawful act in an electioneering attack, N-faction filed a law suit in the district court. Since 'E', against whom this suit was brought, was a relative of the Pradhan under attack, this was used as an attacking propaganda saying:

> "The present Prahdan is making improper use of his power for the benefit of himself and his relatives"
> "This Pradhan brings no benefits to the people of the village".

This case continued in the court with no relationship to the election results. In this way, trifling matters, but unlawful deeds, which had so far been overlooked were used for an attack on the opposing faction and also to increase one's own benefit and to achieve one's own objects.

Incidents cited at (a) to (c) would occur daily. This was the type of electioneering in Cakra and the fight between the factions. As the voting day approached, the opposition and strife intensified. Two days before the election police patrol appeared, and the tension mounted to a higher degree, and finally very tense and stiff opposition at the dawn of the election day came up.

V. Trends on Election Day

The election for the Pradhan and the Gram Panchayat members was held simultaneously on June 4, 1982.

The method of election has already been described above. The election booths were set up in the local elementary school, but the officials handling election were teachers of public elementary schools from the other villages. A police party was sent to the village for maintaining peace.

Both the J-faction and N-faction had to educate their members collectively as how to vote, and to avoid the obstruction of the opposing faction. First of all every member had to learn how to correctly stamp the seal against the election symbol on the ballot paper. Then all members had to be sent to the polling booths and also take care of any improper or obstructive actions by the opposing faction.

Days before the election day, the core organizing members of both the factions visited each house repeatedly to instruct voters as to how they should stamp the vote-casting seal and against which symbol on the ballot paper.

Since the candidates' symbols would vary according to the Sector (in the case of Gram Panchayat elections) even though they may belong to the same faction, the symbol was to be remembered by the voters.

The members of N-faction had a fear that since the candidate of J-faction was the present Pradhan, the official machinery would be used in malpractices during election. But in spite of serious patrolling by police parties, members of N-faction stopped over as agents at polling booths to witness and keep watch over the trends and movements of J-faction. The Chamars who worked at the houses of the members of J-faction as agricultural labourers were not allowed to go for their normal work on election day to prevent any pressure or obstruction from others.

For all members of both factions, victory in the current elections was a necessary pre-condition and hence every effort was made to ensure that all voters were present at the polling booths. The candidates of both the factions for the Gram Panchayat visited each house, appealed and requested the head, convincing members of the respective houses to go for voting.

The J-faction distributed Rs.11 to each house to get assurance of their votes for them. N-faction also distributed the same amount as was done last time.

It was expected that there would be a serious clash between the factions concerned, as they had already fought amongst themselves with arms. Through the meditation of the Gram Secretary, an inter-faction meeting was held three days before election to prevent bloodshed.

Members of both factions were not to go to the election booths individually, but in groups according to the north Indian custom and to prevent clashes and fights. Further, to prevent the meeting of members of one faction with each other, care was taken to allot different voting time.

After the announcement of elections, both the opposing factions met for the first time and decided the bifurcation of voting time.

During the period of voting time 6 a.m. to 6 p.m., J-faction was to vote up to noon, and N-faction in the afternoon.

People who had gathered the previous night in front of the houses of each faction candidates, started their activity. They started moving about here and there, so that they could ensure votes for their faction.

The greatest problem confronted by both factions was how the ladies could be sent to the polling booths. Young and adult women would not normally go out of their houses, and there was "*purdah*" (veil) system which forbade women from showing their faces to men. For this reason, women would not normally go out during the day. Hence both factions made use of a custom among women for community singing for going to the polling booth. The women belonging to the houses of candidates would call the women of their faction, and proceed to the booth in a procession singing songs.

Men also would go to the polling booth in a group. This was, however, resorted to, to prevent attacks from the members of the opposing faction on the way. The Chamars were on leave from their work that day. They all went to poll in a group fearing retaliation as they supported N-faction.

Polling was carried out peacefully. Both factions had already estimated the polling and forecast that N-faction would win the Pradhan elections, i.e., S.N.Singh would obtain the majority of the votes. J-faction did not foresee a large number of votes, unexercised, and if there were no question of a number of people changing sides, then it was clear that numerically a new person would be elected. Further, it was expected that in the case of Gram Panchayat members' election also, N-faction candidates would obtain a majority in Sector I and II.

Although such results were expected, there was severe opposition right up to election day. The individual opposition for the post of Pradhan, spread over to opposition and strife among the two factions. This shows that it was not the winning or losing of the election alone that was at stake.

With the advance of the election period, the emphasis shifted from the victory in election of the Pradhan to other factors. Among the various factors and conditions the emphasis shifted to delivering a direct rude shock to the opposition faction and its members. Even though the members of J-faction expected that they would poll less votes than the opposing faction, they continued their attacks on the opposing faction.

The movement to secretly induce members of the opposing faction to one's own side continued. Even though one went to the polls along with one's own faction, it was a fact that many persons had changed sides at the time of polls. This is further clear from the polling results, as it did not reflect simply the number of voters that each faction held.

In this way the election was over at Cakra. The tension and opposition within the village now advanced to the next stage.

VI. Results of the Election

The opening and counting of the ballot boxes of the Pradhan and Gram Panchayat election was carried out three days later under tight security of the B.D.O.'s officials.

The result of these two elections were as follows:

Election of Pradhan

Total number of votes	828
Valid votes cast	814
Rate of polling	74.0%

S.J. Singh	411	-Elected-
S.N. Singh	403	

Election of Gram Panchayat members

Sector I (number of members : 4)

Total number of votes	342
Valid votes cast	325
Rate of polling	79.9%

— Elected

A (Thakur)	-N-	223
B (Chamar)	-N-	223
C (Thakur)	-N-	214
D (Thakur)	-J-	178

— Defeated

E (Chamar)	-N-	126
F (Thakur)	-J-	118
G (Thakur)	-J-	112
H (Thakur)	-J-	106

Sector II (number of members : 4)

Total number of votes	267
Valid votes cast	234
Rate of polling	75.4%

— Elected

A (Thakur)	-J-	213

B (Thakur)	-J-	206
C (Thakur)	-J-	205
D (Thakur)	-J-	204
— Defeated		
E (Chamar)	-N-	55
F (Thakur)	-N-	53

Sector III (number of members : 3)

Total number of votes		262
Valid votes cast		239
Rate of polling		77.5%
— Elected		
A (Ahir)	-N-	141
B (Chamar)	-N-	127
C (Thakur)	-J-	116
— Defeated		
D (Chamar)	-N-	114
E (Thakur)	-J-	111
F (Thakur)	-J-	108

In the Gram Panchayat elections, the voters were required to stamp the seal against only that number of symbols as were the number of members to be elected (for example in Sector I each voter could stamp the seal against four symbols, that is the number of members to be elected). Therefore, the number of valid votes divided by the number of members to be elected would give the number of votes polled in each sector.

I shall now try and analyse the election results.

The person elected as Pradhan was S.J. Singh, a surprise reversal victory for J-faction. The valid voters of both the factions were as follows:

J-faction   487 persons

N-faction   632 persons

Naturally, it was expected that the candidate S.N. Singh of N-faction would win. In fact it was expected that it would be an easy win. But the result was a surprise reversal.

The share of votes obtained by both factions (as related to the total number of voters and the number of valid votes), and its comparison is given in Table 6, which reveals a close competition among the two factions for the valid votes cast.

Table 6. Share of Votes Obtained by Two Factions (in %)

	Pradhan		Sector I		Sector II		Sector III	
	J	N	J	N	J	N	J	N
(1)	84.4	63.8	93.1	67.8	81.5	27.0	117.5	52.6
(2)	50.5	49.5	39.5	60.5	88.5	11.5	46.7	53.3

(1) : Share for total number of voters

(2) : Share for the number of valid votes

If one studies the number of votes cast, one can find that there is no large difference in the power or influence of the two factions, the difference in the number of votes being only 8. But N-faction holding 145 more voters, their polling percentage was only 63.8% of the electorate while J-faction obtained as much as 84.4%. This means that either many N-faction people did not exercise their franchise or crossed over to J-faction.

The voters cast one vote each in the Pradhan elections. Here there was repeated severe opposition and fighting where full efforts were exercised, where political influence and power was displayed by both the sides. As a result of this the predominance of N-faction collapsed against expectations. N-faction which came into being making use of the internal split groups failed to exhibit its influence and power and was defeated.

The large scale non-exercise of franchise or the crossing over of its members showed the fragility and weakness of the internal unity of the N-faction. If one considers the fact that all members, except those who were sick or those who were away from the village, went to the polls in a group, the result was mostly because of switching loyalty of the members rather than the non-exercise of franchise.

This can also be illustrated by the following calculation. With the number of voters and the share of polling of each faction, one can obtain the estimated number of persons who cast their votes.

If one compares this with the actual polling results, one can study the variation (faction's number of voters × rate of polling, equal to actual votes obtained). According to this calculation, it is +51 for J-faction and −64 for N-faction.

This means that although the N-faction voters went together to the polling booths, an unusually large number switched allegiance at actual polling. It can therefore be said that the strong bindings of J-faction had its effect and many switched loyalty at the polling booths. It is also a symbol of weakness of internal unity in N-faction compared to J-faction; the unity in N-faction was weaker, and it is clear that cohesion among J-faction members was stronger.

The weakness of N-faction was that its participating members belonged to different jati groups. This was the explanation of the people of the village. It was further pointed out that "many Thakur families of N-faction did not vote for S.N. Singh but voted for the opposition candidate". This was understandable because some Thakurs belonging to N-faction had a subconscious distrust of their own N-faction because of participation of Chamars, and other groups. N-faction had a serious problem regarding unity, internal unity as it functioned with members of different jati groups with cooperation and tie across jati frame.

If one would consider the unity among the members, it looked that horizontal tie within the faction took priority over vertical unity. Let me further examine this problem in the context of Gram Panchayat election results.

Among the eleven members elected to the Gram Panchayat, six were of J-faction (all Thakurs) and five were of N-faction (three Chamars and one Thakur and Ahir each). Thus the result was close.

The J-faction which had its Pradhan re-elected, managed to get a majority in the Gram Panchayat elections with a nominal margin as the difference in votes obtained by 'C' and 'D' of Sector III would show. The consequence of a slight shift would have been that N-faction would have grasped the initiative.

The largest Sector, namely Sector II (with four members) had mostly Thakur residents and the trend set by this Sector could be said to be decisive for the final results. This Sector was dominated by Thakurs belonging to J-faction, and the members had a strong unity amongst themselves. The power and influence of the majority group after the split is directly reflected in the election results of Sector II.

In Sector I and II the election pattern was influenced by the unique characteristics of certain candidates, and this had distorted the internal voting patttern. For example, in Sector I, 'D' of J-faction obtained 178 votes and was elected; 'F', 'G' and 'H' of the same faction obtained less than 120 votes and were defeated and the other three persons of N-faction were elected. If each voter had applied his/her stamp against the symbol of all candidates belonging to own faction, this kind of variation would not have occurred. If the voting had been consolidated within each faction, there would not have been such a large variation in the election. Although the unity within each faction seemed to be strong, but it finally became clear that it was unexpectedly weak.

Further, out of the voters of N-faction in Sector I at least 40-50 persons did not vote for their own candidate but voted for 'D' of the opposition faction. In means out of the four seats, they gave three to their own faction and one to another faction. This further under girds the fact of the weakness within the faction groups. The reasons for such occurrences, were explained by members of N-faction as follows: "Many Thakur families of N-faction did not vote for a particular Chamar candidate, but voted for a Thakur of the opposition faction". As 40-50 persons would include a number of families and also since 'E' was a Chamar, this explanation can be accepted as plausible.

Cooperation with a different jati group cutting across the jati framework shows that some members have a strong animosity towards other jati groups. More so in the case of the dominant groups, the Thakurs would certainly have resistance to vote for the lowest ranked group in society, i.e. Chamars.

These election results show that even though a small number of Thakurs joined N-faction, it weakened the unity of the faction. This reversed the trend in the elections, and it also clarifies the victory of J-faction.

This election which brought strong opposition and strife, was based on the political influence exercised by the small groups. When there was no stable group in the village, severe political tensions occurred in the village, increasing opposition and strife. The people of the village moved about in excitement in support of their faction.

It was due to the conditions within Thakurs – the higher and dominant caste – and the Chamars – the socially and deprived caste but predominant in population patterns and trends in village politics were decided.

VII. Trends after the Election

On the evening of June 7 when the election results were declared a grand victory feast was held at the house of the Pradhan for members of J-faction. And with this the election of the Pradhan and Gram Panchayat members came to an end.

The feeling of enmity and strife brought about by the elections, did not, however, end.

Even after the elections, the opposition between the two factions continued. The faction which came to be formed through elections, reflected not only the victory in the elections, but made a primary object of defeating the opposite faction. This developed a trend to increase the benefits for its members. Even when victory or defeat had been decided in the elections, the enmity and strife continued until the next new bone of contention.

The political conditions in Cakra were set by the trends in opposition and strife among the faction groups. Let me look into the concerned cases of trends in both factions after the election.

(i) Among the 11 Gram panchayat members elected, 5 members belonged to N-faction. All these 5 members ignored the oath that they had to take, and gave up the rights and privileges as elected members, and did not attend the Gram Panchayat meetings even once. N-faction completely boycotted and ignored the newly formed Panchayat. At the same time, J-faction on its part went its own way in the village politics and administration. The Panchayat of Cakra started its activities with the support of the group supporting the Pradhan with a majority of one member. This was unprecedented and it was a biased Panchayat.

(ii) A few days after the declaration of the election results, the defeated candidate S.N. Singh filed a law suit in a District Court against the Pradhan for malpractices in the elections. The contents of this law suit were; J-faction falsely polled votes, using the names of dead persons. The instructions for these malpractices came from S.J. Singh.

In this way the invalidation of the election was strongly called for. The court opened proceedings; both sides employed lawyers. This court case has further spoilt the relationship between the two factions and as the elections ended, this court case became the new cause for fresh opposition.

Of course, this was a court case between the two faction leaders, but both the factions consolidated to support their respective leaders and the fight took the shape of a fight between factions. The personal relationship between the two persons concerned was completely reversed: (there was no association; they were not even on talking terms). Further there were no mutual visits between the families.

(iii) The people belonging to the two factions, however, got over the severely strained conditions during that elections, and got back to their normal daily routine. But every small fight or dispute that occurred would develop into a fight with the support of the factions. If any incident occurred, opposition and strife would spread. Among the Thakurs the opposition became at one stage more severe, because the break away Thakur group was now in cooperation with the Chamars.

The disputes involving money and law compared to the period before the election became more severe. Complete non-cooperation between the N-faction and the Pradhan and Gram Panchayat took place. Thus the administration within the village became stagnant.

Since there were many cases of members of N-faction voting for the opposition, a search began for those who had betrayed the faction. Since the voting was secret, no clear proof was available. On the surface, however, there were no changes and the faction shortly made up.

These troubled conditions were symbolic of the armed clash in November 1982 over a law dispute. Among Thakur families there was a dispute over distribution of inherited land, and there was a clash during broad daylight. 10 persons on each side clashed with rods and agricultural implements. It was a serious fight where many were injured. Both groups had the backing of a faction, and the whole village became tense.

After the elections, except a minor dispute, all seemed to be peaceful but in reality the matter was smoldering and a danger of bursting out at any time existed.

(iv) The Chamars on their part collectively stayed away form work during the election period and also demanded higher emoluments.

Even after the elections the Chamars started a collective campaign for increase in wages with the support of Thakurs of N-faction. This took the shape of Chamars who worked in the house of J-faction Thakurs taking repeated leave without prior intimation and then making their demands on their employers. The Thakurs of N-faction who had acceded to the demands of the Chamars came in as mediators, and carried out negotiations between Chamar labourers and the Thakurs of J-faction. In these collective negotiations, sharp words were exchanged as it was a fight between N-faction and J-faction. As a counter measure to the Chamar campaign of taking leave and not coming to work, the Thakurs of J-faction could not find substitute workers, and hence had to accede to their demands. In this way the Chamars consolidated themselves and attacked the Thakurs who were now out of step because of the internal split. The economic struggle between the jati groups now transformed into rivalry and struggle between the factions. It can be said that this situation further spread and deepened in course of time.

At the same time, the Chamars of Cakra prevented work from being carried out at the house of S.J. Singh. Although this campaign was carried out during election time, S.J. Singh, as a result of this, had to employ labour from a neighbouring village at higher wages. Besides this, labour was brought in from other districts to work and this labour had to live in Cakra. It may be taken that agricultural labour relationship is a hereditary set up according to tradition. Hence it is notable that labour in the north Indian village refused to work only because of political objectives.

As explained, the tension and opposition among both the factions continued after the elections (after June 1982). The formation of faction for the village elections brought about great changes and agitation. Further, the horizontal tie within the Thakur jati group was destroyed. But re-grouping took place in the political fighting of the faction cutting across the framework of the jati group and also had a vertical tie. Thus the society and politics of the village came to a turning point.

Notes

[1] In the Thakur group. S.J. Singh got 80.4% support and S.N. Singh got only 19.6%.

[2] See Table 3.

[3] See M.N. Srinivas [1955, 1962, 1966] and Yogendra Singh [1973, 1977].

[4] Jagjivan Ram, who was the most famous politician in the Central Government, had received moral support from Chamars of Cakra.

[5] Special fee of Rs. 5 was paid to each Chamar labourer.

[6] Leader of faction is called a *agua*. Also see, Sharma Miriam, [1979: 110].

[7] See Table 3. Midde and lower groups except Chamars are only 22% of total village population.

[8] Out of 68 Ahirs, votes given to S.J. Singh were 35 (51.5%) and to S.N. Singh 33 (48.5%).

[9] Records and documents of B.D.O. office.

GENERALIZATION AND CONCLUSIONS

I. Conceptualization of a Faction

An overview and basic frame of processes of factions in the elections of the Panchayati Raj (especially the Pradhan) in Cakra, which ultimately led to tension are presented here, in addition to some actual examples of strife. Emphasis has been laid on a comparison between theory and analysis.

In supporting the candidates for the Pradhan election, there was internal opposition in the dominant caste of Thakurs which resulted in their split into two factions. Even before India's Independence, the Thakurs controlled the political power within the village, and stood in a dominant position as compared to other groups because of their unity and stability. But all the unity and stability collapsed instantly with an internal split.

With the internal split among the Thakurs, and in an atmosphere of tension and strife, the Chamar group came out conspicuously on the scene. The Chamars formed the group that was most discriminated in the village besides being the lowest in socio-religious status. They were employed by Thakurs as landless agricultural labourers, but now they started their political activities taking advantage of the fact that they were the second largest population group.

With elections, which only take congnizance of the number of people (i.e. voter), the Chamars came to make their numerical strength felt in the village scene. They formed a faction with the cooperation of a Thakur splinter group and fought against the Thakur majority group.

In the elections of Cakra the emphasis was now on the small political fighting groups called '*parti*' by the villagers which is the result of the faction and began to play a vital role in the village political structure.

Here, it is necessary to further analyse the activities of the political fighting among the small groups and within the jati group and between the jati groups. The activities of the factions in Cakra, and the political trends resulting from these activities are summarized here.

1. Faction is a Group

The faction is formed by members with a common will and collective action, and can be defined as a small group. This is not a formal institutionalized group with written constitution and regulations, but is an informal group. The faction is regulated in the relationship with members of the faction and in the common aims regarding special problems and object now currently pursued. The collective action of the members is developed to get benefits and to activate the faction as a group. In this study, the faction made use of the Panchayati Raj elections in the village to obtain benefits; this being the implementation of common will. The people who had these objectives formed small groups.

2. Factional Fight

The main objective of each faction in an election is to fight against the rival faction which threatens and harms the candidate. The second special characteristic of the faction is that it has strife as its objective.

The cause of the birth of a faction is the tension, opposition and fight with other factions. In the process of resolving some special problem, or point of dispute, complete consent is not reached within the jati group and thus members scatter in different groups. Thus faction is formed as a small fighting group. Since these fighting small groups use different methods for solving problems, they oppose each other leading to repetition of fights. At this stage, fighting with the other faction becomes the major objective and to achieve the objective small groups carry on their activities.

By defeating the opposing faction the small fighting group,

namely the faction, achieves its special objective, solves problems, and provides benefit to each of its members. Each member of the faction is required "to fight" and the interest of the members in the increase or decrease of benefits is directly related to the result of the fight with the other group. Since more than two factions try to obtain political gains in the limited and narrow confines of the village society, the distribution of power and rights opens with a fight among factions. This means that there can be no "peaceful consistence" or "neutrality" among the factions. Basically faction is a fighting small group that fights as a result of tension and opposition.

The opposition and fighting among the factions in Cakra is a true example pertaining to village elections. Both factions backed rival candidates, and to get their own candidates elected, they started fights to defeat the candidates of the opposition faction. The regular members continued their activities as fighting personnel and consolidated themselves as a small group. They aimed to reap large benefits for themselves by defeating the enemy, i.e. the opposition candidates. "Large benefits" in this case would mean the monopolized distribution of the limited social and political resources. It also meant the winning of elections, and the exercise of ones' rights to run a Panchayati Raj to ones' own benefit.

Giving a shock to the members of the opposing faction satisfies the factional groups. Opposition and fighting in the small limited human grouping of a village, affect the social relationship within the village. The evolution of all this among the jatis, the family and relatives too would vary according to the issues of disputes among the factions and their result. Sometimes personal rivalry and opposition in daily life develop into a fight between factions.

3. The Period of Factional Disputes as a Period of Activity

A faction is formed over some special point of dispute and so it starts its activity consequently. The period of activity in a faction exists only as long as the dispute continues and so it would be essentially short. The faction has no historical permanence, but exists temporarily upto the end of the dispute. A number of factions come into existence, the cause of the same being various problems and incidents. These problems repeatedly are diffused or consolidated. In other words, when one dispute ends, new points of disputes arise, and thus the faction gets re-formed.

Members of a faction, following a particular direction and pursuing a set objective would not continue to be members of the same faction, instead they would have to join another faction to gain maximum benefits for themselves. Moreover, it is possible that a faction formed over a particular dispute could continue with the same structure and with another dispute. The faction's objective is the pursuit of its members' interests and winning the dispute; hence the membership is fluid and continuity of membership is short.

During the period of consolidation, if a group is off for a short period, the level of relief will be maximum at that end. The next stage is dispersion and consolidation. The fluidity and cross-voting of the members during voting as seen in the result of the election, are closely related to the circumstances mentioned above.

The short existence and the fluidity of the faction, have a close connection. Since the existence of the small group is only temporary, for this very reason the fluidity is high. It is further clear that the wave of consolidation and unity is also large.

4. *The Faction as a Political Small Group*

The faction which fights for political authority within the village is a political small group. The social and political resources, like power and prestige, available in a village are limited. While there is a close relationship between these two factors, they are often crystallized in a particular social status or position. The ones who are in this social position, monopolize and hold more social and political resources than the others. Hence, they seem to exercise power and control both. The social status built up by social and political resources, restricts members which in turn leads to control of power. Power always develops in relationship with power and control of others. This activity of political power supports and maintains social status, and finally overwhelms the other members and helps gain supremacy over them.

Exercising political power as a small group, in other words reaping benefits after attaining social and political status, is the objective of the faction. To attain this objective, fighting develops. The members of the opposing factions are pressurized and frightened down by the political power. To make use of such a controlling power a faction comes into being and goes into action.

The factions in Cakra, came into being in a span of time and started their activities to crush the opposing faction, ultimately bringing them to obedience and control by means of their own political power. The fight was made use of for this exercise in tense conditions when two factions functioned cutting across the barriers of jati groups.

Because the factions strived for political power, they were a political small group. Their existence as a political small group was because of the rivalry in village elections, to handle village elections, to take care of water, land, inheritance, money, housing disputes, etc. The factions are political because they fight for political power in the village. As the faction is political, many problems and conditions developed into a struggle and thereafter the faction took action as a political fighting small group.

5. Recruitment of Faction Members by the Leader

The faction formed to achieve a particular object and to obtain certain benefits, is established through members who have a common will and wish to carry out their activities together. When there are multiple factions the decision to join a particular faction depends on the members. But at the same time canvassing by the leader is also vigorous.

In the results brought out by this study also, it is obvious that the daily contact between the leader and the members (or the family/jati group) had various objects of different members, the leader who can support and cooperate in achieving these objects in the best possible manner will be selected.

The leader forms the core and nucleus of the faction. It is by linking up with the leader that the members form their group. The internal unity and cooperation within the faction is really a matter of the relationship between the members and the leader. In other words, though the members of a faction may not be intimate amongst themselves, it would be enough if close relationship between the leader and the member was maintained.

The members are called for open gathering by the leader. The members of both the factions were recruited by their leaders S.J. Singh and S.N. Singh through individual (or family) relationship. S.N. Singh particularly made use of his profession as a doctor, and got the support of the Chamars. With the use of professional services he also made Thakur members as part of his faction. From the fact that N-faction cut across different jati groups for its organization, one can understand that unity was built up with the leader at the core. Therefore, the overwhelming priority was achieving an object and gaining benefits rather than keeping within the jati framework. Further, by supporting the leader and by obeying him the faction was formed and the activities of the faction continued.

6. *Formation of the Faction vs. the Dominant Caste*

For the faction to be formed and for its activities to continue, no group should exist in a village which was stable and had a high capacity to control the villagers. If the Thakurs, the dominant caste, had maintained strong unity among themselves, and if no serious opposition or a strife had occurred, political in-fighting of small faction groups could not have been formed. In fact, when the stability of the Thakurs collapsed, the activities of the faction started.

The stability of group is fully based on the internal unity and the common consensus, control and exercise of power over other groups and in such a case there would not be large opposition and strife among themselves. Even if problems and points of strife occurred, the discipline within the faction would adjust, and maintain the stability; the latter were usually practised by the Thakurs.

The stability that existed among the Thakurs in this way sometimes collapsed because of a particular point of self-centred quarrel and may be exemplified with the current example. As a jati group having strong horizontal ties, it was overwhelmed by other groups. But with the internal split, they had followed other directions. Opposition started within the dominant group resulting in split, and in turn it led to ties and cooperation with other jati groups. Now the development was in a vertical direction.

The dominant caste was in a position of permanent control in the village but they could maintain their superiority for so long as the other groups might recognize their dominance.

Due to internal split, the unity within the group was lost, and the internal strife based on the point of dispute continued and spread. This was due to the aspiration to achieve the set aims that cooperation with other jati groups may be resorted to. The weakening of the dominant caste and the collapse of its internal cohesion was clearly the root cause of the activity of the faction.

The deterioration of the cohesion in the dominant caste, and the resultant split, provided the opportunity to the middle and lower jati groups to increase their influence and power. The Thakurs had overwhelmingly controlled the other groups upto now, but the recent weakening of the Thakurs paved the way to encourage other factions to appear on the stage. The weakening of the cohesion among the Thakur group brought about a consolidation in the other jati groups. The middle and lower class groups took the place of the dominant caste to gain and use political power and influence. Towards this end they tried to strengthen unity amongst themselves.

In this study of Cakra, the economically sound middle and lower jati groups formed an unity as against the internal split in the Thakur group. It is worth considering that the lower and middle class groups came up to the level of activity among the Thakurs. This was specially seen in the case of Chamars as they closed up their ranks to forge unity and became extremely active.

The small political fighting group, the faction, came into being while dividing the dominant caste. The collapse of their stable control created the political activity of the faction.

For the faction to achieve its objects and reap benefits through the common will of its members, there had to be mutual cooperation, promoting coordinated action among them. The members of the dominant caste were dislodged from the horizontal tie of their jati group. The other jati groups also at the same time strengthened their own group and further went on to consolide the political small fighting group, the faction.

I have so far clarified some special characteristics of factions in village Cakra, viz.: (i) The faction is a group, (ii) The faction fights, (iii) The active period of faction is a period of strife, (iv) Faction is a political small group, (v) Members of the faction are collected and organized by the leader, (vi) The split among the dominant caste is the cause for the formation of the faction.

II. Sociological Interpretation

Assuming that "there are no controversies where there is nothing to quarrel about" and that "community disagreement is also a measure of community life" [Coleman, 1957: 3], the two most self-evident conclusions which can be drawn from the case presented in the preceding chapters are that Cakra is a very lively community and that the people who live there have a deep sense of belonging. The intensity and the vigour with which the Cakra residents engage in protracted controversies, as well as the fact that many a time such controversies are created out of seemingly non-controversial issues, bear sufficient testimony to the above conclusions. It is clear that Cakra is not merely a place where its residents happen to live. They "participate" in its life, they "belong" to it, and events that take place there excite their interest. As a result, Cakra is a constantly vibrating community; recording contrasts, uniqueness and similarities of the "village life world".

Let me begin with the village itself. It was argued in chapter 2 that much of the political behaviour of the people assumes meaning and relevance only in the context of the village society in which it takes place. For this, the village was viewed as a viable sociological entity, providing its own political arena within which people encounter each other as they seek their political goals. The determination of political goals, too, was seen as a function of the context provided by the village.

In the next section, therefore, an attempt will be made to examine, in view of the case materials, the extent to which Cakra constitutes a significant sociological entity, as well as the way in which it provides context and relevance for the political behaviour of its residents. Following this, I shall see how this context defines the political goals.

1. *Cakra: a Sociological Entity and a Context of Political Behaviour*

Cakra is related to the outside world through numerous ties, yet it remains a distinct entity. It has its own name and identity; its records are separately maintained by the revenue department; its territorial boundaries are clearly defined. In recent years, it has organized a separate panchayat as an institution of local self-government. All these administrative aspects make Cakra a distinct community. But its autonomous distinctiveness is shown not only by these overt manifestations but also by the fact of collective consciousness, shown often in the behaviour of its residents, which further shapes it as a sociological entity. In view of the common ancestry claimed by the landowning group of the Raghubanshi Thakurs, this collective consciousness may not be surprising. Moreover, the almost absolute dominance which this group has traditionally enjoyed in the economic and political life of the village, as well as the element of interdependence caused mainly by the *jajmani* system, have perhaps together helped this collective consciousness to encompass the remaining sectors of the village population.

Thus, it seems that Cakra does constitute a sociological unit as shown in the collective consciousness of its residents, as well as in their efforts to present a joint front when confronted with an external "threat". There have been occasions, of course, when the two processes have not worked.

Some of the historical cases in Cakra show how the community failed to present a joint front in the face of external pressure not only from the block officials, but also from the neighbouring villages. That their community's prestige was at stake was known to all Cakra residents. However, in these and other similar cases, various other factors seemed to have intervened. Whether it was effective or not, the fact that the villagers did invoke the principle of village prestige sufficiently at this point suggests the presence of community consciousness in Cakra, thereby giving it a sociological reality.

The role of the village as a sociological entity becomes still more pronounced when I note that it provides the context and relevance to most of the political behaviour and processes which take place there. I shall refer to this role of the village through the analysis, where two interrelated factors may be noted at this stage.

When it is argued that the village provides the context for the political behaviour, the implication is that it is the structural arrangement of the village, the pre-existing pattern of inter-personal and inter-group relationships, and the village-based symbols of power, dominance and prestige which provide this context. The different sets of norms followed by the villagers are also part of this context. It is only when the diverse political actions of the Cakra dwellers are viewed in this perspective that they become meaningful phenomena.

Here one could argue that there is nothing unique about this. Every political arena, whether it is a peasant village, a tribal hamlet, a small town in the western countries, a nation state, or even the United Nations, has its own context as defined by the society of which it is an immediate part. Yet, this is exactly the point which is being emphasized. Cakra provides its own political arena, and to understand the political behaviour of its residents, I shall have to view it within the overall context of village society.

The second related factor makes the point clearer: an external impingement on the village does not affect its residents directly but only after it has been "translated" in terms of the local context, as outlined earlier. The constitutional provision to abolish untouchability in India was one thing in the statutory book, but by the time it reached the village scene it became another by being "translated" in terms of the established patterns of inter-jati relations, economic and political dominance, and so on. The same was true of them and reform legislation which aimed to provide ownership rights and to make them aware of the intended meaning of the legal provisions, yet it was the meaning they themselves assigned which were regarded as important. Similarly, the government might have had its own rules yet in the implementation of such rules, the villagers applied their own judgement.

And, in this way, the village has collectively tended to absorb most of the external impingements and to convert them into issues negotiable within its own general framework. All this should not, however, imply that individual actors did not made use of external resources and apparatus to meet their goals. As seen in the present case, they did so quite frequently. The heavy reliance on court litigation to settle internal disputes is an example. Yet, at best, it was only as "means" that these external resources and legal apparatus were viewed. The "goals" continued to be village based. When they were not so, they were not regarded significant in the internal politics of the village.

But before I deal further with the goals, let me re-examine one of the major theoretical assumptions; that "political goals" are not only determined by the context by the village but also are based on an individual's self-interest as a main motivating force behind his political actions.

2. Self-Interest

In what sense could it be correct to assume that an individual's political behaviour is mainly motivated by his "self-interest"? One could, of course, take a position that theoretical assumptions, after all, are only points of orientation, and do not, therefore, necessarily call for defence. Still, in chapter 2, with the help of several empirical illustrations from various studies of the Indian village society, an attempt has been made to show that political actions are, by and large, determined by self-interests as perceived by the actors. The case material presented in this study supports, among other things, this basic assumption. Practically in every case, almost every actor seemed to be working to maximize his own gains. The actual goals varied from situation to situation and from person to person, depending upon the issues involved and the positions occupied by the actors. Yet, the underlying principle appeared to be the same, as explained in the sequel.

On the basis of my case material it is, indeed, possible to argue that one's interests were not always rightly perceived. At times, both ignorance and wrong perception, perception of one's own strength as well as that of the opponent, seemed to have influenced the judgement. But it would be admitted that the above statement is based more upon the knowledge of the situation of a certain action than upon the initial comprehension of the situation by the actor himself.

It seems that the final outcome of an action should not be taken as the main criterion. The basic fact remains that the Cakra dwellers did have some conception of their self-interests at the time of taking action.

It is, however, necessary at this point to mention that self-interest was not always the main motivating force behind people's actions. As argued in chapter 2, and dealt with subsequently in a section entitled "Conflict and Continuity in Cakra", many a time behaviour was simply normative, habitual, and spontaneous, Due to the particular nature of the event, or because of the force of momentum caused by the event, or because of certain traditions or conventions associated strongly with certain aspects of village life, people did not always act strictly in accordance with their self-interests. But, then, such actions did not strictly fall within definition of political behaviour.

3. Political Goals

Political behaviour was defined in this study as "... those activities through which a man, in competition with others, attempts to retain or enhance his public power. Since 'power' implies control over resources, whether human or material, political behaviour includes all those activities whereby a man tries to achieve or retain control over resources or over men or both".

It may seem that the above conception of political behaviour is too broad and general, subsuming under it a wide range of human actions, some of which may not be of political nature. If political actions include, for example, achieving and retaining command over resources, how, then, are they different from economic activities? Substantively, perhaps, there is no difference. Still the difference lies in the total context in which the action takes place. Let me present, in view of my case material, the major political goals which Cakra dwellers pursued, and the significance of these goals in the context of the village. This, it is hoped, will substantiate the conception of political behaviour.

4. The Achievement and Retention of Control over Resources

The main resource in Cakra, the achievement and retention of which occupied most of people's attention, had been land.[1] Many of the village conflicts were centred around this factor. The numerous battles – physical, legal and tactical – which followed the introduction of the land reform legislations, involving not only the usual tenant-landlord relationship but also struggle between close agnates, the disputes between the richest and one of the poorest people in the village over the latter's house site, all these cases showed that the actors involved were either trying to retain command over their own land, or were trying to achieve command over land which did not rightfully belong to them, or were trying to prevent others from achieving such command.

Land, being scarce, was a much sought after resource in Cakra. There were more claimants than those who already had command over it. As a result, the achievement or retention of land was a competitive activity; one owned land at the cost of depriving others who were equally interested in it. To this extent only, this was an economic, and not a political activity. But there were other factors also involved therein.

It is suggested here that if a given resource is either a symbol or a source of political power in a society, the need of achieving or retaining command over it assumes political dimensions. Moreover, if the achievement or retention of command over a resource requires the use of means such as political power, influence, mustering support of others, etc., such action by very definition becomes political.

In Cakra, ownership of land was both a symbol as well as a source of political power. In fact, it had been traditionally a symbol of Thakurs' dominance and status. Within the group of the Thakurs, because of the system of ancestral co-proprietorship, it symbolized the relative inter-jati position of such structural units as the family, *kunba* or *tola*. Besides being a symbol of power and dominance, ownership of land in Cakra also came to signify social prestige. Therefore, a gain or loss of land was not always seen in economic terms alone. In fact, economic considerations were hardly ever brought up when the ownership of land was the issue. When social prestige was at stake, no effort to save it was regarded too big. Expenses incurred on prolonged court litigation, on repeated visits to the city, on bribing the officials, or bringing witnesses, etc., were often far out of proportion to the initial economic consideration involved. Any means, including false promises, physical force, and manipulation of land records, were in order.

It was in this sense that achievement or retention of command over resources was a political activity in Cakra. But land was not the only resource to which the Cakra dwellers aspired, although it was, by far, the most important one.

Hence, it is interesting to note that in order to seek this goal many people were willing even to forego a part of their land. Is there a contradiction here? Not necessarily. Besides the consideration of priority between two resources, which was perhaps in people's mind, as well as the fact of inevitability (after all, some people had to give up their land) there was another important factor. Losing land in this case did not mean someone else within the village gaining it. It, thus, did not signify competition within the framework of the village setting.

5. *The Achievement and Retention of Power over Men*

Another political goal seemingly pursued by the Cakra dwellers was the acheivement and retention of power over men, or negatively avoiding being controlled by others. The most evident example of this was seen at the time of the contest for public office - 1982 Panchayati Raj election of the Pradhan and the Village Panchayat members. The two cases also provide a useful contrast, denoting the relative power and also the prestige associated with these public offices. But more important were the new statutory powers vested with the panchayat office. To win a panchayat office, thus, meant achieving power over others. However, the general public, the voting population, looked at it differently. For them, mostly, it was a question of avoiding being controlled by those who they feared were likely to use the new prerogatives against them.

Seeking formal offices was not the only indication of Cakra dwellers' attempt to achieve and retain power over men. My case meterials show many other ways in which this goal was sought. Sometimes it simply took the form of displaying one's superior power. At other times, this goal took the form of asserting one's power over others. Still another and a more direct indication of this power seeking goal in Cakra was often in the favours bestowed by some of the larger land-owners on others. Sometimes such action took the form of offering financial, tactical, or simply moral support to the known foes of one's opponents. The only consideration in offering such help was extending one's power.

As far as the receivers of these favour were concerned, the case posed a conflict of goals; avoidance being controlled by others, on one side, and achieving or retaining command over resources, on the other.

Incidental to the two political goals, I have so far considered as achieving and retaining command over resources, and power over men; there is still another goal which was often being sought by the Cakra residents. This had prevented others from achieving either of the above two goals. The reason for calling it incidental to the other two is because that one normally prevents the other from seeking something because he himself may be seeking it. This process is particularly evident when the resources are limited and claimants many. And, of course, when there is a competition for power as such; the very process of achieving power for oneself tends to deprive others of it.

Yet, many times in Cakra the two processes, a "positive" and a "negative" power, were independent of each other. Often one person prevented another person from achieving command over a resource or from achieving power over others without necessarily getting the benefit himself. "I may neither gain nor lose it, but I am not going to let him get it", was the underlying attitude.

As pointed out earlier, the village as a social unit not only provided a context and an arena for the political behaviour of its members, but through this context also defined the political goals which they sought. In fact, any goal external to the village setting, as it signified power or command over resources, was regarded as of greater significance in the internal politics of the village. For example, of course S.J. Singh's Pradhanship was a factor of great political relevance in the village, his being a member of the Kshetriya Samiti and the chairperson of one of its task committees, together carried great weight in the society of Cakra.

An action or an issue assumed political dimensions in Cakra only when it affected power relations or distribution of resources within the local community.

6. Achievement of Political Goals

As the goals had relevance only in the village context, the data show that the means used to seek them were not necessarily limited to the rules and principles internal to the village alone. Depending upon a person's perception of self-interests, and upon the range of choices open to him, the latter being determined by his structural position and the resources at his command, the means varied from person to person and from situation to situation. Each conflict situation, thus, was not only a conflict of goals but also a conflict of means. Each conflict situation involved the use of different, and other mutually contradictory, sets of rules.

The contradiction was not between the external and internal rules alone. The internal organization of the village, based upon the structural arrangement and the normative order, had its own inherent contradictions. Normally speaking, land, for example, was a prestigious resource, besides being the major economic asset. Yet, structurally, its ownership was limited to only one group. Within the landowning group of the Raghubanshi Thakurs, the agnatic bond among its members (a structural feature) gave them a status of equality. While the uneven distribution of land, also a consequence of the structural arrangement, caused much of the economic disparity. The closer the structural (agnatic) bond between persons, the greater was the normative expectation for them to have a mutually amicable relationship. Yet, the structurally determined system of succession whereby the property of an heirless persons would be inherited by his closest agnates, was a cause for suspicion and enmity between them. The ritually superior status of the Brahmans, which brought them deference from every member of the community, was in contradiction with their lower economic and political position. The obligations to one's jati group and those to one's *jajman*, or to the political patron, or to the economic "benefactor", were not always in harmony. In this way, the internal organization of the village provided numerous contradictions to be faced by its residents. The number of such contradictions is greatly increased when I take into account several sets of rules which the external world brought into Cakra. Almost invariably these new rules were in conflict with one or the other organizational principle of the village.

But while these various contradictions caused conflict situations, they had also provided different sets of rules to be invoked by the villagers to meet their political goals. Interestingly, a person invoked a set of rules in one setting and violated it in another. And, in this way, in one case after the other the same process seemed to be repeated: actors trying to legitimate their goal seeking behaviour under one or the other system or rules.

In cases where the disputes were brought to legal courts, the rules consisted not of the actual provisions of the related laws but how they were interpreted. Lawyers, witnesses, bribes, manipulation of records, all were part of the same framework. It was not a question of showing on whose side did the law stand. It was rather a matter of bringing the law to one's side. All this was not a creation of the villagers' ingenuity. They were simply making use of the legal administrative system that existed; their ingenuity lay in adapting themselves to this and exploiting it for their own ends.

How about the physical violence reported in many cases? To which system or "rules", if any, did it belong? In a sense it was perhaps an example of what is popularly known as the rule of "might is right". In many cases, it was the more powerful and resourceful people who used physical force against the weaker and poorer ones to get whatever they otherwise were not able to get. Also, the fact that often such force was used through hired professionals, which only the resourceful could acquire, supports the above observation. The belief that due to their superior resources, they could easily "get away with it" without serious legal consequences, was another supportive factor.

There was yet another factor. The use of physical force for one's safety to resolve one's grievance against the other was a part of the general ethos not only in Cakra but in the entire Thakur dominated culture. During the period of field work the villagers often said, in jest as well as in earnest that when everything else failed, the staff came to rescue. The ultimate law among the Thakurs, they would say, lies in the strength of their staffs. This applied not only to cases where a person had reasons to be genuinely aggrieved against someone but also when the claims made were not genuinely "legitimate".

It should be noted that in neither of these cases, the use of physical force was applied by the more powerful and more resourceful persons against the weaker ones. It was rather between agnatic equals, which suggests that it was not simply a rule of "might is right". Thus, it would seem that physical violence was part of the general normative pattern which regulated political life in Cakra. It was one of the many means available to Cakra dwellers through which to carry on their struggle for political goals.

This should not, however, imply that the society in Cakra was regulated by the "rule of the jungle", nor does it mean that the use of violence was not disapproved by the people in general. For one thing, this was only one among the many means. Moreover, at least as far as the relations among the Thakurs were concerned, the use of violence was not only publicly disapproved but also often widely condemned.

In view of the above facts, it is perhaps reasonable to conclude that there was a contradiction between social norms. There was a general feeling of disapproval towards the use of physical violence as well as some sanctions against it while politically its use to achieve goals was considered legitimate. Or, it could be said that while the several contradictions in the society generated friction and conflict, the resolution of which sometimes necessitated the use of violence, the general disapproval towards it and the social sanctions against it were the mechanisms used by the society to prevent it from becoming too disruptive.

Another means widely used by the Cakra dwellers and crucial to many of their goals was to seek and retain support of their fellow villagers. So widespread was this activity that often it itself appeared to be a goal that was being pursued. There was an element of competition in securing support, most clearly seen at the time of panchayat election, when the chief contenders looked around for suitable running-mates. For the chief contenders, these running-mates were primarily a means to widen the area of their own support. The support itself was not the goal but a means to achieve power as symbolized in the elective office.

A careful examination of the case study shows that seeking and giving support was a two-way process. It is here that the notion of exchange as a social process becomes most relevant.

The case of political support I have discussed so far is one among the more important and relatively steadier ones. The same principle of reciprocity — of mutuality of interests — however, seemed to underlie practically every other political relationship, regardless of how "insignificant" or short-lived it was. In fact, most of these other relationships were generally unsteady and short-lived. They lasted so long as they served the purpose which had initially brought them into effect.

Thus, seeking or giving political support was a major two-way political process in Cakra through which people tried to achieve their political goals, and out of which grew various forms of political alliances. Factionalism as an aspect of village politics was a direct result of this process.

7. *The Nature of Factionalism in the Politics of Cakra*

On the basis of the evidence provided by several empirical studies, an attempt was made in chapter 2 to show that factionalism is processual, and not a structural phenomenon in the internal politics of the Indian village. Factions, when they emerge, do not represent corporate entities. Their boundaries are fluid. They are transient in nature. Factional conflict is not a conflict between "haves" and "have-nots". The case of Cakra seems to support all these empirical generalizations about the nature of factionalism.

Despite the many disparate hostilities which existed in Cakra during the time span covered by the case material, it is probably safe to conclude that the dominant theme in the recent history of village politics was the history of the conflict between S.J. Singh and S.N. Singh, the two richest and the most influential persons of Cakra. They provided the central, core elements to what often appeared as the two factional cleavages in the village. It was only when the other disparate hostilities were tied up with the hostility between S.J. Singh and S.N. Singh, that they assumed factional character.

Factionalism as a political phenomenon can be termed structural if it meets at least one of the two conditions: first, if its emergence and continued existence is contingent upon and coincidental with the already existing structural categories, such as, in Cakra, the jati, *pana* and other units of lineal segmentation, neighbourhood, etc.; and second, if in itself it assumes structural properties, such as becoming a corporate entity with clearly defined boundaries, regular membership, and common and ostensible goals.

None of these two conditions were met by the two factions existing in Cakra. The factional cleavage was not a cleavage along any structural categories in the village. It was not a conflict between jati groups, nor between *pana* or neighbourhood units. People joined factions in defence of the agnatic bonds. S.J. Singh and S.N. Singh, who constituted the core elements of the two factions were close agnates within a major lineal branch of the Raghubanshi Thakurs.

Let me now turn to the second necessary condition. Did the factions in Cakra assume structural properties of their own? In other words, did there exist corporate units of permanent standing, with clearly defined boundaries, regular membership, and common and ostensible goals?

The answer is "no". The evidence is clear. The two factions in Cakra were not permanent corporate units. The only relatively stable things in the recent history of factional politics in Cakra were a few different hostilities, initially unrelated to each other. Occasionally these hostilities merged together to provide a broader base to the two factions. There was also, to a large extent, a set pattern of alliances between the core and the major support elements of the two factions. Yet, it was not always definite.

Thus, it was not the alliance which determined the course of events. It was rather the course of events which determined the nature of the alliance. The very character and composition of the two factions depended upon the issues involved and the interests at stake. Also factions, when they existed, did not have corporate goals. It was only the diverse political goals of the constituent members which, within a given situation, brought them together. If the goals changed, or the situation altered, the faction, too, did not remain the same.

In view of all the above consideration, one can say that factionalism is a highly dynamic process, as the relatively short history of Cakra shows. It is not something which exists; it is something which occurs. As it moves, it feeds itself on the events as they take place, sometimes engulfing the entire village scene, at other times withdrawing into the background. But whether it spreads or shrinks, or it is active or dormant, is not the result of its own self-propelling force as is sometimes referred to by the observers of the Indian village scene. It rather moves by the force of will provided by the key political actors. These actors themselves are not consciously "creating" factions. They are simply doing what seems to be appropriate for their political goals within the context of a village society. Factionalism is only one of the outcomes of this goal-seeking activity.

But then, the question remains why was factionalism so rampant and pronounced in Cakra, when it is, assuming that this observation is correct, relatively unnoticed in some other communities. Also, in Cakra itself, why did factionalism prove to be so pronounced at certain times that a stalemate was created, while at other times it was not so?

It is suggested that there are two important factors underlying the differences in the intensity of factional conflict between one community and another, as well as such differences between one situation and the other in the same community. The relative bargaining positions occupied in a community by the main contenders for political goals, and, secondly, the relative number of issues present in any given situation on which bargaining is possible. These are perhaps not the only factors which account for such differences. Among other things, the unique historical experiences of a community, its general ethos and traditions, its level of structural differentiation, the sequential development of one conflict issue to the other, etc., are also likely to influence the intensity of factional conflict. Yet, it is suggested that the two factors mentioned above provide useful distinction and insights in the phenomenon under study.

If, for example, a community's structural organization places one person in a relatively advantageous bargaining position over the rest, and in every significant area of life; there would be no competition for political goals on a community scale, no need for seeking support, or for allying with others. As a result of these, the community would be free from factional conflicts. Needless to say, such conditions are rarely, if ever, found. In Cakra, the two main contenders for political gains were not only "equals" on agnatic grounds, their economic positions were also very similar. In this situation if one of the two tried to assert his position over the other, or sought gains which were likely to place the other in a less advantageous position, the other was likely to resent it. This situation was further compounded by the fact that although there were great economic disparities among the Raghubanshi Thakurs, because of the agnatic nature of their relationship each one of them tended to regard himself as equal to everyone else. Thus, the chances for political competition were large. And since the two main contestants were more or less on an equal footing, a major way to improve one's bargaining position over the other was through seeking support of people who, in turn, were similarly motivated. Thus factionalism became unavoidable.

The second factor is the number of issues present in a given situation on which bargaining is possible. This, it is believed, would help to understand why certain issues in Cakra were more easily resolved than others.

And in this way, final agreement was possible between the key actors. The most important factor in this was the possibility of bargaining between the parties concerned.

8. Faction Dynamics in Cakra

In the Panchayati Raj election of 1982, special characteristics of faction have already well discussed. Their characteristics are very close to investigations of special qualities and analysis of factions during 1950s to 1960s. The study was carried out in the first half of 1980s. Even though there is a time difference of more than 20 years, it suggests that the small groups formed a basic structure of the Indian village. In both cases, the same kind of political fights of small groups were prevalent. The existence of the faction with the aim of political strife in an Indian village is clearly one of the special features in the rural scene. The characteristics of the faction had greatly changed – socially and economically.

The study carried out in the 1950s and 1960s showed the factions beginning their activity of opposition and resistance within the dominant caste. In other words, within the dominant caste which controlled and dominated other jati groups in the village, there was a split and collapse of stable unity and cohesion; at this time factions appeared on the scene. The opposition with the dominant caste deteriorated into tension and conflicts. The other jati groups which were controlled by the dominant caste were now mobilized to aid their internal fight and the activity of the faction which is actually the internal fight within the dominant group.

In comparison with the above, the factions described in this study bring the entire village into focus. Not only that, in this case, all the jati groups were involved in fights for political power. Although the basic conditions for the formation of the factions were the same as in 1960s, the middle and lower jati groups came to participate positively in the village politics, and they were a vital factor in these activities. In the political movement in the village, they displayed a participation of the same level as the Thakurs, and in this case the internal split among the Thakurs had a close tie with the trends of activity of middle and lower groups.

The middle and lower groups now made their existence greatly felt because they now consolidated themselves; number dominancy of population is a weapon in voting, especially where there is large population. Indeed, the internal split in the Thakur group came about because the trends in the middle and lower groups had an influence over the election results. By cooperating and having ties with the middle and lower groups, who made up a large portion of the population, the Thakurs had an internal split.

Although faction leads to political fighting within small groups it is also used to denote the entire range of political tendency of the village encouraging consolidation of different groups and establishing a vertical combination.

The model of the dominant caste was emphasized and was indeed central to this research. The core faction accelerated the collapse of the unity, the horizontal tie, and the internal stability of the dominant caste. Afterwards the faction went on to form a united new group in a new combination, for the politically fighting small group. The model of the dominant group emphasized the horizontal tie among the upper class, while the faction clearly went in for a vertical tie, cutting across different political conditions in the village. Recombination with a vertical cutting across, means going beyond the jati groups, establishing internal discipline and framework structure forming a new union of members. The vertical set up in the village collapsed, and there was re-organizing of members of all upper, middle, and lower jati groups.

The recombination with a vertical crossing between groups brought about an internal split in the upper jati groups and also strengthening of unity in the middle and lower jati groups. Unity and consolidation among Thakurs, the dominant caste, took a sudden turn for the worse, because of the development of a multiple sense of values and increasing gap between the rich and the poor. This in turn developed into separate actions on the part of individuals.

The consolidation and cooperation among the middle and lower jati groups was further strengthened to reap even more benefits.

The present political conditions in the north Indian village indicate dis-unity among the upper jati groups, while there exists consolidation of the middle and lower jati groups.

In the rural scene of North India, the question is whether the present consolidated middle and lower jati groups and their members will maintain their solidarity in future also, or whether the upper jati groups will once again revive their unity? If one concludes from the fact that the jati groups are fast losing their functions as a group, I feel that on the whole village scale, there would be a transformation to individual assertion. This may be called as family centred individuality. While there is a wave towards revival of old trends (reverting to jati groups), perhaps there will be an evolution from jati groupism to faction, and then on to individualism centred around a family.

9. *Conflict and Continuity in Cakra*

With a virtual deadlock on most of its political front, with so many internecine conflicts that characterized inter-personal relations, and with perfidy and treachery a commonplace phenomenon, the picture of Cakra which emerges from the present narrative is perhaps a sordid one, contradicting perhaps the very idea of "community". Yet, the important fact remains that life in Cakra continues. At the surface level one can still notice "tranquility" of which a few glimpses are presented at the beginning of chapter 6. Despite the fact that the paths were slushy, the panchayat crippled, and many of the inter-personal relations strained and bitter, people continued to live in the village with remarkable ease and casualness.

But it was not merely the surface-level tranquility which showed continuity in Cakra. Nor was it simply a matter of "forced coexistence"; people did not just "live together" while carrying on as atomized units, their own personal daily businesses. They lived in Cakra as "the members of a community", giving it what was its due and receiving from it what they thought was theirs.

One may well wonder how this continuity was possible with so much conflict in the village. As to how "community life" could be maintained when the inter-personal relations were marked with so much mutual distrust and vindictive animosity?

The answer lies partly in the fact that conflict and continuity were not necessarily mutually exclusive and dichotomous phenomena in Cakra. In fact, one could even argue that inter-personal hostilities and factional conflict were contributory factors in the very process of Cakra's continuity. As was pointed out at the beginning of this chapter, these conflicts showed the vigour with which Cakra residents participated in community life. By using every possible means to achieve goals which had relevance only in the village context they showed the intensity of their commitment for the village society. By undermining each other's interests, and by asserting one's power and challenging that of the others, they subscribed to the symbols of relative success or failure in the village. These acts, thus, had the effect of upholding and also reinforcing some of the basic organizing principles of the village, thereby insuring its continuity.

It is furthermore necessary to remember that, the aspects of village life which people were primarily concerned with, constitute only a fraction of its totality. The political scene of the village was, as some of the case materials show, that the villagers seemed to make a clear distinction between issues which they regarded crucially important for their survival and collective continuity, and those which were not regarded so important.

This does not mean that the people did not try to resolve these problems. These issues were of a nature where, if serious resistance arose, decisions and actions could be deferred. These issues could also be allowed to be played up for political tension.

There were numerous other instances, not recorded in my case materials, where behaviour was simply habitual, spontaneous, and in conformity with a single established set of rules. It has the effect of either warding off "threats to the collective survival" or strengthening these bonds which insured continuity in the village. The underlying principle was again the same; how crucially important was the issue!

When the villagers once noticed, for example, that a herd of wild cattle was roaming around the countryside, and it was necessary to protect the ripening wheat crop, it did not take long for them to assign by rotation two persons each night to guard not only their own fields but also those of others, including, at times, their political foes. Political considerations were also subordinated when serious sickness or other personal calamities arose in a family. Help, cooperation, and sympathy on such occasions were rendered in the most human, neutral and spontaneous manner.

In these numerous ways, the village of Cakra was able to maintain its continuity while allowing its members to engage in prolonged and at times bitter political conflicts. These conflicts might sometimes appear to be very disruptive, but so far they have not deprived Cakra of those basic ingredients which made it an on-going community. In fact, it was mostly due to the quality of these basic elements that the political conflicts I have described were possible and meaningful.

Note

This is one of the basic causes of faction in the village, as says a proverb: "For quarrels there appear three issues: wealth, women, and land" [see Singh and Singh, 1981: 59].

BIBLIOGRAPHY

Baden-Powell, B.H.

1892 *The Land Systems of British India,* (3 Vols.). Oxford: The Clarendon Press.

1894 *Land Revenue and Tenure in British India.* Oxford: The Clarendon Press.

1896 *The Indian Village Community: Examined with Reference to the Physical, Ethnographic, and Historical Conditions of the Provinces.* London: Longmans.

1899 *The Origin and Growth of Village Communities in India.* London: S. Sonnenschein and Co.

Bailey, F.G.

1959 For a Sociology of India? *Contributions to India Sociology,* No. 3, pp. 88-101.

1960 *Tribe, Caste and Nation.* Manchester: Manchester University Press.

1964 The Study of Politics in Village India. Paper presented at the Annual Meeting (16th) of the Association for Asian Studies, Washington, D.C., March, 1964. (Memeo).

1965 Decisions by Consensus in Councils and Committees: With Special Reference to Village and Local Government in India. In *Political System and the Distribution of Power.* ASA Monograph No. 2, Michael Banton (ed.), New York: Frederick A. Prager.

1968   Parapolitical Systems. In *Local Level Politics*. Marc. J. Swartz (ed.), Chicago: Aldine Publishing Co. pp. 281-294.

1969   *Stratagems and Spoils*. Oxford: Blackwell.

Banfield, Edward C.

1958   *The Moral Basis of a Backward Society*. Glencoe: The Free Press.

Barth, Fredrick

1959   *Political Leadership Among Swat Pathans*. London School of Economics Monographs in Social Anthropology, No. 19. London: University of London.

1963   *The Role of the Entrepreneur in Social Change in Northern Norway*. Bergen-Oslo: Norwegian University Press.

1967   On the Study of Social Change. *American Anthropologist*, 69, pp. 661-669.

Baviskar, B.S.

1971   Factions and Party Politics. *Economic and Political Weekly*, 3 (12).

1974   Sociology of Politics. In *A Survey of Research in Sociology and Social Anthropology*, Indian Council of Social Science Research (ed.), Bombay: Popular Prakashan. pp. 431-507.

Beals, Alan R.

1954   *Culture, Change and Social Conflict in a South Indian Village*. Unpublished Ph.D. Dissertation, University of California, Berkeley.

1959   Leadership in a Mysore Village. In *Leadership and Political Institutions in India*. Richard Park and Irene Tinker (ed.), Princeton: Princeton University Press. pp. 427-437.

1961   Cleavage and Internal Conflict: An Example from India. *Journal of Conflict Resolution*, Vol. 5, No. 1, pp. 27-34.

1962   Pervasive Factionalism in a South Indian Village. In *Intergroup Relations and Leadership*. M. Sheriff (ed.), New York: John Wiley & Sons.

Beals, Alan, R. and B.J. Siegel

1966   *Divisiveness and Social Conflict*. Stanford: Stanford University Press.

Beidelman, T. O.

1959   *A Comparative Analysis of the Jajmani System*. Monograph of the Association for Asian Studies. No. 8. Locust Valley, N.Y.: J.J. Augustin Inc. Publishers.

Benedict, Burton
1957 Factionalism in Maurition Villages. *The British Journal of Sociology*, Vol. 8, No. 4, pp. 328-342.

Berreman, G.D.
1963 *Hindus of the Himalayas*. Berkeley: University of California Press.
1979 *Caste and Other Inequities; Essays on Inequality*. Issued in Kirpa Dai Series in Folklore and Anthropology, as No. 2. New Delhi: Manohar Publications.

Beteille, André
1965 *Caste, Class and Power*. Berkeley: University of California Press.
1969 *Castes: Old and New*. Bombay: Asia Publishing House.
1972 *Inequality and Social Change*. Delhi: Oxford University Press.
1974a *Studies in Agrarian Social Structure*. Delhi: Oxford University Press.
1974b *Six Essays in Comparative Sociology*. Delhi: Oxford University Press.
1983 *Equality and Inequality: Theory and Practice*. Delhi: Oxford University Press.

Bhargava, B.S.
1979a *Panchayati Raj Institutions: An analysis of issues, problems and recommendations of Ashok Mehta Committee*. New Delhi: Ashish Publishing House.
1979b *Panchayati Raj; System and Political Parties*. New Delhi: Ashish Publishing House.

Blau, Peter
1964 *Exchange and Power in Social Life*. New York: John Wiley & Sons.

Balu, P.M. and W.R. Scott
1966 *Formal Organization*. London: Routledge and Kegan Paul.

Blau, P.M. and R.C. Schoenherr
1971 *The Structure of Organization*. New York: Basic Book, Inc.

Blunt, E.H.A.
  1987 *Census of India 1911*. United Provinces of Agra and Oudh,
         (First Published in 1911), New Delhi: Usha Publications.
Biossevain, Jeremy
  1964 Factions, Parties and Politics in Malta. *American Anthro-
         pologist*, 66, pp. 1275-1287.
  1968 The Place of Non-groups in the Social Sciences. *Man*, No.
         3, pp. 542-556.
  1974 *Friends of Friends*. Oxford: Blackwell.
Boulding, Kenneth
  1962 *Conflict and Defence*. New York: Harper and Row.
Brass, Paul. R.
  1965 *Factional Politics in an Indian State*. Berkeley: University
         of California Press.
  1968 Uttar Pradesh. In *State Politics in India*. Myron Weiner
         (ed.), Princeton: Princeton University Press. pp. 61-166.
  1984 *Caste, Faction and Party in Indian Politics*. 2 Vols., Delhi:
         Chanakya Pub.
Breman, Jan
  1974 *Patronage and Exploitation*. Berkeley: California Univer-
         sity Press.
Burger, Angela Sutherland
  1969 *Opposition in a Dominant Party System*. Berkeley: Univer-
         sity of California Press.
Carvas, Mary C.
  1972 *The Dynamics of Indian Political Factions*. Cambridge:
         Cambridge University Press.
Carstairs, G. Morris
  1955 A Village in Rajasthan. In *Indian Village*. M.N. Srinivas
         (ed.), Bombay: Asia Publishing House.
  1957 *The Twice Born*. London: Hogarth Press.
Chakravarti, Anand
  1975 *Contradiction and Change*. Delhi: Oxford University Press.
Chance, Normana
  1962 Factionalism as a Process of Social and Cultural Change.
         In *Intergroup Relations and Leadership*. M. Sheriff (ed.),

New York: John Wiley & Sons. pp. 267-273.

Chavannes, Akbert

1901 *Studies in Sociology,* 2nd Ed., Knoxville: New Thought Library.

Choudhary, R.K.

1987 *Caste and Power Structure in Village India.* New Delhi: Inter-India Publications.

Cohen, Roland

1970 The Political System. In *A Handbook of Methodology in Cultural Anthropology.* Raoul Naroll and Ronald Cohen (eds.), Garden City, N.Y.: The National History Press.

Cohn, Bernard S.

1954 *The Chamar of Senapur.* Unpublished Ph.D. Dissertation, Cornell University.

1955 The Changing Status of a Depressed Caste. In *Village India.* McKim Marriott (ed.), Chicago: Chicago University Press. pp. 53-77.

1959 Some Notes on Law and Change in North India. *Economic Development and Cultural Change,* 8, pp. 79-93.

1965 Anthropological Notes on Disputes and Law in India. *American Anthropologist,* 67, pp. 82-122.

1979 Structural Changes in Indian Rural Society. In *Land Control and Social Structure in Indian History.* Frykenberg, Robert Eric (ed.), New Delhi: Manohar Publications.

Coleman, James S.

1957 *Community Conflict.* Glencoe: The Free Press.

1964 Collective Decisions. *Sociological Inequity,* Vol. XXXIV, No. 2, pp. 166-181.

1966 Foundations for a Theory of Collective Decisions. *The American Journal of Sociology,* Vol. LXXI, No. 6 (May 1966), pp. 615-627.

Coser, Lemis

1956 *The Functions of Social Conflict.* Glancoe: The Free Press.

Dahrendorf, Ralf

1959 *Class Conflict in Industrial Societies.* Stanford: Stanford University Press.

Desai, A.R.

 1969 *Rural Sociology in India.* Bombay: Popular Prakashan.

Desai, Vasant

 1988 *Rural Development.* 6 Vols., Bombay: Himalaya Pub. House.

Dhillon, H.

 1955 *Leadership and Groups in a South Indian Village.* New Delhi: Planning Commission, Government of India Press.

D'Souza, Victor

 1982 *Inequality and its Perpetuation: A Theory of Social Stratification.* New Delhi: Manohar Publications.

Dube, S.C.

 1968 Caste Dominance and Factionalism. *Contributions to Indian Sociology,* (n.s.), 2, pp. 58-81.

Domont, Louis

 1962 Kingship in Ancient India. *Contributions to Indian Sociology,* 6. pp. 48-77.

 1972 *Homo Hierarchicus.* Chicago: University of Chicago Press.

Domont, Louis and David Pocock

 1957 eds. *Contributions to Indian Sociology,* No. 1, Paris: Mouton and Co.

Easton, David

 1959 Political Anthropology. In *Bienniel Review of Anthropology 1959.* Bernad J. Siegel (ed.), Stanford: Stanford University Press. pp. 210-262.

 1965 *A Framework for Political Analysis.* Englewood Cliffs, NJ: Prentice Hall, Inc.

Elliott, Corolynm

 1970 Caste and faction among the Dominant Caste. In *Caste in Indian Politics.* Rajni Kothari (ed.), New Delhi: Orient Longmans, pp. 121-172.

Epstein, T. Scarett

 1962 *Economic Development and Social Change in South India.* Manchester: Manchester University Press.

 1967 Productive Efficiency and Customary Systems of Rewards in Rural South India. In *Themes in Economic Anthropology.*

Raymond Firth (ed.), ASA Monograph No. 6. London: Tavistock Publications.

1973 *South India.* New York: Holmes and Meier Publishers.

Etienne, Gilbert

1968 *Studies in Indian Agriculture.* Berkeley: University of California Press.

Fenton, William N.

1955 Factionalism in American Indian Society. *Ethnologica,* 2, pp. 330-340.

Firth, Raymond

1951 *Elements of Social Organization.* London: Watts and Co.

1954 Social Organization and Social Change. *Journal of the Royal Anthropological Institute,* Vol. 84, Pts. I and II.

1955 Some Principles of Social Organization. *Journal of the Royal Anthropological Institute,* Vo. 85, Pts. I and II.

1957 Introduction to "Factions in Indian and Overseas Indian Societies". *The British Journal of Sociology,* Vol. 8, No. 4, pp. 291-295.

Fortes, Mayer and E. Evans-Pritchard

1940 eds. *African Political Systems.* London: Oxford University Press.

Foster, George M.

1960-61 Interpersonal Relations in Peasant Societies. *Human Organization,* Vol. 19, No. 4, pp. 174-178, (followed by Comments pp. 179-184).

1962 *Traditional Cultures and the Impact of Technological Change.* New York: Harper and Row.

1963 The Dyadic Contract in Tzintzumtzan. *American Anthropologist,* 65, pp. 1280-1294.

Frankel, Francine R. and Kari Von Vorys

1972 *The Political Challenge of the Green Revolution.* Policy Memorandum, No. 38. Princeton: Center for International Studies, Princeton University.

Freed, Ruth, S. and Stanley A. Freed

1966 Unity in Diversity in the Celebration of Cattle - Curing Rites in a North Indian Village. *American Anthropologist,* 68, pp. 673-692.

Freed, Stanley A.
  1963a Fictive Kinship in a North Indian Village. *Ethnology*, Vol. II, No. 1, pp. 86-103.
  1963b An Objective Method for Determining the Collective Caste Hierarchy of an Indian Village. *American Anthropologist*, 65. pp. 879-891.

Fukunaga, Masaaki
  1985 "The Concept of Space and Boundary in North Indian Village". *Journal of Indian and Buddhist Studies*, Vol. XXXIII, No. 2. pp. 869-862.
  1989 Faction Dynamics in a North Indian Village. Ph.D. Dissertation, Department of Sociology. Varanasi: Banaras Hindu University.

Gallin, Bernard
  1968 Political Factionalism and its Impact on Chinese Village Social Organization in Taiwan. In *Local Level Politics*, Marc J. Swartz (ed.), Chicago: Aldine Publishing Company, pp. 377-400.

Gamsopn, Williama
  1961 A Theory of Coalition Formation. *American Sociological Review*, 26. pp. 373-382.

Gardner, Peter M.
  1968 Dominance in India: A Reappraisal. *Contributions to Indian Sociology*, (n.s.), 2. pp. 82-97.

Ghurye, G.S.
  1950 *Caste and Class in India*. Bombay: Asia Publishing House.

Gluckman, Max
  1954 *Rituals of Rebellion in South East Africa*. Manchester: The University Press.
  1955 *The Judicial Process Among the Barotse of Northern Rhodesia*. Manchester: The University Press.
  1956 *Custom and Conflict in Africa*. Oxford: Basil Blackwell.
  1965 *Politics, Law and Ritual in Tribal Society*. Chicago: Aldine Publishing Company.

Gough, Kathleen
  1960 Caste in a Tanjore Village. In *Aspects of Caste in South*

India, Ceylon and North-West Pakistan. E.R. Leach (ed.), Cambridge: Cambridge University Press. pp. 11-60.

1970 Social Structure of a Tanjore Village. In *Change and Continuity in India's Village.* K. Ishwaran (ed.), New York: Columbia University Press.

1973 Harijans in Thanjavur. In *Imperialism and Revolution.* Kathleen Gough and Hari P. Sharma (eds.), New York: Monthly Review Press. pp. 222-245.

Gould, Harold

1967 Priest and Contrapriest: A Structural Analysis of Jajmani Relationships in the Hindu Plains and Nilgiri Hills. *Contributions to Indian Sociology,* (n.s.) 1, pp. 26-55.

1969 Toward a 'Jati' Model for Indian Politics. *Economic and Political Weekly,* 4, pp. 291-297.

1970 Is the Modernity Tradition Model All Bad. *Economic and Political Weekly,* Special No. V, (29-31) July.

Gouldner, A.W.

1960 Norms of Reciprocity: A Preliminary Statement. *American Sociological Review,* Vol. 25, No. 2, pp. 161-178.

Government of India

*Planning Commission, New Delhi :

1952 *First Five Year Plan.*

1957 *Second Five Year Plan.*

1961 *Third Five Year Plan.*

1970 *Fourth Five Year Plan.*

1974 *Fifth Five Year Plan.*

*Ministry of Community Development and Cooperation:

1957 *Report of the Study Team for Community Projects and National Extension Service.*

1958 *The Fifth Evaluation Report on Working of Community Development and National Extension Service book.*

*Ashok Mehta Committee:

1959 *Report of the Working Group on Panchayat.*

1961 *Report of the Working Group on Panchayat.*

1978 *Recommendations of the Ashok Mehta Committee on Panchayati Institutions.*

Government of Uttar Pradesh

 1947   *U.P. Panchayati Raj Act. 1947.* Allahabad; Superintendent
        of Printing & Stationary, U.P.

 1952   *U.P. Panchayati Raj Act, 1952 (Amendment).*

 1955   *U.P. Panchayati Raj Act, 1955 (Amendment).*

 1957   *U.P. Panchayati Raj Act, 1957 (Amendment).*

 1961   *U.P. Kshetra Samitis aur Zila Parishad Adhiniyam, 1961
        (Amendment).*

Graham, B.D.

 1968   The Succession of Factional System in Uttar Pradesh
        Congress Party 1937-66. In *Local Level Politics.* Marc J.
        Swartz (ed.), Chicago: Aldine Publishing Company. pp.
        323-360.

Gupta, A.K.

 1988   *Sociological Implications of Rural to Rural Migration: a
        case study of rural migration in Punjab.* Allahabad: Vohra
        Publishers' Distributors.

Harper, Edward

 1968   Social Consequences of an 'Unsuccessful' Low Caste
        Movement. In *Social Mobility in the Caste System in India.*
        James Silverberg (ed.), *Comparative Studies in Society and
        History Supplement,* 3, pp. 36-65.

Hitchcock, John T.

 1956   *The Rajputs of Khalapur: A Study of Kinship, Social
        Stratification and Politics.* Unpublished Ph.D. Dissertation,
        Cornell University.

Hitchcock, John T. and Leigh Minturn

 1963   The Rajputs of Khalapur, India: The Ethnographic Back-
        ground. In *Six Cultures: Studies of Child Rearing.* Beatrice
        B. Whiting (ed.) New York: John Wiley & Sons.

Homans, George C.

 1958   Social Behaviour as Exchange. *The American Journal of
        Sociology,* Vol 63, pp. 597-606.

 1961   *Social Behaviour: Its Elementary Forms.* New York:
        Harcourt Brace and World.

 1964a Commentary. *Sociological Inequality,* Vol. XXXIV, No. 2,
        pp. 221-31.

1964b Bringing Men Back. In *The American Sociological Review*, Vol. 29, No. 5, pp. 809-818.

Institute of Development Studies
1976 *Village Studies - Data Analysis and Bibliography - Vol. I India 1950-1975.* Essex: Bowker Publishing Company.

Iswaran, K.
1966 *Tradition and Economy in Village India.* Delhi: Allied Publishers.

Jain, R.B. (ed.)
1981 *Panchayati Raj.* New Delhi: Indian Institute of Public Administration.

Jannuzi, F. Tomasson
1974 *Agrarian Crisis in India.* Austin: University of Texas Press.

Jayaram, K.
1947 *A Study of Panchayats in Madras.* Bombay: Indian Society of Agricultural Economics.

Jones, Edward E.
1964 *Ingratiation: A Social Psychological Analysis.* New York: Appleton - Century - Crafts.

Karve, Irawati and Y. B. Damle
1963 *Group Relations in Village Community.* Poona: Deccan College Post Graduate and Research Institute.

Khare, R.S.
1962 Group Dynamics in a North Indian Village. *Human Organization,* Vol. 21, No. 3, pp. 201-14.

Knox, John
1963 The Concept of Exchange in Sociological Theory. *Social Forces,* Vol. 41, No. 4, pp. 341-45.

Kohli, Atul
1987 *The State and Poverty in India; the politics of reform.* Cambridge South Asian Studies, 37. Cambridge: Cambridge University Press.

Kolenda, Pauline, M.
1966 Toward a Model of the Hindu Jajmani System. In *Contours of Cultural Change in South Asia.* William L. Rowe (ed.), Human Organization Monograph, No. 9, pp. 11-31.

Kothari, Rajni
  1970 Introduction. In *Caste in Indian Politics*. Rajni Kothari (ed.), New Delhi: Orient Longmans. pp. 3-25.
Leach, E.R.
  1954 *Political Systems of Highland Burma*. London: Bell and Co.
  1960 Introduction: What Should We Mean by Caste. *In Aspects of Caste in South India, Ceylon and North-West Pakistan*. E.R. Leach (ed.), Cambridge: Cambridge University Press. pp. 1-10.
Lewis, Oscar
  1954 *Group Dynamics in a North Indian Village*. New Delhi: Planning Commission, Government of India.
  1955 Peasant Culture in India and Mexico. In *Village India*. M. Marriott (ed.), Chicago: University of Chicago Press.
  1958 *Village Life in Northern India*. Urbana: University of Illinois Press.
Lynch, Owen
  1969 *Politics of Untouchability*. New York: Columbia University Press.
MacDouall, J.
  1980 The Models of Power in Contemporary Rural India. *Contributions to Indian Sociology*, (n.s.), 14, No. 1, pp. 77-94.
Madan, T.N.
  1969 *Changing Pattern of Rural Administration in Uttar Pradesh*. Bombay: All India Institute of Local Self-Government.
Maddick, Henry
  1970 *Panchayati Raj; a study of rural local government*. London: Longman.
Majumdar, D.N.
  1958 *Caste and Communications in an Indian Village*. Bombay: Asia Publishing House.
Mandelbaum, D.G.
  1970 *Society in India*. Vol. I-II. Berkeley: University of California Press.
Marriott, McKim
  1952 Social Change in an Indian Village. *Economic Development*

and *Culture Change*, Vol 1. No. 2.

1955a Little Communities in an Indigenous Civilization. In *Village India*. M. Marriott (ed.), Chicago: University of Chicago Press.

1955b Social Structure and Change in a U.P. Village. In *India's Village*, M. N. Srinivas (ed.), Bombay: Asia Publishing House.

Mason, Philip

1967 ed., Unity and Diversity: An Introductory Review. In *India, and Ceylon: Unity and Diversity*. Oxford: Oxford University Press. pp. 1-29.

Mayer, Adrin C.

1957 Factions in Fiji Indian Rural Settlements. *The British Journal of Sociology*, Vol. 8, No. 4, pp.317-328.

1958a The Dominant Caste in a Region of Central India. *South-western Journal of Anthropology*, Vol. 14, No. 4, pp. 407-427.

1958b Local Government Elections in a Malwa Village. *Eastern Anthropologist*, Vol. 11, pp. 189-202.

1960 *Caste and Kinship in Central India*. London: Routledge and Kegan Paul.

1966 Significance of Quasi-groups in the study of Complex Societies. In *Anthropological Approach to the Study of Complex Societies*. ASA Monograph No. 4, London: Tavistock Publications. pp. 97-122.

1967a Caste and Local Politics in India. In *India and Ceylon: Unity and Diversity*. Philip Mason (ed.), Oxford: Oxford University Press.

1967b Patrons and Brokers: Rural Leadership in Four Overseas Indian Communities. In *Social Organization: Essays Presented to Raymond Firth*. Maurice Freedman (ed.), London: Frank Cass and Co. Ltd. pp. 167-188.

McCormack, William C.

1956 *Changing Leadership of a Mysore Village*. Unpublished Ph.D. Dissertation, University of Chicago.

1959 Factionalism in a Mysore Village. In *Leadership and Political Institutions in India*. Richard Park and I. Tinker, (eds.), Princeton: Princeton University Press.

Meillassoux, Claude

1973   Are there Castes in India? *Economy and Society*, 2, pp. 89-111.

Mencher, Joan P.

1974a The Caste System Upside Down, on the Not-So-Mysterious East. *Current Anthropology*, 15, pp. 469-493.

1974b Conflict and Contradiction in the 'Green Revolution': The Case of Tamilnadu. *Economic and Political Weekly*, 9, pp. 309-323.

Miller, D.B.

1975   *From Hierarchy to Stratification.* Delhi: Oxford University Press.

Miller, D.F.

1965   Faction in Indian Village Politics. *Pacific Affairs*, Vol. 38, No. 1, pp. 17-31.

Morris-Jones, W.H.

1963   India's Political Idioms. In *Politics and Society in India.* London: George Allen and Unwin Ltd. pp. 133-154.

1964   Politics and Society. In *The Government and Politics of India.* London: Hutchinson University Library, pp. 48-72.

Nicholas, R.

1963   Village Factions and Political Parties in Rural West Bengal. *Journal of Commonwealth Political Studies,* Vol. II, No. 1, pp. 17-31.

1965   Factions : A Comparative Analysis. In *Political Systems and the Distribution of Power*, M. Banton (ed.), ASA Monograph No. 2. New York: Frederick A. Praeger. pp. 21-62.

1966   Segmentary Factional Political Systems. In *Political Anthropology,* Marc Swartz, V. Turner and A. Tuden (eds.), Chicago: Aldine Publishing Company. pp. 49-59.

1968   Structures of Politics in the Villages of South Asia. In *Structure and Change in Indian Society.* Milton Singer and Bernard S. Cohn (eds.), Chicago: Aldine Publishing Company. pp. 243-284.

1968b Rules, Resource and Political Activity. In *Local Level Politics*. Marc J. Swartz (ed.), Chicago: Aldine Publishing Company. pp. 295-321.

Opler, Morris E.

1956 The Extensions of an Indian Village. *The Journal of Asian Studies,* Vol. XVI, No. 1, pp. 4-10.

1959a Factors of Tradition and Change in Local Election in Rural India. In *Leadership and Political Institutions in India.* R. Park and I. Tinker (eds.), Princeton: Princeton University Press.

1959b Family, Anxiety and Religion in a Community of North India. In *Culture and Mental Health.* Marvin Opler (ed.), New York: The Macmillan Co. pp. 273-289.

1960 Political Organization and Economic Growth: The Case of Village India. *International Review of Community Development,* No. 5, pp. 187-197.

Opler, Morris and R.D. Singh

1948 The Division of Labor in an Indian Village. In *A Reader in General Anthropology.* Carleton S. Coon (ed.), New York: Holt Rinehart and Winston. pp. 464-496.

1952 Economic, Political and Social Change in a Village of North Central India. *Human Organization,* Vol. 11, No. 2.

Orenstein, Henry

1965 *Gaon: Conflict and Cohesion in an Indian Village.* Princeton: Princeton University Press.

Parthasarthy, G.

1971 *Green Revolution and the Weaker Sections.* Bombay: Thacker & Co. Ltd.

Pocock, D.F.

1955 The Movement of Castes. *Man,* Vol. LV, pp. 79-80.

1957 The Bases of Factions in Gujarat. *British Journal of Sociology,* Vol. 8, No. 4, pp. 295-307.

1962 Notes on Jajmani Relationships. *Contributions to Indian Sociology,* 6, pp. 78-95.

Pohekar, G.S.

1970 *Studies in Green Revolution.* Bombay: United Asia Publications Pvt. Ltd.

Powell, John Duncan
 1970 \Peasant Society and Clientelist Politics. *American Political Science Review*, 64, pp. 411-425.

Pradhan, M.C.
 1966 *The Political System of the Jats of Northern India.* Bombay: Oxford University Press.

Rangnath
 1967 Rural Leadership Old and New. In *Leadership in India.* L.P. Vidyarthi (ed.), Bombay: Asia Publishing House. pp. 267-276.

Rao, M.S.A.
 1963 Rural Development Programmes: A Sociological Analysis. In *Problems of Rural Change.* M.S. Gore (ed.), Delhi: Delhi School of Social Work, University of Delhi.
 1978 ed. *Social Movements in India.* Vol. I, New Delhi: Manohar Publications.
 1979 ed. *Social Movements in India.* Vol. II, New Delhi: Manohar Publications.
 1984 ed. *Social Movements in India.* (Two Volumes bound in One), Paperback Edition, New Delhi: Manohar Publications.

Rastogi, P.N.
 1964 Factionalism, Politics and Crime in a U.P. Village. *Eastern Anthropologist*, Vol. 17, No. 2, pp. 168-182.
 1967 Anatomy of Factional Conflict. *Sociological Bulletin*, Vol. 16, No. 1, pp. 17-32.

Retzalaff, Ralph H.
 1962 *Village Government in India.* Bombay: Asia Publishing House.

Rosenthal, D.B.
 1966 Factions and Alliances in Indian City Politics. *Midwest Journal of Political Science*, 10, (3).

Roy, Ramashray and V.B. Singh
 1987 *Between Two Worlds: a Study of Harijan Elite.* Delhi: Discovery Pub. House.

Rowe, William L.

1960a *Social and Economic Mobility in a Low Caste North Indian Village Community.* Unpublished Ph.D. Dissertation, Cornell University.

1960b The Marriage Network and Structural Change in North Indian Community. *Southwestern Journal of Anthropology,* Vol. XVI, pp. 291-311.

Rudolph, Lloyd and S.H. Rudolph

1960 The Political Role of India's Caste Associations. *Pacific Affairs,* 33, pp. 5-22.

1987 *In Pursuit of Lakshmi: The Political Economy of the Indian State.* Hyderabad: Orient Longman.

Rudolph, Susanne H.

1961 Consensus and Conflict in Indian Politics. *World Politics,* 13, pp. 385-399.

1969 *The Modernity of Tradition.* Bombay: Orient Longman.

Schapera, I.

1956 *Government of Politics in Tribal Societies.* London: Watts and Co.

Schwartzberg, Joseph E.

1968 Caste Regions of the North Indian Plains. In *Structure and Change in Indian Society.* Milton Singer and B.S. Cohn (eds.), Chicago: Aldine Publishing Company. pp. 81-113.

1978 ed. *A Historical Atlas of South Asia.* Chicago: University of Chicago Press.

Sengupta, N.

1982 Caste as an Agrarian Phenomenon in Twentieth Century Bihar. In *Agrarian Relation in India.* Arvind N. Das and V. Nilkant (eds.), New Delhi: Manohar Publications.

Sharma, H.P.

1973 The Green Revolution in India: Prelude to a Red One? In *Imperialism and Revolution in South Asia.* Kathleen Gough and H.P. Sharma (eds.), New York: Monthly Review Press. pp. 77-102.

Sharma, K.L.

1986 ed. *Social Stratification in India.* New Delhi: Manohar Publications.

Sharma, Miriam
  1979 *The Politics of Inequality.* Delhi: Hindustan Publishing Co.
Sharma, Mohan .L.
  1984 *Dynamics of Rural Power Structure: A Study of Rajasthan.*
         Jaipur: Aalekh Publishers.
Sharma, R.N.
  1979 *Indian Rural Sociology.* New Delhi. Munshiram Manohar-
         lal.
Shepperdson, M.J.
  1969 Political Conflict in Ten Villages in India, Pakistan and
         Ceylon. *Contributions to Indian Sociology,* (n.s.), 3, pp. 45-
         75.
Shivaiah, M., K.V.N. Rao, L.S.N. Murty, G. Mallikajuniah
  1976 *Panchayati Raj. An Analytical Survey.* Hyderabad: National
         Institute of Community Development.
Siegel, B.J. and A. Beals
  1960a Conflict and Factionalist Dispute. *Journal of Royal Anthro-
         pological Institute,* 90, pp. 107-117.
  1960b Pervasive Factionalism. *American Anthroplogist,* 62, pp.
         394-417
Simmel, George
  1955 *Conflict.* (translated by Kurt Wolff and R. Bendix). Glen-
         coe: The Free Press.
Singer, Milton
  1964 The Social Organization of Indian Civilization. *Diogenes,*
         Vol. 45, Winter, pp. 84-119.
  1972 *When a Great Tradition Modernizes.* New York: Praeger
         Publishers Inc.
Singh, Baljit
  1961 *Next Step in Village India.* Bombay: Asia Publishing House.
Singh, Dinesh Kumar
  1977 *Rajput Clan Settlements in Jaunpur District (Middle Ganga
         Valley).* Unpublished Ph.D. Dissertation in Geography.
         Varanasi: Banaras Hindu University.
Singh, G.S.
  1982 *Dobhi Ka Itihas.* (in Hindi). Dobhi: Daroga Singh.

Singh, Rana P.B.
  1975 Distribution of Castes and Search for a Theory of Caste Ranking. *National Geographical Journal of India*, 21, (1), pp. 20-40.
  1977 *Clan Settlements in the Saran Plain (Middle Ganga Valley): A Study in Cultural Geography*. Varanasi: National Geographical Society of India, Pub. No. 18.

Singh, Rana P.B. and R.B.Singh
  1981 *Changing Frontiers of Indian Village Ecology - Majhanpura*. Varanasi: National Geographical Society of India, Pub. No. 27.

Singh, R.L., Rana P.B. Singh and D.K.Singh
  1976 Mechanism of spatio-temporal diffusion of a clan-settlement in a part of Middle Ganga Valley: Some Comparisons and Corelates. In *Geographic Dimensions of Rural Settlements*, R.L. Singh, et al., (eds.) Varanasi: National Geographical Society of India, pp. 19-32.

Singh, Rudra Datta
  1956 The Unity of an Indian Village. *The Journal of Asian Studies*, Vol. XVI, pp. 10-19.

Singh, Srinath
  1976 *Modernization of Agriculture: A Case Study in Eastern U.P.* Delhi: Heritage Publications.

Singh, Tarlok
  1955 The Village Panchayat and the Pattern of Village Development. (memo. quoted by H. Tinker, 1963).

Singh, Yogendra
  1973 *Modernization of Indian Tradition*. Faridabad: Thomson Press Private Ltd.
  1977 The Changing Pattern of Social Stratification in India. In *Dimensions of Social Change in India*. M.N. Srinivas, S. Seshaiah, V.P. Parthasarathy (eds.), New Delhi: Allied Publishers.

Smith, Marian W.
  1952 The Misal: A Structural Village Group of India and Pakistan. *American Anthropologist*, 54, pp. 41-56.

1953   Structure and Unstructured Class Societies. *American Anthropologist,* 55.

Somjee, A.H.

1964   *Politics of a Periurban Community in India.* Bombay: Asia Publishing House.

1971   *Democracy and Political Change in Village India.* Delhi: Orient Longman.

Srinivas, M.N.

1955   The Social System of a Mysore Village. In *Village India.* McKim Mariott (ed.), Chicago: University of Chicago Press. pp. 1-35.

1959   The Dominant Caste in Rampura. *American Anthropologist,* 61, pp. 1-16.

1962   *Caste in Modern India and other Essays.* Bombay: Asia Publishing House.

1966   *Social Change in Modern India.* Berkeley: University of California Press.

1979   *The Remembered Village.* (Second Impression, First Published in 1976), Delhi: Oxford University Press.

Srinivas, M.N., S. Seshaiah, V.S. Parthasarathy

1977   (eds.) *Dimensions of Social Change in India.* New Delhi: Allied Publishers.

Swartz, M., V. Turner, and A. Tunden

1966   eds., *Political Anthropology.* Chicago: Aldine Publishing Co.

Swartz, Marc J.

1968   ed. *Local Level Politics.* Chicago: Aldine Publishing Co.

Terence, J. Byress

1988   Charan Singh (1902-87): An Assessment. *The Journal of Peasant Studies,* Vol. 15, No. 2, January.

Thibaut, John W. and Harold H. Kelley

1959   *The Social Psychology of Groups.* New York: John Wiley & Sons.

Thorner, Daniel

1956   *The Agrarian Prospect in India.* Delhi: Allied Publishers.

Tinker, Hugh
  1963 The Village in Framework of Development. In *Administration and Economic Development in India*. Ralph Baraibanti and Joseph Spengler (ed.), Durham: Duke University Press.

Turner, A.C.
  1987 *Census of India 1931*. United Provinces of Agra and Oudh (First Published in 1931), New Delhi: Usha Publications.

Turner, Ralph H.
  1962 Role-Taking: Process Versus Conformity. In *Human Behavior and Social Processes*. Arnold Rose (ed.), Boston: Houghton Miffin Co. pp. 20-40.

Turner, Victor W.
  1957 *Schism and Continuity in an African Society*. Manchester: Manchester University Press.

  1966 Ritual Aspects of Conflict Control in African Micro-Politics. In *Political Anthropology*. M.J. Swartz, V.M. Turner and A. Tuden (eds.), Chicago: Aldine Publishing Company.

Ullah, Inayat
  1958 Caste Patti and Faction in The Life of a Punjab Village. *Sociologues*, Vol. 8, No. 2, pp. 170-186.

Vidyarthi, L.P.
  1969 ed., *Conflict, Tension and Cultural Trend in India*. Calcutta: Punthi Pustak.

  1978 *Rise of Anthropology in India*, Vol. II, Delhi: Concept Publishing Co.

Yadav, J.S.
  1968a Factionalism in a Haryana Village. *American Anthropologist*, 70, pp. 898-910.

  1968b Group Dynamics and Panchayat Elections in a Punjab Village. *Journal of Social Research*, Vol. 2, No. 2, pp. 58-72.

Wallance, Anthony F.C.
  1956 Revitalization Movements: Some Theoretical Considerations for their Comparative Study. *American Anthropologist*, 58, pp. 264-281.

Weiner, Myron
  1965a Party Politics and Panchayati Raj. In *Studies in Indian*

Democracy. S.P. Ajyar and R. Srinivasan (eds.), Bombay: Allied Publishers, pp. 405-411.

1965b Village and Party Factionalism in Andhra: Pannur Constituency. In *Indian Voting Behavior*. M. Weiner and Rajni Kothari (eds.), Calcutta: Firma K.L. Mukhopadhyya, pp. 177-202.

Wiser, W.H.

1936 *The Hindu Jajmani System*. Lucknow: Lucknow Publishing House.

Wood, Evelyn

1959 Patterns of Influence within Rural India. In *Leadership and Political Institutions in India*. R.L. Park and I. Tinker (eds.), Princeton: Princeton University Press.

Zaheer, M. and J. Gupta

1970 *The Organization of the Government of Uttar Pradesh: A Study of State Administration*. Delhi: S. Chand and Co.